How can we motivate ourselves to do what we think we ought; how can we deliberate about personal values and priorities? Because Helm argues that standard philosophical answers to these questions presuppose a sharp distinction between cognition and emotion that undermines an adequate understanding of values and their connection to motivation and deliberation. Rejecting this distinction, Helm argues that emotions are fundamental to any account of value and motivation, and he develops a detailed alternative theory of both of emotions, desires, and evaluative judgments and of their rational interconnections. The result is an innovative theory of practical rationality and of how we can control not only what we do but also what we value and who we are as persons.

BENNETT W. HELM is Assistant Professor of Philosophy at Franklin & Marshall College, Pennsylvania. He has published articles in Home Studies Advanced Philosophical Quarterly, Pacific Philosophical Quarterly, Southern Journal of Philosophy, and Noûs.

CAMBRIDGE STUDIES IN PHILOSOPHY

Emotional reason

CAMBRIDGE STUDIES IN PHILOSOPHY

General editor ERNEST SOSA

Advisory editors

JONATHAN DANCY *University of Reading*
JOHN HALDANE *University of St. Andrews*
GILBERT HARMAN *Princeton University*
FRANK JACKSON *Australian National University*
WILLIAM G. LYCAN *University of North Carolina, Chapel Hill*
SYDNEY SHOEMAKER *Cornell University*
JUDITH J. THOMSON *Massachusetts Institute of Technology*

RECENT TITLES

PAUL HELM *Belief policies*
NOAH LEMOS *Intrinsic value*
LYNNE RUDDER BAKER *Explaining attitudes*
HENRY S. RICHARDSON *Practical reasoning about final ends*
ROBERT A. WILSON *Cartesian psychology and physical minds*
BARRY MAUND *Colours*
MICHAEL DEVITT *Coming to our senses*
SYDNEY SHOEMAKER *The first-person perspective and other essays*
MICHAEL STOCKER *Valuing emotions*
ARDA DENKEL *Object and property*
E. J. LOWE *Subjects of experience*
NORTON NELKIN *Consciousness and the origins of thought*
PIERRE JACOB *What minds can do*
ANDRE GALLOIS *The world without, the mind within*
D. M. ARMSTRONG *A world of states of affairs*
DAVID COCKBURN *Other times*
MARK LANCE & JOHN O'LEARY-HAWTHORNE *The grammar of meaning*
ANNETTE BARNES *Seeing through self-deception*
DAVID LEWIS *Papers in metaphysics and epistemology*
MICHAEL BRATMAN *Faces of intention*
DAVID LEWIS *Papers in ethics and social philosophy*
MARK ROWLANDS *The body in mind*
LOGI GUNNARSSON *Making moral sense*

Emotional reason

Deliberation, motivation,
and the nature of value

Bennett W. Helm

Franklin & Marshall College, Pennsylvania

CAMBRIDGE
UNIVERSITY PRESS

PUBLISHED BY THE PRESS SYNDICATE OF THE UNIVERSITY OF CAMBRIDGE
The Pitt Building, Trumpington Street, Cambridge, United Kingdom

CAMBRIDGE UNIVERSITY PRESS
The Edinburgh Building, Cambridge CB2 2RU, UK
40 West 20th Street, New York NY 10011–4211, USA
10 Stamford Road, Oakleigh, VIC 3166, Australia
Ruiz de Alarcón 13, 28014 Madrid, Spain
Dock House, The Waterfront, Cape Town 8001, South Africa

http://www.cambridge.org

First published 2001

Printed in the United Kingdom at the University Press, Cambridge

Typeface Bembo 10/12 pt   *System* 3b2   [CE]

A catalogue record for this book is available from the British Library

Library of Congress Cataloguing in Publication data
Helm, Bennett W.
Emotional reason: deliberation, motivation, and the nature of
value / Bennett W. Helm.
p.   cm. – (Cambridge Studies in Philosophy)
Includes bibliographical references and index.
ISBN 0 521 80110 9
1. Emotions (Philosophy).   2. Reasoning.
3. Free will and determinism.   4. Ethics.
I. Title.   II. Series.
B105.E46   H45   2001
128′.37 – dc 21   00–045555

ISBN 0 521 80110 9 hardback

To Karen

Contents

Acknowledgements

I began thinking systematically about the topic of this book in 1997 during Simon Blackburn's National Endowment for the Humanities Summer Seminar, "Objectivity and Emotion in Practical Reason." Thanks to Simon and the other participants in that seminar, especially Justin D'Arms and Daniel Jacobson, for their thoughtful criticisms. Thanks also to Yaroslava Babych and Aleksandra Markovic who, under the aegis of the Franklin & Marshall College Hackman Scholar's Program, provided helpful discussion of the issues raised in §4.3. An initial draft of this book was written with the financial support of a National Endowment for the Humanities Summer Stipend (1998) and an American Council of Learned Societies Fellowship (1998–99); I am grateful to these institutions as well. Finally, thanks to Michael Murray for providing comments on an early draft of the complete manuscript.

Parts of this book have appeared in embryonic form elsewhere. The discussion of freedom of the heart in §6.4 derives from my "Freedom of the Heart," *Pacific Philosophical Quarterly*, 77 (1996), pp. 71–87; the example of Betty in §5.2 and its moral are based on my "Integration and Fragmentation of the Self," *Southern Journal of Philosophy*, 34 (1996), pp. 43–63; and a simplified version of chapter 7 was published as "Emotional Reason: How to Deliberate about Value," *American Philosophical Quarterly*, 37 (2000), pp. 1–22. I am grateful to the editors and publishers of these journals for their permission to use material from these essays.

1

Two problems of practical reason

The idea that a person is a rational animal, as a formula for understanding what is distinctive about persons, has been enormously influential in attempts to understand ourselves as human agents. Of course, insofar as we recognize other animals like dogs and cats as agents, we thereby implicitly understand them as rational in a certain way, for psychological explanation is essentially explanation in terms of reasons. What make us different from mere animals, however, are the distinctive abilities to reason we exhibit. Thus, roughly, our reasons are at least potentially articulate and informed by linguistic concepts, and it is because of our abilities to articulate, clarify, and criticize these reasons that we can self-consciously choose what to believe, do, and value, and why. The possibility of such choice brings with it the possibility for distinctive kinds of freedom: freedom not only to act but also to choose our visions of the good, visions which partly define the kind of persons we are. Moreover, such articulateness and freedom make intelligible our being responsible not only for what we do, but also (and more importantly) for who we are.

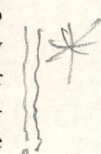

In this brief description, I have already laid out some important features of the kind of reason that defines us as persons: it is linguistically informed, articulate, self-conscious, critical, and *reflexive* – i.e., about not only the world but also ourselves. Merely to identify these features is not, of course, to have a complete account of the nature of human reason, let alone of what it is to be a person, for many puzzles remain. Two such puzzles will be my primary concern. The first, the motivational problem, is a puzzle about the connection between our choosing something as the outcome of deliberation and our being motivated to pursue it. The other, the deliberative problem, concerns the nature of our deliberation about personal values, deliberation which can seem paradoxical insofar as

1

what values we decide upon both is a matter of individual choice (and so is something we freely invent) and is simultaneously accountable to standards of reason (and so is something we can discover). Solving these problems is a necessary step in understanding the kind of reason that defines us as persons. The trouble is, these problems have proved extraordinarily recalcitrant.

As I shall argue in this chapter, such recalcitrance has its source in common philosophical ways of understanding these problems, ways that are rooted in commonly accepted conceptions of rationality (as either epistemic or instrumental) and the nature of the mind quite generally (as divisible into the cognitive and the conative). In §1.2, I shall articulate these common conceptions, arguing in §§1.3–1.4 roughly and in outline how they result in an understanding of the motivational and deliberative problems that blocks any satisfactory solution. This motivates my central claim that if we are to solve these problems we must rethink this common understanding of the mind, rejecting the sharp divide between cognition and conation and the correlative conception of rationality as either epistemic or instrumental. Instead, I shall offer an alternative conception of reason that accords desire and emotion a more central place, an alternative I sketch in §1.5 by way of a preview of the rest of the book. As I shall ultimately argue, this alternative enables me to formulate the motivational and deliberative problems in a way that makes them more tractable and so provides a better understanding of human practical reason as well as of persons.

Insofar as my aim is to understand persons and our mental lives, however, it presupposes a general conception of the nature of the mind and psychological explanation, which I shall now make explicit. Rationality, Donald Davidson rightly claims, is the constitutive ideal of the mental.[1] Part of the point of this claim is to identify a form of explanation distinctive of mental phenomena. Thus, whereas explanation in the physical sciences works by locating physical phenomena within a broader context of other physical objects and events related by laws, explanation of mental phenomena proceeds by locating these phenomena within a broader context of other mental states or events (including intentional action) in such a way as to reveal their rationality. So whereas physical explanation reveals the explanandum as to be expected given the

[1] "Mental Events," in *Essays on Actions and Events* (Oxford: Clarendon, 1980), pp. 207–25, at p. 223. See also Daniel Dennett's "True Believers," in *The Intentional Stance* (Cambridge, MA: MIT Press, 1987), pp. 13–42.

antecedent conditions, psychological explanation reveals the explanandum as what rationally ought to happen.[2]

The claim that rationality is the constitutive ideal of the mental, however, does not concern merely the nature of psychological explanation, for the possibility of explanation in terms of rationality is a condition of the intelligibility of the mental as such. Again, compare this to analogous claims about the physical. We could not make sense of something as physical unless we are potentially willing to locate it within a broader pattern of law-governedness in terms of which it can be explained. Thus, numbers (or, as Davidson has argued, mental phenomena) are not governed by strict laws and so are not physical. If some apparently physical object were consistently to behave in ways that manifestly violate the physical laws as we understand them, our first inclination would be to dismiss it as not real: as an illusion or hallucination. Of course, our first inclination may turn out to be wrong, and so the object may force us to revise, even substantially, our conception of the relevant laws, but this only reinforces the point: the intelligibility of something as physical presupposes that it fits within a pattern of law-governedness, and it is this fact that guides revisions in our understanding of the relevant laws. Hence, law-governedness is the *constitutive ideal* of the physical in that the possibility of explanation in terms of laws is a condition of the intelligibility of the physical as such. Likewise, mental phenomena are intelligible only as located within a broader pattern of rationality in terms of which they can be explained; rationality in this way is constitutive of the mental as such. This needs further clarification.

It would be clearly false to claim that every particular mental state must be identifiable as rational in order to be a mental state at all: irrational beliefs, desires, emotions, etc. are all too common. Rather, rationality is the constitutive ideal of the mental in the sense that a creature is intelligible as an agent, as having various mental capacities, only if its exercise of those capacities is for the most part rational. This "looseness" in the constitutive ideal of the mental therefore makes possible isolated instances of irrationality, but only if they are isolated: too much irrationality destroys the essential background that makes agency possible. Thus, it is possible for a person irrationally to believe falsehoods even when the truth is staring her in the face; yet, as the number of false beliefs and failures to be responsive to manifest truth

---

[2] Cf. William Dray, *Laws and Explanation in History* (Oxford University Press, 1957), especially chapter 5.

increases, it becomes increasingly difficult to make sense of her as understanding the content of what she professes to believe and so as having any beliefs at all about the relevant domain. (Witness, for example, my lack of understanding of or even belief about esoteric areas of theoretical physics.) Too many false beliefs, too many failures of responsiveness to the truth, spread widely enough through the person's system of beliefs therefore erodes the background of epistemic rationality against which her having the capacity for belief at all is intelligible. Likewise, it is possible for someone irrationally to fail to take obvious means to his ends; yet too many such failures, widespread throughout his practical activity, erodes the background of instrumental rationality against which his having the capacity for desire at all is intelligible.

In short, a creature's generally being rational is a condition of the possibility of its being a subject of mental states and so having various mental capacities, though this allows for isolated instances of irrationality. To articulate various kinds of rationality more clearly, such as epistemic or instrumental rationality, is therefore to understand better what it is to be an agent and so to have the relevant mental capacities. It is in this sense that rationality is the constitutive ideal of the mental. Moreover, we can identify and distinguish different kinds of agents by identifying and distinguishing differences in the kinds of rationality proper to them. Thus, to understand the kind of rationality distinctive of persons is nothing other than to understand the nature of personhood itself: a person just is a distinctive kind of rational animal.

1.2 THE COGNITIVE–CONATIVE DIVIDE

Ordinary philosophical understandings of intentional mental states divide them into cognitions and conations. The fundamental difference here is typically captured in terms of the notion of a direction of fit as a way of thinking about the conditions of success of these intentional mental states.[3] Thus, our cognitions, such as belief and judgment, have a *mind-to-world direction of fit* in the sense that when there is a conflict between what we cognize to be the case and what really is the case, it is our cognitions that ought to change in order to conform to the world in order for these cognitions to be successful – to be true. This is because cognitive states are about how things are and so are to be assessed in

---

[3] See, e.g., John Searle's *Intentionality: An Essay in the Philosophy of Mind* (Cambridge University Press, 1983) for a clear account of the notion of a direction of fit.

terms of standards of truth; the world, as that which is true or not, is consequently the source of these standards. By contrast, our conations, such as desire, have a *world-to-mind direction of fit*, for when a conation is unfulfilled, it is the world that ought to be changed in order to conform to our minds in order for our conations to be successful – to be satisfied. Thus, conation is the source of the standards by which we assess the state of the world as satisfactory or not. In each case, it might be thought, the direction of fit provides motivation for change in cases of mismatch: to change one's mind in cases of cognitions, and to change the world in cases of conations. Such motivation for change is rationally required by the kinds of intentionality these states have; consequently, that one generally is motivated in these ways is a condition of the possibility of one's having the capacities for cognition and conation.

Clearly, it seems, these two directions of fit are mutually exclusive. For if the world is the source of the relevant standards for assessing the fitness of the connection between mind and world, as is the case with mind-to-world direction of fit, then the world must have a kind of rational priority over our cognitions; as such, the world cannot simultaneously be liable to correction by our minds, on pain of giving up this priority and so the idea that cognitions are at issue. The converse is true for world-to-mind direction of fit. Consequently, cognitive and conative states seem to be fundamentally different kinds of mental states. Moreover, these two directions of fit seem exhaustive, for the notion of a direction of fit is the notion of the source of a normative standard, and there seems to be no alternative source of such standards than either the mind or the world. Consequently, any intentional mental state must be either a cognition or a conation but not both.

This understanding of cognition and conation as fundamentally different both reinforces and is reinforced by a common conception of reason according to which reason is in general a matter of figuring out how to achieve the requisite correspondence between mind and world, given the appropriate direction of fit; differences in kinds of reason therefore correspond to differences in the requisite direction of fit. Thus, in *theoretical reason* we try to figure out how things are by articulating and applying the norms of epistemic rationality so as to get our thoughts to correspond to the world with the sort of mind-to-world direction of fit characteristic of cognition. Likewise, in *practical reason* we try to figure out how to get the world to correspond to our thoughts by articulating and applying the norms of instrumental rationality; by acting in the ways prescribed by practical reason, we thereby impose on the world the sort of world-to-mind direction of fit characteristic of conation. As with the distinction in kinds of direction of fit, this distinction of reason into theoretical and practical is typically understood to be mutually exclusive and exhaustive.

It might be thought, however, that emotions are exceptions to this claim that all contentful mental states must be either cognitions or conations, with either one or the other direction of fit. Consider even a simple emotion like fear. Fear is a response to one's situation being of a certain kind: something is dangerous. As such, the rational appropriateness of fear depends on the situation really being that way: fear is in part a cognitive state, having a content with mind-to-world direction of fit. Yet fear is also evaluative and motivating. The content of fear is not merely that something is about to be destroyed or harmed, but that this is a bad thing, and as a result one is motivated to do something to prevent or mitigate that harm. In this way, fear is a conative state, with world-to-mind direction of fit. So in a sense fear involves both directions of fit.

Nonetheless, according to philosophical orthodoxy, emotions can be easily accommodated within the theory if we understand these directions of fit as issuing from conceptually separable components of the emotions. Thus, emotions should be understood as compound states and so as consisting of both cognitive and conative states somehow bundled together in a unitary package. This is the idea behind cognitivist theories of emotions, which understand emotions to be reducible to beliefs (as the prototypical cognitive state), desires (as the prototypical conative state), and perhaps some bodily sensation. (So as to avoid confusion of cognitivism about the emotions with cognitivism about values, I shall refer to the former as "*emotional cognitivism.*") Fear, therefore, can be understood as a belief that danger looms, the desire to avoid that danger, and, perhaps, the sensation of a knot in one's stomach.[4] Moreover, this basic reductivist strategy can be applied to all our complex mental states

---

[4] Not all theories of emotions can comfortably be understood as cognitivist in the sense of reducing emotions to beliefs and desires. Robert Roberts and Patricia Greenspan each reject the idea that fear, for example, involves the belief that a danger looms, arguing that we can make better sense of the conflict within a person who is both afraid and believes that there really is no danger if we understand the fear to involve merely the appearance of danger. Nonetheless, the fundamental strategy of understanding emotions in terms of distinct cognitive and conative states remains. (For details, see Roberts' "What an Emotion Is: A Sketch," *Philosophical Review*, 97 (1988), pp. 183–209; and see Greenspan's *Emotions and Reasons: An Inquiry into Emotional Justification* (New York: Routledge, 1988).)

and attitudes, including caring, valuing, loving, trusting, and respecting. Hence, the mind is understood to be fundamentally composed of three kinds of mental state: cognition and conation, as well as non-intentional qualia.

Both this conception of rationality as either epistemic or instrumental (but not both) and the conception of contentful mental states as either cognitions or conations (but not both) seem inevitable. The result is that cognition comes to be seen as intrinsically more rational than conation in two ways. First, we can understand only our cognitions as fully rational in that they are always subject to correction because of the norms of theoretical rationality in light of the mind-to-world direction of fit they display. Conations, with their world-to-mind direction of fit, cannot be rationally assessed in this way, and so are intrinsically less rational than our cognitions. Of course, our conations are "correctable" insofar as we can subject them to norms of consistency and coherence, especially in light of instrumental rationality, but there is nothing outside conation to which they must be answerable, on pain of giving up the idea that these are conations and not cognitions. Second, insofar as reasoning is a matter of figuring out how to achieve the relevant correspondence between mind and world and so issues in a practical or theoretical judgment, our ability to reason is a cognitive rather than a conative ability. For, as a result of deliberation, we come to articulate in judgment our best understanding of how things are or of what to do, an understanding that, because it can be explicitly confronted with the world through the application of epistemic and instrumental reason, has a claim to objectivity. By contrast, our emotions and non-instrumental desires are subjective and less rational: to the extent that our emotions and desires are merely affective, they do not reflect at all how things objectively are and so cannot be held to rational standards except those of consistency and coherence.[5]

This account of cognition and conation as mutually exclusive and exhaustive categories of intentional mental states, together with the correlative account of epistemic and instrumental rationality, I shall call the "*cognitive–conative divide*." Of course, the cognitive–conative divide is somewhat of a caricature; nonetheless, the basic view is extremely seductive and is deeply entrenched in philosophical thinking about the

---

[5] Of course, to the extent that our emotions have a cognitive element and so are about the world, they are answerable to judgment, which always rationally trumps them in cases of conflict.

mind quite generally and moral psychology in particular. As I shall now (in §§1.3–1.4) suggest more than argue, this cognitive–conative divide underlies our ordinary understanding of the motivational and deliberative problems and makes the solutions to these problems intractable. This makes way for my central claim, sketched in §1.5, that the real solution is to reject the cognitive–conative divide and thereby reconceive the motivational and deliberative problems in a way that makes their solutions more readily apparent.

1.3 THE MOTIVATIONAL PROBLEM

As I indicated in §1.1, the motivational problem is a problem about the connection between deliberative choice and motivation. On the face of it, it seems there must be a tight connection between the decisions we make as the result of deliberation about what to do and what we are motivated to do, for it is by making such decisions that we exercise control over our motivations. Indeed, it can seem, somewhat naïvely, that to make such a decision just is to be motivated to act accordingly. The difficulty arises, however, when we are confronted with phenomena like those of weakness of the will and listlessness, which seem to undermine any straightforward conceptual connection between our considered evaluative judgments and motivation.

To see this, consider the following standard example. You can look at the chocolate cake, decide that, all things considered, it is best not to have a second piece right now, but nonetheless take and eat it, even while saying to yourself, "I shouldn't be doing this," and trying not to. Here you evaluate more cake as bad, struggle not to eat any, but end up doing so anyway: you suffer from *weakness of the will*. In extreme cases, you can make this evaluation that having more cake is bad but not feel at all motivated to act in accordance with it and so not struggle at all to overcome your akratic appetite; such complete failures of motivation are cases of *listlessness*. On the face of it, the risk of weakness or listlessness is ever present, and this is what makes it so philosophically troubling. For such a risk seems completely to sever any conceptual connection between evaluation and motivation, between practical reason and action. The naïve view of evaluative judgment as itself essentially motivating must simply be wrong, for the connection between evaluation and motivation seems to be, even when it is in place, only contingent and fortuitous. Consequently, the *motivational problem* emerges as the problem of understanding how, in the face of the possibility of phenomena like weakness of the will and listlessness, it is possible to have control over what we do.

In response to the motivational problem, a common strategy is simply to accept the division between our practical, evaluative judgments and motivation, evidenced in these cases of weakness of the will and listlessness, as a persistent feature of our psychological heritage: there is an *inevitable motivational gap* between practical judgment and desire, a gap that must somehow be bridged by something other than further deliberation and judgment if such deliberation is to have an effect on our actions.[6] The motivational problem is thereby conceived as the problem of how it is possible to bridge this inevitable motivational gap in cases in which we are not listless or weak willed, and it can be solved, therefore, only by postulating some contingent mechanism outside deliberation that connects the two.

Indeed, such a strategy seems to be forced on us by the assumption of the cognitive–conative divide, for our practical judgments, it seems, cannot themselves be conations, or listlessness – our making practical judgments but being wholly unmoved by them – would be impossible.[7] Yet if our practical judgments are cognitions, then, according to the cognitive–conative divide, they must be conceptually distinct from particular conations: cognitions and conations are mutually exclusive. Consequently, it might seem, one can always have the cognition without having any of the relevant conations motivating one to act accordingly, and one can always have the conation without making any corresponding practical judgment. To be committed to some content having one direction of fit in no way requires or presupposes that one is committed to a similar content with the opposite direction of fit. Cognitions and conations are, in this sense, *distinct existences*, and it is precisely for this reason that the motivational gap between them seems inevitable.[8]

---

[6] Michael Smith, for example, adopts this strategy; see his *The Moral Problem* (Oxford: Blackwell, 1994). I shall discuss Smith, and motivational externalism more generally, in more detail in §6.2.1.

[7] Actually, this strategy is not forced on us: some motivational internalists who accept the cognitive–conative divide do not adopt it. I shall discuss motivational internalism in more detail in §6.2.2.

[8] Notice that in understanding cognition and conation to be distinct existences, those who accept the cognitive–conative divide need not understand our capacities for cognition and conation to be conceptually independent. As Carl Hempel has argued, we must at least accept an epistemic interdependence: we cannot know what cognitions a creature

9

I shall now suggest that this account of the motivational problem, in light of the assumption of the cognitive–conative divide, makes its solution impossible. Part of the problem lies in understanding the relevant kind of control in question. Consider, by way of comparison, the way in which I can exercise control over a remote-controlled car. When I control the car, I do so by exploiting the causal connections between the positions of the various switches and dials on the control box and what happens in the car. Thus, to make the car go straight, I must continually make readjustments to the dials on the control box so as to overcome extraneous causal influences on the car: a bumpy road, a strong cross-wind, etc. Such an exploitation of causal connections is the nature of my control over the car, and in the absence of these causal connections I lose control entirely.

By contrast, the exploitation of such causal connections cannot be the whole story about how we can exercise control over our motivation. For, in controlling my motivation, I exploit not merely contingent causal connections between my practical judgments and my desires but also rational connections between the contents of my judgments and the objects of my desires: I exploit my appreciation of the reasons my judgments provide for having and acting on these desires. Thus, faced with the possibility of a second piece of chocolate cake, I judge that I should not have one now because, although eating it would be pleasurable, my concern to eat well outweighs the momentary pleasure I would get here and now from eating it. It is my appreciation of this reason that can motivate and ought to motivate me to resist the cake or even no longer to find it tempting. Hence, the relevant kind of control we can have over our motivations is *rational control* – control by virtue of an appreciation of reasons – and should not be assimilated to the kind of causal control we can have over ordinary physical objects.[9]

The trouble is, such distinctively rational control is incompatible with the assumption of the cognitive–conative divide. For this assumption, by

---

has without also knowing what conations it has, and vice versa. (See his "Aspects of Scientific Explanation," in *Aspects of Scientific Explanation and Other Essays in the Philosophy of Science* [New York: The Free Press, 1965], pp. 331–496, especially §10.3.2.) Moreover, it is consistent with the cognitive–conative divide to take this interdependence of the capacities to be ontological, a condition of the possibility of having the capacities at all. That is why I put the claim of conceptual distinctness at issue in the cognitive–conative divide in terms of any two particular instances of cognition and conation.

9 Cf. Susan Wolf's *Freedom Within Reason* (New York: Oxford University Press, 1990), especially chapter 3.

forcing us to conceive of cognition and conation as distinct existences, separated by an inevitable motivational gap, requires that we somehow bridge the gap. But what bridges the gap cannot be either a cognition or a conation, for these merely stand on opposite sides of the gap. This means that what bridges the gap cannot be intentional, for intentional states must be, given the assumption, either cognitive or conative. Yet, if it is not intentional, then it is mysterious how it could be properly responsive to the reasons we have for acting, and any coincidence between our reasons and our motivation would then only occur by chance or good fortune. At best, therefore, what bridges the gap seems to present merely the illusion of control and not genuinely rational control. That is not so much a solution to the motivational problem as capitulation in the face of it.

As I shall suggest in §1.5, the real solution is to reject the assumption of the cognitive–conative divide and so to reconceive the relation between practical judgment and desire: what is needed is a conception of desires as themselves susceptible to the reasons for action we come to accept in judgment and so as more than mere conations. Of course, what I have offered here is far from a complete argument against this assumption, and I shall, in chapter 6, discuss a variety of specific positions, both internalist and externalist, on how control over our motivations is possible given the assumption of the cognitive–conative divide. Nonetheless, we already have one reason motivating a reconsideration of this assumption. Another stems from the deliberative problem.

1.4 THE DELIBERATIVE PROBLEM

As I suggested in §1.1, part of what is definitive about persons is our ability to deliberate about and so choose our visions of the good, our values, which partly define the kind of persons we are; the possibility of such reasoning, therefore, enables us to have a say in, and so be responsible for, who we are. The questions at the heart of the deliberative problem are: how is such deliberation possible and what is the source of the norms governing both how we deliberate and the conclusions we reach?

In asking these questions about how deliberation about value is possible, I have in mind primarily personal values rather than moral values. That is because my concern is with how practical reasoning

11

enters into our freedom to define ourselves and so our responsibility for who we are. For *personal values*, unlike moral values, are values that are relative to the individual in the sense that what personal values it is right for me to hold may well differ from those it is right for you to hold, and so personal values are what make a distinctive contribution to my identity as a person. Henceforth, when I speak of values, I shall intend personal values unless explicitly noted otherwise. (Nonetheless, I shall also be concerned with how we can reason about those cares and concerns that are not so "deep" as personal values insofar as they do not enter into one's conception of the kind of person it is worth being.)

In general, questions about what is worth pursuing or who it is worth being cannot be answered by appealing to instrumental reasoning. For *instrumental reasoning* is simply a matter of figuring out how to attain a given end; as a result, the value of the means we discover by instrumental reasoning derives from the antecedent value of that end, which is simply presupposed. However, because deliberation about value, especially at the deepest level, is concerned precisely with the value of these "ultimate" ends, instrumental reasoning alone is not sufficient as an account of such deliberation. What, then, can we add to instrumental reasoning to fill in this gap and so provide an account of how deliberation about value, with its requisite normative force, is possible?[10]

What makes this question so difficult to answer is that our understanding of personal value is pulled in seemingly opposed directions of objectivity and subjectivity. On the one hand, a person's values are at least in part up to her, and are in this sense subjective: she can have a say in creating or *inventing* the kind of person it is worth her being. To be able to invent ourselves in this way is to have a kind of freedom that is distinctly human: a freedom not merely to control our actions but more

---

[10] Recent interpreters of Aristotle, such as John Cooper (*Reason and Human Good in Aristotle* [Cambridge, MA: Harvard University Press, 1975]), Miles Burnyeat ("Aristotle on Learning to Be Good," in Amélie Rorty, ed., *Essays on Aristotle's Ethics* [Berkeley: University of California Press, 1980], pp. 69–92), David Wiggins ("Deliberation and Practical Reason," *Proceedings of the Aristotelian Society*, 76 [1975–76], pp. 29–51), and John McDowell ("The Role of *Eudaimonia* in Aristotle's Ethics," *The Proceedings of the African Classical Associations*, 15 [1980]) have thought that he distinguishes instrumental reasoning from *constitutive reasoning*, which concerns how more completely to articulate vaguely specified ends such as that of a good vacation or a good life (*eudaimonia*). Merely to speak of constitutive reasoning, however, is so far merely to provide a label for a kind of reasoning rather than a clear account of how such reasoning can proceed or of its normative foundations. Thus, "How is constitutive reasoning about eudaimonia possible?" is just another way of formulating the problem.

fundamentally to govern ourselves; call this freedom *"autonomy"*. Thus it is inconsistent with our autonomy that the source of the norms at issue in the kind of person it is worth our being be wholly external to us; rather, to be autonomous is for the source of those norms to be at least partially within one's understanding of who one is to be. In being autonomous, therefore, we can choose certain values, and by making these choices we determine our reasons.

On the other hand, there seems also to be an element of objectivity in what values a person holds in that she can deliberate about them correctly or incorrectly. Deliberation is a matter of choosing for reasons, thereby making possible the articulation of why one course of life is better than another, so that it is not intellectually arbitrary which values we choose. Hence through deliberation we can *discover* the values things really have and so the kind of person it is worth our being, potentially overcoming delusions or misunderstandings about ourselves. The possibility of such discovery means that there are rational constraints on which values we can autonomously choose. The claim here is not merely that there are some values it is (perhaps morally) impermissible to choose, such as the value of bigotry; nor is it that the constraint is merely that of internal consistency. If those were the only constraints, we could view the choice of personal values as one of selecting arbitrarily from among the many internally consistent, morally permissible values. Yet our choice of personal values and so our understanding of the kind of person it is worth each of us being is not arbitrary in this way. For we think it is possible to have better or worse reasons for such choices, reasons we might discover only through much effort and soul-searching. The demand for discovery and objectivity is a demand to rule out this kind of arbitrariness. This means that the relevant reasons must govern our choices not merely in the sense that we happen to feel compelled to choose in accordance with these reasons (because, perhaps, they merely seem to justify our choices), but that these reasons succeed in justifying those choices, for it is only this success that can ground the relevant kind of objectivity.

These pulls toward autonomous invention and rational discovery seem, on the face of it, to be equally essential to our understanding of ourselves as persons. On the one hand, to give up on the pull toward invention is to give up on our autonomy, our ability to have a say in the kind of person it is worth our being and thereby to take responsibility for who we are. Yet this ability both to call our lives into question and, having done so, to determine what life it is worth leading is fundamental to distinguishing ourselves as persons from the animals. There are, surely, other differences between persons and animals, such as our linguistic ability and our self-consciousness, but autonomy is fundamental insofar as it is because we are autonomous that we can understand how these other differences contribute to a distinction in kind and not merely in degree. On the other hand, to give up on the pull towards discovery is to concede that our choices of values are arbitrary, lacking any rational justification. Yet an arbitrarily chosen life lacks the kind of grounding that is precisely the point of our deliberation about value: to attain through the discovery of such grounds a depth of meaning in our lives that would be wholly lacking in a life chosen arbitrarily. Consequently, to give up on either invention or discovery is to give up on a dimension of ourselves that diminishes our status as persons.

The problem is that such talk of rational discovery seems to leave no room for autonomous invention, and vice versa. How can we make sense of the possibility of getting our values (objectively) right or wrong when we are the ones (subjectively) determining the standards of correctness? This difficulty, which I shall call the *apparent paradox of simultaneous autonomous invention and rational discovery*, seems to under-mine our best attempts at getting clearer on the kind of deliberation at issue here. This apparent paradox therefore seems to force us to give up on one or the other of these dimensions of our understanding of persons, both of which seem essential. The *deliberative problem*, then, emerges as the problem of understanding how deliberation about value is possible while both finding a way out of this apparent paradox and maintaining a reasonably robust conception of ourselves as persons.[11]

I shall now suggest more than argue that the deliberative problem is unsolvable if we make the assumption of the cognitive–conative divide.[12] This assumption forces us to conceive our deliberation about values in one of two ways, depending on whether the task is understood as a cognitive or a conative matter. First, according to *cognitivist theories of value*, there are facts about the values things really have that are

[11] In setting up the deliberative problem in this way, I have been strongly influenced by Charles Taylor; see especially his *Human Agency and Language: Philosophical Papers 1* (Cambridge University Press, 1985).

[12] Once again, my aim here is only to motivate a careful re-examination of the cognitive–conative divide; clearer arguments will be provided in chapter 7 in light of a detailed examination of the literature.

ontologically prior to what we think these values to be.[13] Consequently, the task in deliberation is a cognitive task: one of getting our evaluative beliefs accurately to mirror the world in light of evidence that justifies those beliefs epistemically. Except insofar as they can serve as a source of evidence, emotion and desire are therefore simply irrelevant to the task of deliberation. Second, according to *non-cognitivist theories of value*, ontologically prior to conation there is no fact about what values things have; rather these values are intelligible as existing in the world only as projected there by our evaluative sensibilities, paradigmatically our emotions and desires.[14] Given this ontological priority, the non-cognitivist claims, we cannot appeal to these projected values in order to explain or justify our sensibilities. The task of deliberation, therefore, is to get our evaluative sensibilities somehow into good shape, for example in light of non-epistemic demands of consistency.

Cognitivist theories may seem clearly able to make good sense of the idea that we discover value, for discovery is fundamentally a cognitive affair, a matter of getting our minds to conform to the world. This might be thought a strength of the view when it comes to moral value, the primary target of cognitivism, for we do not think moral values are simply up to each of us to choose individually. It is, however, problematic when we consider personal value, for it is precisely because of its construal of discovery that cognitivism cannot make sense of the idea that we invent value, that we can have a say in defining the kind of person it is worth being. If discovery were understood as the confrontation of an antecedent fact of the matter concerning what values we should adopt, there would simply be no room for our input; rather we would simply have to conform our evaluative attitudes to these facts on pain of irrationality. To be a cognitivist about personal values, therefore, is to give up on the conception of ourselves as autonomous, as able to have a say in the kind of life it is worth our living, and, as I argued above, this is to give up too much. Cognitivism therefore fails as a solution to the deliberative problem.

---

[13] See, for example, Peter Railton, "Moral Realism," *Philosophical Review*, 95 (1986), pp. 163–207, and Richard Boyd, "How to Be a Moral Realist," in Stephen Darwall, Allan Gibbard, and Peter Railton, eds., *Moral Discourse and Practice* (Oxford: Clarendon, 1997), pp. 105–35. I shall discuss cognitivist theories of value more thoroughly in §7.1.1.

[14] See, e.g., Allan Gibbard, *Wise Choices, Apt Feelings: A Theory of Normative Judgment* (Cambridge, MA: Harvard University Press, 1990), and Simon Blackburn, *Ruling Passions: The Theory of Practical Reason* (Oxford: Clarendon, 1998). I shall discuss non-cognitivist theories of value more fully in §7.1.2.

Of course, a cognitivist might try to make room for the idea of invention in one of two ways. First, a cognitivist might attempt to accommodate this idea by noting that which values we discover depends on the particular route we take in deliberation. Since we can control the course of our deliberation, we can therefore control which values we discover thereby and in this way have a say in defining the kind of person it is worth our being. However, this tack leaves us with too thin a notion of discovery, of objectivity. For it conceives of deliberation as a matter of coming across only some values out of the total range of values there are, such that our input to deliberation is merely a matter of selecting some subset of these values as properly ours. Yet this selection is itself merely arbitrary: we can offer no reason for adopting the values thereby selected over other values other than that we happened across these first. The point of the requirement of objectivity, however, is precisely to rule out such arbitrariness so as to be able to attain a depth of meaning in our lives. The first tack therefore fails.

A second way in which a cognitivist might try to make room for invention is this. Insofar as we can act so as to change the world, we can change in particular those aspects of the world that have a bearing on what values there are so that, when we go to discover these values, we discover different values than we otherwise would have. In this way, it might be thought, we can have a say in what these values are and thereby accommodate the idea of invention. However, this accommodation either is an illusion or gives up too much by way of objectivity. For, in acting so as to change the values things have, we either act for a reason or not. If we act for a reason, such a reason – to change the values things have – must itself be a value and so (on the cognitivist conception) must be a potential object of discovery over which we have no control; thus, the idea that we can by so acting invent value must be only an illusion. If we act for no reason, then we reveal our choice of which values to invent to be merely arbitrary, and we have thereby lost the relevant notion of objectivity. This second tack therefore fails as well.

If cognitivism fails to solve the deliberative problem because of its emphasis on discovery at the expense of invention, it may seem that we are forced to non-cognitivism in order to make sense of that invention. After all, insofar as, according to non-cognitivism, values are projected by our evaluative sensibilities, we are the ones who determine what values things have for us. How, then, can non-cognitivism handle the idea that our evaluative sensibilities can go right or wrong, that there are rational standards at issue here? We cannot understand our values to serve as the relevant standard, for that would be to understand our sensibilities as answerable to the world, as on the cognitivist account. Rather, non-cognitivism understands our sensibilities to be ontologically prior to the values things have, and that is what the metaphor of projection is meant to convey. Consequently, to make sense of such a standard, non-cognitivism can appeal only to the sensibilities we actually have and to standards of rationality internal to these sensibilities themselves: standards of coherence and, perhaps, the stability of these sensibilities in the face of pressures to change them. This would mean that deliberation can go right or wrong in the sense that it attains or fails to attain a pattern of sensibilities that is stable and coherent; when it goes right, a non-cognitivist can say, we have discovered the values things have for us.

This account of discovery, however, is too weak to ground the relevant kind of objectivity our values can have. For presumably there will be many stable and coherent patterns of sensibilities we could have, and so many systems of values that can be understood as correct for us to adopt. On what basis, then, is a person to choose from among these systems of values the one that defines the kind of person it is worth his being? To this question the non-cognitivist can have no answer: each is as fully "right" as any other, and you simply have to pick arbitrarily among them. Again, such arbitrariness is at odds with the robust notion of objectivity and discovery at issue in our conception of ourselves as persons. Put another way, the objection is this: in response to the question of why you value something, it is insufficient to answer that this value figures in a stable and internally coherent system of sensibilities. For such a formal requirement on our sensibilities does not address the question, which is after the content of the value: what is so valuable about it? The demand for objectivity is the demand that the value something has itself serve as a justification for our evaluative sensibilities, and this is precisely what the non-cognitivist rules out by the appeal to conation. Non-cognitivism can therefore offer only a thin and seemingly inadequate surrogate for discovery, and this pushes us back to cognitivism as an account of the element of discovery.

In short, if we accept the cognitive–conative divide, we must understand the discovery of value in cognitive terms as a matter of matching our thoughts to a mind-independent world, and we must understand the invention of value in conative terms as a matter of projecting our evaluative attitudes onto the world. Autonomous invention and rational discovery are therefore mutually exclusive and exhaustive: we must either accept the priority of value over our thoughts (and so be cognitivists) or accept the priority of our evaluative sensibilities over value (and so be non-cognitivists), but not both. Consequently, the deliberative problem is thereby conceived as a genuine paradox of simultaneous invention and discovery, thus forcing us to choose (as cognitivists and non-cognitivists do) discovery instead of invention or vice versa, thereby giving up part of what is fundamental to personhood.

It should be clear that these are not by any means knock-down arguments against cognitivism or non-cognitivism. More sophisticated versions of these doctrines purport to answer the objections I have just raised, and I shall consider these views in more detail in chapter 7. My aim here, however, is merely to outline the difficulties for each view and to suggest the following diagnosis: what forces the choice between a robust notion of invention and a robust notion of discovery is the assumption of the cognitive–conative divide on which these two doctrines depend; we can avoid having to make the choice, and so the difficulties that choice presents, by rejecting that divide in the first place.

This can be seen in light of the following objection. It may seem that I am illegitimately casting the deliberative problem in terms of a contrast between invention and discovery. Really, one might say, the issue ought to be cast in terms of autonomy and rational constraint, and here it might seem that there is no conflict: our freedom to determine the kind of person it is worth being is not at all undermined by the presence of reasons supporting one view of the matter over another. Indeed, following Descartes' account in the 4th Meditation, we might say that we are most free precisely when our decisions are made in the light of substantive reasons rather than arbitrarily. Consequently, it might seem, the deliberative problem is merely the result of my miscasting of the issues.

So far, I think this view of autonomy and reason is exactly right, though I do not think it renders the deliberative problem moot. The difficulty arises when we notice that the relevant kind of autonomy at issue in the deliberative problem is in effect freedom to determine what our reasons are. To have a say in the kind of person it is worth my being is not merely to defer to pre-existing reasons and shape my life accordingly; it is, rather, to shape the reasons and so the worthiness of this kind of life themselves. So the problem becomes one of how, given this conception of autonomy, we can be under substantive rational constraint in determining what our most basic reasons are. Indeed, given the cognitive–conative divide, this can only be paradoxical in precisely the way the image of simultaneous invention and discovery suggests: either we alone determine what our reasons are by virtue of conation, in which case we are not subject to any substantive rational constraint while doing so, or, if we are subject to such constraint, then it is cognition that is so constrained and so its object, as ontologically prior to that cognition, is not something we have a say in determining. Consequently, one who accepts the cognitive–conative divide must cast the issue in terms of a contrast between invention and discovery: either these reasons must be potential objects of cognition and, because of its mind-to-world direction of fit, discovery, or they must be potential objects of conation and, because of its world-to-mind direction of fit, invention, but not both. Once again, the apparent paradox at the heart of the deliberative problem has become a genuine paradox given this acceptance of the cognitive–conative divide.

If we reject the cognitive–conative divide, however, we can thereby reject the implicit assumption that either the values things have or our evaluations must be ontologically prior to the other. Thus, we can say that the kind of person it is worth our being is subjective and so potentially an object of autonomous invention insofar as there is no fact independent of the evaluative perspectives we actually adopt as to what this kind of person is. This is a denial of the ontological priority of value over our sensibilities, though it does not amount (as it would if we assumed the cognitive–conative divide) to an affirmation of the reverse priority. Likewise, we can say that the kind of person it is worth our being is nonetheless objective and so potentially an object of discovery insofar as we cannot make out what that kind of person is without appealing to the values things actually have. Once again, this is the denial of the ontological priority of our sensibilities over the values things have, and it is a denial wholly consistent with the above conception of subjectivity and invention.[15]

This understanding of simultaneous invention and discovery of value

---

[15] Such a "no-priority view" is roughly the sort of view advocated by John McDowell ("Values and Secondary Qualities," in Ted Honderich, ed., *Morality and Objectivity: A Tribute to J. L. Mackie* [London: Routledge & Kegan Paul, 1985], pp. 110–29), David Wiggins ("A Sensible Subjectivism," in *Needs, Values, Truth: Essays in the Philosophy of Value*, 2nd edition [Oxford: Blackwell, 1991], pp. 185–214), and Charles Taylor (*Human Agency and Language*); I shall discuss these authors in more detail in §7.2.

is, therefore, circular, but that does not mean that the circularity is vicious. (Indeed, what would make the circularity seem vicious is the assumption of the cognitive–conative divide – that there must be ontological priority one way or the other.) The trouble is that to make such an account convincing we need to provide a clear understanding of our mental states and their connection to value that is an alternative to those permitted by the cognitive–conative divide (i.e., cognitivism and non-cognitivism), for it is only in light of such an account that the charge of vicious circularity can be rebutted. To a large extent, that is my aim in this book.[16]

1.5 REJECTING THE DIVIDE: A PREVIEW

I have suggested that the assumption of the cognitive–conative divide and of the corresponding conception of rationality as either epistemic or instrumental underlies our conceptions of the motivational and deliberative problems and so has resulted in an unsatisfactory understanding of ourselves and how we can reason practically. Thus, on the one hand, the split between cognition and conation results in an understanding of the motivational problem as that of how to bridge the inevitable gap between cognition and conation. As I argued, this understanding of the problem seems to force us to see practical reason as only contingently and fortuitously connected with motivation, thereby undermining any resulting account of how we can rationally control what we do. On the other hand, this split results in an understanding of the deliberative problem in terms of a genuine paradox of simultaneous invention and discovery, a paradox which forces the choice between cognitivism and non-cognitivism, between an emphasis on the cognitive and the idea of rational discovery and an emphasis on the conative and the idea of autonomous invention. No matter which of these options we choose, it seems, we are led to give up an important dimension of our understanding of ourselves: as autonomous and so responsible for the kind of persons we are, or as able non-arbitrarily to reason about who to be and so to discover what has meaning in our lives.

In spite of their entrenchment in philosophical understandings of the mind, these conceptions of cognition, conation, and rationality are not

---

[16] Indeed, part of my complaint about McDowell's, Wiggins', and Taylor's theories is that they fail to present their views in light of an explicit account of what our mental states would look like once we reject the cognitive–conative divide.

obligatory. My aim in this book is to argue for an alternative conception of evaluative judgment, desire, and emotion as each being essentially both cognitive and conative in a way that cannot be analyzed into separable components. In essence, this is to undercut the traditional cognitive–conative divide in a way that enables me to reconceive both the motivational and deliberative problems. As a result, we should not conceive of the motivational problem as that of figuring out how to bridge an inevitable gap between evaluation and reason on the one side and motivation on the other. Rather, I shall argue, potential (but not inevitable) gaps between evaluation and motivation can arise entirely within reason, so that nothing extra-rational is required to bridge such gaps. Moreover, once we reject the cognitive–conative divide, we should not conceive of the deliberative problem as simply a choice between cognitivism and non-cognitivism. Rather, we can understand the standards of deliberation about value as partially within our evaluative sensibilities and so as in a sense invented by us, while still being genuine standards that enable us to discover personal value.

In each case, the reconception of the problem and so of what is needed in order to solve it depends on an understanding of our emotions and desires as making a distinctive contribution to reason, thus enabling us to see rationality as more than just epistemic or instrumental. In Part I, I aim to provide an account of our emotions and desires that makes this possible. My aim in chapter 2, "Emotions and the cognitive–conative divide," is essentially to clear the ground of competing accounts of emotion and desire so as to make room for the kind of account I shall offer. In attempting to solve the mind–body problem, philosophers of mind typically offer accounts of the intentionality of desire that ignore a central feature of desire, namely that it views its object as worthy of pursuit or avoidance – as having import. Making sense of such import, therefore, is central to solving the mind–body problem, though this is a problem that is typically simply ignored within philosophy of mind. I suggest that we can achieve an account of import if we turn to a rather natural understanding of emotions as essentially pleasures and pains: to feel such a pleasure or pain is to "feel" an evaluation of one's situation, where such an evaluative feeling seems to be an appropriate source of the imports things have for us. This account of emotions, however, conflicts with standard cognitivist theories of emotions, which presuppose the cognitive–conative divide. I argue that such accounts fail to be accounts of emotions, ultimately diagnosing their failure to lie with that

21

presupposition. Consequently, I argue, solving the problem import presents is impossible under the assumption of the cognitive–conative divide.

In chapter 3, "Constituting import," I fill in the account of emotions sketched in chapter 2 in terms of a more fundamental notion of a *felt evaluation* in such a way as to solve the problem of import. At the core of this account is a distinctive analysis of the notions of pleasure and pain. Emotions are pleasures and pains not in that they somehow involve bodily sensations; rather, I argue, emotions can be redescribed as pleasures and pains: to feel fear just is to be pained by danger. The point of this redescription is twofold. First, it highlights the idea that emotions are evaluations. I argue that such evaluations are best made sense of as a kind of intentional awareness of import, for the rational warrant of emotions depends in part on whether they are properly responsive to the imports things have. Consequently, import must have a kind of objectivity that is presupposed by particular emotions. Second, the redescription of emotions as pleasures and pains makes intelligible the fact that emotions motivate us in certain ways. I argue that talk of pleasure and pain in these two contexts of evaluation and motivation is univocal, for to feel pleasure and pain – to feel the import of one's situation in this way – just is to feel a motivational pull. In this respect, emotions involve both cognitive and conative elements, though these elements are not intelligible as isolable components. Indeed, I argue, this same account applies as well to desires and, surprisingly, to bodily pleasures and pains. This understanding of emotions, desires, and bodily pleasures and pains as simultaneously responsive to import and motivating in a way that rejects the cognitive–conative divide is part of what I intend in calling them "felt evaluations."

I have said that particular felt evaluations presuppose import as a feature of the world to which they can be correctly or incorrectly responsive. Yet import is also subjective insofar as my cares and personal values need not be shared by others. How is this dual objectivity and subjectivity possible? The answer lies in understanding import as emerging in part out of patterns of felt evaluations. Such patterns should not be understood as mere dispositions to feel emotions or desires; rather, the patterns are *rational* both in that they are imposed by rational commitments among emotions and desires and in that they are partially constitutive of the warrant of their constituents. In this way, import is both *objective* insofar as it is ontologically prior to particular felt evaluations, which are responsive to it, and nonetheless *subjective* insofar as it is partly constituted by the rational patterns of one's felt evaluations; indeed, this is another fundamental feature of felt evaluations made possible by the account I provide of their mutual rational commitments. (Of course, this account of felt evaluations has not yet made intelligible a deeper level of objectivity needed for a solution to the deliberative problem, namely that it is possible to discover what imports things should have for you. More on that in Part II.)

In chapter 4, "Varieties of import," I extend this account of import in two ways. First, I articulate more clearly the intuitive distinction between our cares and values and offer an account of this distinction, and so of the relative "depth" of values, in terms of a distinction between reflexive and non-reflexive felt evaluations, which define different kinds of rational patterns. Second, I examine the ways in which the imports of different things are related to each other, both instrumentally and in terms of degree of import. In part, the notion of degree of import can be understood in terms of the strength or intensity of the desires and emotions that constitute the relevant pattern, thereby complicating our understanding of the kind of rationality these patterns involve. Yet relative importance involves more than just a difference in intensity, and I argue that it can be properly understood only by expanding our understanding of felt evaluations to include a sense of relative import as a distinctive kind of responsiveness to particular situations.

The upshot of Part I, therefore, is a new conception of emotion and desire as neither cognitions nor conations (nor compound states of cognition and conation). Rather, given their connection to import, emotions and desires share features of both cognition and conation in a way that requires rejecting those categories of mental state and replacing them with a new one: felt evaluations. It should be clear, however, that this new understanding of emotions and desires as felt evaluations requires as well a new understanding of the kinds of rationality that apply to them. In articulating the kinds of rational patterns of felt evaluations constitutive of import, I am in effect articulating a distinct kind of rationality: a rationality of import.

In Part II, I turn my attention to our ability to reason about what to do and who to be and so to the ways our understanding of this ability has been transformed by the account of felt evaluations, import, and the rationality of import. As I indicated above, the account of import offered so far is incomplete. For, we cannot yet make sense of there being reasons to change what has import for you and so of what should have import; this is, in essence, the deliberative problem. Moreover, we cannot yet make sense of how we can have control over what we do, for the account of motivation, tied as it is to seemingly passive states of emotion and desire, so far makes no room for deliberation; this is, in essence, the motivational problem. Remedying these deficiencies requires examining how evaluative judgment is connected to the sort of felt evaluations discussed so far.

In chapter 5, "Single evaluative perspective," I argue that emotions and evaluative judgments are rationally interconnected in that each can, in a way, correct the other. In particular, a general failure of the sort of emotional response called for by evaluative judgment tends to undermine the rationality of that judgment and so make it that one ought to reconsider that judgment. In virtue of these rational interconnections, I argue, emotions must be understood as concept-laden, passive assents, and evaluative judgments must be understood as having (or lacking) a kind of emotional depth; evaluative judgments and emotions therefore normally constitute a single evaluative perspective. In this way, evaluative judgment is brought into the same rational pattern of felt evaluations constitutive of import.

I exploit this account of a single evaluative perspective in chapter 6 ("Rational control: freedom of the will and the heart") in offering a solution to the motivational problem. For, other things being equal, having deliberated and arrived at an evaluative judgment, the evaluative perspective that judgment provides will *ipso facto* be an emotional perspective as well, on pain of undermining the rationality of that judgment. Insofar as emotions (and desires) are felt evaluations, they are in part motivational states. So there is a conceptual, rational connection between deliberative judgment and motivation, a connection that enables us to exercise rational control over our motivations by deliberating and judging.

Of course, the devil is in the details, for the brief description of the account I have given so far makes it look as if weakness of the will – being motivated to act contrary to your deliberate choice – is impossible. By exploiting features of the precise nature of the rational interconnections among evaluative judgments, emotions, and desires, I show how it is possible for our evaluative perspective to be divided in such a way that we are motivated contrary to our deliberative judgment. Attaining rational control, therefore, is in large part a matter of being able to regain a single evaluative perspective (and not by merely capitulating in judgment to our emotions and desires). This requires an account of the nature of the will – of how through evaluative judgment we can control our actions directly – and, more fundamentally, of how we can thereby rationally control our emotions and desires and so achieve a kind of freedom, distinct from freedom of action and freedom of the will, which I call "freedom of the heart." Consequently, the idea that we generally have rational control over what we do is not threatened by the possibility of weakness of will, and the motivational problem is thereby solved.

In chapter 7 ("Deliberation about value"), I turn to tackle the deliberative problem. Here I exploit the account of the rational interconnections among emotions and evaluative judgments, including the account of the concept-ladenness of emotion, to provide an account of import as an evaluatively thick property, and so as a potential object of discovery, that nonetheless is not rationally prior to the rational patterns of our judgments and emotions and so is also an object of invention. Central to the account is an understanding of how we can elucidate and refine the evaluative concepts in terms of which we deliberate about, criticize, and justify what has import to us. For, given the rational interconnections among emotions and judgments, such a refinement must ultimately be answerable to how much sense it is able to make of our emotional responses partially constitutive of import. Insofar as the patterns of our emotions do not cohere with our understanding in judgment of the values things have, we have reasons to rethink our deliberative conclusions and the concepts on which they are based. Consequently, the standards of criticism are in this way partially internal to our evaluative sensibilities.

The upshot is a radically new account of the nature of practical reason and of our mental states quite generally. Although, in presenting the case for this account, I try to present clear reasons for each step along the way, in the process criticizing alternative accounts and responding to imagined objections, these reasons taken one by one are not likely to satisfy my opponents, given the fundamental nature of the dispute. In the end, the best justification for the view I present is the way the whole view hangs together and enables us to resolve persistent and seemingly intractable problems.

PART I

Felt evaluations

2

Emotions and the cognitive–conative divide

Philosophical accounts of freedom, practical reason, and moral or personal value typically presuppose that we already understand what it is for us to have the capacities for desire and evaluative judgment, capacities that are typically understood in light of the assumption of the cognitive–conative divide. Consequently, these accounts proceed without questioning that assumption or the resulting understanding of these capacities; this is, I believe, a mistake. In this chapter, I shall bring this assumption into question, arguing that an adequate account of our evaluative attitudes, and therefore of value itself, requires that we reject the assumption. In its place I shall offer an account of value as constituted in large part by what I shall call "felt evaluations," a notion I use to provide a distinctive kind of account of emotion and desire. This account will be sketched here, and developed in more detail in chapters 3–4.

2.1 THE PROBLEM OF IMPORT

The picture physical science paints of nature is one of pure mechanism, devoid of any kind of meaning whatsoever. As mechanistic, nature operates according to laws that specify how things will happen or generally tend to happen; consequently, the possibility of there being normative standards of correctness in these physical processes is simply unintelligible from within this picture. On the face of it, such a picture of nature seems at odds with the existence of minds like ours, for minds essentially involve meaning and representational states and therefore standards of correctness in terms of which these states are to be assessed. Moreover, minds seem essentially to involve conscious states with a kind of subjectivity and potential for freedom that again seem not to fit into our understanding of mechanism. Given the seeming correctness of this

29

broadly mechanistic picture of nature, and given the obvious fact of the existence of minds, how do the two fit together? This is the *mind–body problem*.

Recent attempts in philosophy of mind to solve the mind–body problem have focused on two main issues, both of which are central to our understanding of minds: intentionality and consciousness. The thought is that by addressing consciousness we can come to an understanding of the essential subjectivity of minds, and by focusing on intentionality we can come to an understanding of the nature of meaning and standards of correctness. To provide an account of intentionality and consciousness, therefore, can seem to be to provide a solution to the mind–body problem, at least in its essential outlines.

There are, of course, other ontological problems involving the mind, though these problems are thought to be solvable in light of the general account of the mind provided by these accounts of intentionality and consciousness. One such problem relevant here is that of the ontological status of moral or personal value: once again, there seems to be a conflict between the existence of moral value and the scientific picture of nature as the *locus* of empirical fact, which is apparently devoid of value. In general, many meta-ethical accounts of moral value are given at least in part in terms of conation – especially desire as the paradigm conative state. What motivates such an appeal to desire in giving an account of value is the intuitive sense that there is a conceptual connection between desire and what is good or worth pursuing, though the exact nature of that connection varies from one account to another.

The trouble is that accounts of the mind and its place in nature, focused as they are on intentionality and consciousness, are unable to provide an account of desire that is rich enough to do the job. The real issue here is intentionality, for desire is essentially an intentional state, even if it is not always conscious. In focusing exclusively on intentionality, philosophers of mind conceive the task of understanding the nature of desire as that of providing an account of what it is for a creature to represent something as a goal and so to use this representation within a broader system of representations, including cognitive states (e.g., beliefs), to generate a course of action intelligible as appropriate to achieve the goal. Thus, the intentionality of desire is understood in terms of two kinds of standards of correctness: directly in terms of instrumental rationality, for it is this that underwrites the appropriateness of action to goal satisfaction; and indirectly in terms of epistemic rationality, for, even if one's actions are appropriate to achieving the goal in light of one's beliefs, the goal may not be achieved because one's beliefs are false. These two kinds of standards of correctness defining the intentional content of desires, however, are inadequate for understanding a conceptual connection between desire and what is worth pursuing.

To see this, consider a chess-playing computer. To characterize the computer as playing chess is to articulate a goal around which the computer's behavior is organized: its outputs are intelligible as non-random legal moves that make some sense as attempts to win. For all practical purposes, this ability requires that the computer be able to apply at least a rudimentary form of instrumental rationality in order to formulate sub-goals that must be accomplished in order to achieve the highest-order goal of winning the game. This means that we can understand why, in light of this highest-order goal, the computer would make the moves it does, thereby providing at least the beginnings of an account of the computer as having intentional states.[1] However, does the computer *desire* to win? For this to be so, winning itself must be intelligible as worth pursuing for the computer. Yet the appeal to instrumental rationality so far simply presupposes the worthiness of winning and cannot on its own provide an account of it. Because we cannot make sense of winning as worth pursuing by the computer's lights, the best we can say is that the computer exhibits rationally mediated goal-directedness rather than a genuine desire.

By contrast, a dog can desire to go out on a walk.[2] This means not

---

[1] Indeed, Daniel Dennett thinks it is the whole of the account; see his *The Intentional Stance*. Of course, many would object to the idea of a computer having intentional states. The standard motivation for this objection, voiced clearly in John Searle's "Minds, Brains, and Programs" (*Behavioral and Brain Sciences*, 3 [1980], pp. 417–24), is that the symbols computers manipulate do not have intentional content insofar as they fail to be hooked up to the world in the right way. That is, what has gone missing is an understanding of how epistemic rationality applies to the computer. Nonetheless, however this account gets filled in, my basic point remains: instrumental rationality, even when combined with epistemic rationality, as the basis of an account of intentionality is insufficient to account for the conceptual connection between desires and what is worth pursuing.

[2] Once again, this is a controversial claim, for some philosophers have denied that non-linguistic animals can have any mental states at all. (See, e.g., Donald Davidson's "Belief and the Basis of Meaning" and "Thought and Talk," both in *Inquiries into Truth and Interpretation* [Oxford: Clarendon, 1984]; and see R. G. Frey's *Interests and Rights: The Case Against Animals* [Oxford: Clarendon, 1980].) For the moment, I want to sidestep this issue, for my example is intended merely to illustrate the distinction between goal-directedness and desire. Nonetheless, for a detailed defense of the possibility of animal thought, see my "Significance, Emotions, and Objectivity: Some Limits of Animal

merely that the dog is able to behave in ways that are instrumental to its going on a walk by, for example, bringing its leash to its master or scratching at the back door, but also that the dog cares about going on walks: this is something that matters or has significance or importance to it, as is clear in part from its frustration or anger at not being let out and its joy when it finally is. I shall use *"import"* to denote any such worthiness imparted by a subject's concern for something.[3] As such, import provides a non-instrumental reason for the dog's pursuit of the walk and therefore makes intelligible the idea that the dog desires it and finds it worth pursuing. Consequently, the dog is intelligible as a qualitatively different kind of thing than a chess-playing computer: the dog is a potential subject of import and as such has a "stake" in the outcome in a way that is simply unintelligible for the computer.

Desires, therefore, are to be distinguished from goal-directedness in terms of the way in which they involve import.[4] Nonetheless, both desire and goal-directedness are intentional states insofar as they have a kind of representational content that guides subsequent behavior. Insofar as attempts to solve the mind–body problem are focused merely on intentionality and consciousness, this distinction between desire and goal-directedness is simply ignored. Given this distinction, however, we need to ask about the place of import in nature, for import, like moral value, essentially involves a kind of worth that seems to have no place in nature as science conceives of it. This is the *problem of import*, and it is a problem that must be solved in order to distinguish desire from goal-directedness and so to use the resulting account of desire in providing even richer accounts of personal and moral value. By ignoring the distinction between desire and goal-directedness, philosophers of mind have thereby ignored the problem of import and so created a mismatch between the kind of account of desire they offer and the kind of account

---

Thought" (Ph.D. dissertation, University of Pittsburgh [1994]) and "The Significance of Emotions," *American Philosophical Quarterly*, 31 (1994), pp. 319–31.

[3] My use of the term "import" stems from, and is intended to suggest, Charles Taylor's work on the way in which values and the rationality of values enter into an account of what it is to be a person. See his *Human Agency and Language* and his *Sources of the Self: The Making of Modern Identity* (Cambridge, MA: Harvard University Press, 1989). Notice that import, understood this way, is a rather generic axiological term; I shall later (in chapter 4) distinguish different kinds of import instituted by different kinds of concern (caring and valuing), in part as a way of distinguishing persons from animals.

[4] This is a point Michael Smith misses entirely in claiming that "having a goal is being in a state with which the world must fit, [and] being in a state with which the world must fit is desiring" (*The Moral Problem*, p. 118).

presupposed by the richer kind of value that lies at the heart of the motivational and deliberative problems discussed in chapter 1.

2.2 EMOTIONS AS EVALUATIVE FEELINGS

As described above, import is in general a kind of worth imparted by a subject's concern for something. Solving the problem of import therefore requires giving an account of the relevant kind of concern and showing how that concern can give rise to import. Clearly, such concern will involve the kind of goal-directedness described above, but just as clearly such goal-directedness is insufficient. The question is, what more is needed?

In this section, I shall suggest more than argue that to solve the problem of import we must turn to the emotions. In doing so, I shall provide a brief sketch of an account of emotions and their connection to import. However, this kind of account runs counter to standard accounts of emotions because it runs afoul of the assumption of the cognitive–conative divide. In §§2.3–2.4, therefore, I shall discuss these standard, "cognitivist" accounts of emotions, arguing that the assumption of the cognitive–conative divide implicit in these cognitivist accounts prevents an adequate solution to the problem of import. This provides powerful motivation for the kind of theory of emotions I shall sketch here and develop in more detail in chapter 3.

Emotions are essentially feelings of a certain kind, and a large part of the difficulty in articulating an account of emotions is that of understanding the kind of feelings at issue. Such feelings are not reducible to bodily sensations, as is clear when we consider our ordinary descriptions of emotional feelings. In having an emotion, one may feel uncomfortable, uneasy (or at ease), lighthearted, on top of the world, pushed around, or like nothing is going to work. In none of these cases is the feeling a literal description of a bodily sensation. Thus, when I feel uneasy as three young men follow close behind me on a dark, deserted street, my discomfort is not the discomfort I feel with an upset stomach. For to say that I feel uneasy might be taken as an alternative, albeit somewhat vague, way of saying that I am afraid, for fear is, roughly, a feeling of unease because things threaten to go badly. In this way, emotional feelings are something like a sense of how things are going – whether well or poorly. By contrast, to say that I feel queasy in my stomach is not an alternative way of describing my fear, and I can feel afraid without any such sensations. As a result, bodily sensations must be understood as something we feel in addition to our emotions and not as an essential part of those emotions.

Emotional feelings, therefore, are essentially evaluative feelings: feelings of things going well or poorly. This point can be developed more clearly with some technical vocabulary. The *target* of an emotion is the object at which the emotion is directed: when I am afraid of the bear or angry at Agnes, the bear and Agnes are the targets of my emotions. What makes an emotion be the kind of emotion it is and so distinguishes it from other kinds of emotion is the way in which the emotion construes the target as having a kind of import. Thus, fear involves construing its target as dangerous, anger as offensive, satisfaction as a good achieved, etc. Such an evaluative construal, as definitive of an emotion as the kind of emotion it is, is that emotion's *formal object*. Emotions are *evaluative feelings* insofar as their formal objects involve import in this way: to fear the bear or be angry at Agnes is to feel the bear to be dangerous or to feel Agnes to be offensive.

Part of the point of describing emotions as feelings is to highlight their passivity: the capacity for emotion is a kind of receptivity to import. Conversely, we might say, the import of your situation impresses itself on you in your feeling a particular emotion. This has two implications. First, we can assess the emotion for warrant depending on whether its target really has the import defined by the emotion's formal object. For example, after a hard, frustrating day at work I get annoyed at my dog for giving me his usual, exuberant greeting, which I normally enjoy. Here, my emotion of annoyance is unwarranted precisely because it is not properly responsive to the import things have for me. Consider another example: John is afraid as the fire is about to consume his house. If this fear is to be warranted, that can only be because the fire is a threat to something that matters or has import to him; there is something rationally odd about his fear if the house did not have this import to him. Thus, his fear would be unwarranted if he had recently inherited the house from a distant relative he never knew, was trying unsuccessfully to sell it, and was contemplating committing arson for the insurance money anyway. In such a case, apparently, John does not care about what happens to the house so long as he gets his money, and this absence of import undermines the warrant of his fear. In general, therefore, the target must actually have the import defined by the formal object in order for the emotion to be warranted.

34

Second, and ultimately more important, in order to be a standard for the warrant of emotions, import must have a kind of objectivity as existing independently of particular emotions. It is this status as an independent object that enables us to make sense of import as impressing itself on us in feeling emotions.[5]

Another part of the point of describing emotions as feelings is to distinguish the kind of evaluation implicit in them from the evaluations explicit in judgment. For, in having an emotion, one does not make the evaluation of the target dispassionately but rather feels the evaluation of the target. This is part of the point of describing emotions as pleasures and pains. Thus, fear differs from a mere judgment of the presence of danger insofar as one is pained by that danger, and satisfaction differs from a mere judgment of a good achieved insofar as one is pleased by that achievement. Pleasure and pain just are the distinctive kind of passionate feelings of import that emotions are: emotions feel good or bad and in this way are directed at import as their intentional object. Moreover, as I shall argue in chapter 3, it is because emotions are pleasures and pains that they are intelligible as motivating.

In short, emotions are evaluative feelings in that they are pleasant or painful responses to import as an intentional object that impresses itself on us in having the emotion.

Nonetheless, emotions are also an essential part of what constitutes import, as might be suggested by this understanding of emotions as pleasant or painful: pleasure and pain seem to be the right kind of source for the concern that imparts import. Of course, it is not plausible to say that for something to have import to one, one must now have some emotion concerning it. Rather, what is plausible is the weaker claim that something does not have import for one if, no matter what happens, one fails entirely to respond emotionally to it. For example, if in the face of the most malicious, intentional, repeated, and successful efforts by another to thwart your achievement of a goal you fail to be moved to anger or at least annoyance or frustration, it is hard to make sense of that

---

[5] This claim requires further justification, for it is unclear exactly what kind of object import is, especially given import's status as imparted by the individual's concern. I shall return to this issue briefly in §2.4 and more fully in chapter 3. Notice, however, that my claim here is that import is independent only of *particular* emotions, not of emotions generally. My claim in chapter 3 will be that import emerges out of a distinctive kind of pattern of emotions, in keeping with the intuition broached above and sketched below that emotions are partially constitutive of import.

goal as having any import to you. If you do not feel it in your heart, at least on some relevant occasions, then you fail to care about it.

The idea, then, is to appeal not to particular emotions but rather to patterns of emotional response to something as a way of making sense of it as having import. Consequently, we can make sense of particular emotions as themselves being warranted or unwarranted responses to import depending on whether they fit into some such pattern. Moreover, we can make sense of motivational pulls that similarly fit into such a pattern as pulls towards what is worth pursuing – as, that is, genuine desires that are themselves responsive to import. The kind of concern that imparts import, therefore, is not itself a particular mental state but rather this sort of pattern of emotions and desires.

2.3 EMOTIONAL COGNITIVISM

Nonetheless, this account of emotions as evaluative feelings may look inherently confused in two ways. First, as evaluations, emotions are more or less warranted responses to how things are in the world and so involve intentional content; as such, it might seem, they are essentially cognitions. By contrast, the feelings of pleasure and pain involved in emotions seem to be essentially non-intentional and non-cognitive. Consequently, it may look like I am illicitly sliding between a sense of "feels good or bad" that involves qualitative tone (i.e., "is pleasant or painful") as well as, perhaps, motivation, and a sense that involves intentional content (i.e., "looks to be good or bad"). These two kinds of state seem to be fundamentally different, and, insofar as emotions involve both, that is because emotions are composite states of cognition, qualitative feels, and perhaps conation. So, the objection concludes, the very notion of an evaluative feeling, as a unitary state of pleasure or pain at some import, is inherently confused.

The assumption implicit in this first objection is, in effect, that of the cognitive–conative divide, discussed in §1.2: cognitive states, as having mind-to-world direction of fit, must be essentially different in kind from both conative states, which have world-to-mind direction of fit, and qualitative states, which have no direction of fit at all. Given this essential difference, it is illegitimate to slide between talk of pleasure and pain, as qualitative or conative, and talk of evaluation, as cognitive. Insofar as emotions involve evaluations, qualitative feels, and conations, they must be composite states.

Indeed, with the assumption of the cognitive–conative divide in place, a second apparent confusion in my account comes into view, this time concerning the nature of evaluation. I claimed that import is simultaneously both subjective and objective. As subjective, import is a kind of worth constituted by, and relative to, individuals; for example, by desiring some end (we might think) I thereby constitute not only that end but also things that bear on the achievement of that end as having import. In this way, the mental states that constitute import have world-to-mind direction of fit and so are conations, prototypically desires, as with the example just given. However, as objective, import is an entity to which certain mental states must be properly responsive; such states must therefore be cognitions, with mind-to-world direction of fit. Thus, I might come to discover that something is a threat to the achievement of an end I desire and in this way come to discover its import to me. In this way, we can distinguish two kinds of evaluation in terms of their direction of fit: *constituting evaluation*, with its world-to-mind direction of fit, and *discovering evaluation*, with its mind-to-world direction of fit. Yet, on the account I just sketched, emotions must be simultaneously constituting evaluations (insofar as import is subjective) and discovering evaluations (insofar as import is objective), as well as non-intentional qualitative states of pleasure or pain. Given the cognitive–conative divide, however, no unitary state can be both conative and cognitive, let alone qualitative as well; my account therefore involves an unworkable confusion.

If we accept these two objections and the underlying assumption of the cognitive–conative divide (which I do not for reasons to be provided below), the obvious solution is to divide and conquer: we should understand emotions as composite states of cognition, conation, and qualitative feels. This is the fundamental idea behind emotional cognitivism, currently the most popular kind of theory of emotions.

Emotional cognitivism purports to provide a reductive account of emotions in terms of belief, desire, and bodily sensation. The basic motive for this reductivism is something like Ockham's razor: postulate as few basic kinds of entities as possible in order to understand the phenomena. Thus, the idea is that, since we need to postulate beliefs, desires, and bodily sensations anyway, we can and should get away with an account of the intentionality of emotions – of their having targets and formal objects – as well as of their motivational pull and distinctive qualitative feels in terms of these antecedently intelligible states of belief, desire, and bodily sensation. In this way, fear gets understood as the combination of the belief that some danger looms, the desire to avoid it, as well as, perhaps, sensations of queasiness in one's stomach. Likewise, anger is reducible to the belief that one has been offended, the desire to retaliate, and sensations of blood rushing to one's head.

There are, however, serious problems for emotional cognitivism. In the remainder of this section, I shall address two such problems, namely the problem of the emotionality of emotions and the problem of rational conflict with judgment, and I shall argue that these problems require that we give up on emotional cognitivism's reductivism. This will put me in a position in §2.4 to argue in light of the problem of import directly against the assumption of the cognitive–conative divide, which underlies and motivates emotional cognitivism, thereby motivating my alternative account (presented in chapter 3).

2.3.1 *The problem of emotionality*

One standard objection to emotional cognitivism is that it cannot capture the "emotionality" of emotions – what is distinctive of emotions as the kind of mental state they are. Thus, it is commonly noted, it is possible to believe there is a danger present, want to avoid that danger, and feel butterflies in one's stomach without feeling fear. We must, it seems, make a distinction between the emotional evaluation of something as an object of fear and the non-emotional evaluation of it as dangerous, and cognitivists may seem unable to make this distinction; this is the *problem of emotionality*.

To account for the emotionality of emotions, cognitivists have therefore applied one of two basic strategies. The first is to account for emotionality in terms of some special kind of belief or desire. Thus, Joel Marks claims:

what transforms a(n evaluative) judgment into an emotion is "intensity" of some desire with respect to the judgment.[6]

By appealing to the notion of a strong desire, Marks tries to account for the physiological and sensational effects of emotions. We can, he claims, answer the question of why, for example, one felt butterflies in one's stomach by appealing to the strength of one's desire. Furthermore, he claims, a strong desire may well result in other effects of emotions:

---

[6] "A Theory of Emotion," *Philosophical Studies*, 42 (1982), pp. 227–42, at p. 232.

logical missteps and hasty inferences, in part as the result of a failure to notice certain relevant features of the situation.

A central difficulty with this appeal to the strength of desire as an attempt to capture the emotionality of emotions is that it is not clear how we can give an account of the relevant kind of strength. For, on the one hand, it might seem that a desire is strong in the sense that it is colored by emotion, but such an appeal to emotion would be viciously circular. On the other hand, we might avoid this appeal to emotion by understanding the sense in which one desire is stronger than another in terms of a disposition to act on one desire rather than another in cases in which they conflict. However, this account of strength is inadequate to capture the emotionality of emotions, for, once again, it seems we can have a desire that is relatively strong in this sense, along with the requisite belief and bodily sensation, and still not feel the emotion.

Another variant of this first strategy is to account for emotionality in terms of a special kind of belief or judgment; this is the tack taken by Martha Nussbaum.[7] According to Nussbaum, we must distinguish bare assent from full assent. *Bare assent* to an evaluation is merely an intellectual acceptance of it, and this is clearly possible in the absence of any emotion. When an emotion is clearly warranted, as in the case of a judgment concerning the death of a loved one, merely to give bare assent to the evaluation is to be "in a state of denial," failing properly to appreciate the judgment and so failing unequivocally to commit oneself to it.[8] By contrast, *full assent* to an evaluation is an unequivocal commitment: a commitment that moves one metaphorically by resonating cognitively within one (p. 382). Thus, fully to assent to an evaluative proposition is to "allow in" that proposition, to acknowledge it "with the core of my being . . . to realize in one's being its full significance" (p. 381). It is such full assent to an evaluative proposition, Nussbaum claims, that accounts for the emotionality of emotions.

The central difficulty for Nussbaum's account is similar to that for Marks': we cannot give an account of what it is fully to assent to an evaluation without a viciously circular appeal to the emotions. After all,

---

[7] See her *The Therapy of Desire: Theory and Practice in Hellenistic Ethics* (Princeton University Press, 1994). In this work (especially chapter 10), Nussbaum provides a detailed interpretation of Chrysippus' theory of emotions, which she tentatively endorses by calling it "one of the most powerful candidates for truth in this area" (p. 368). For this reason, and because of the originality of her interpretation, I shall simply attribute the theory to Nussbaum herself.

[8] *The Therapy of Desire*, p. 376; see also p. 378.

full assent must be more than decisive assent with a clear (intellectual) appreciation of the implications (cf. Nussbaum's "realize . . . its full significance"). What is needed, and what Nussbaum tries to get with her metaphors of assenting "with the core of my being," is that one feels the evaluation emotionally. Without a specification of how we are to understand such full assent non-metaphorically, Nussbaum is simply begging the question.

One intuitive way to begin to spell this idea out non-metaphorically is to appeal to the notions of pleasure and pain. Thus, to assent "with the core of my being" is to be pleased or pained by the evaluation implicit in the emotion: fear differs from a mere judgment of the presence of danger insofar as in fear one is pained by that danger, and satisfaction differs from a mere judgment of a good achieved insofar as in satisfaction one is pleased by that achievement. On the face of it, given the fundamental assumptions of cognitivism (namely that of reductivism and of the cognitive–conative divide), this intuition might seem to give rise to a second strategy for accounting for the emotionality of emotions, namely in terms of the causes or effects of the relevant beliefs and desires. According to William Lyons:

So, for X to be an emotional state, X must include an evaluation which causes abnormal physiological changes. Both the evaluation and the physiological changes are necessary conditions for X being an emotional state, but neither are separately sufficient. Jointly they are.[9]

Lyons ultimately claims that what is distinctive of emotions is that the relevant beliefs and desires cause a physiological state that is felt, where this feeling, a bodily sensation, we might naturally say, is pleasant or painful.

This appeal to bodily sensations as the effect of certain beliefs and desires fails as a way of capturing the emotionality of emotions for two reasons. First, the appeal to bodily sensations fails to capture the sense in which emotions are feelings of pleasure and pain. For, as I argued in §2.2, what distinguishes an emotion like fear from the judgment concerning the presence of danger is that to feel fear is to be pained by danger – a kind of pain that is essentially intentional and evaluative. Consequently, the kind of feelings emotions essentially are, as intentional and evaluative, cannot be reduced to bodily sensations, which are non-intentional. This means that the kind of feelings that emotions essentially are cannot be understood, as cognitivists like Lyons try to do, as an

[9] *Emotion* (Cambridge University Press, 1980), p. 58.

afterthought, tacked on to the theory after all the evaluative work has been done.

This leads to a second criticism of this appeal to bodily sensations: this appeal makes what is distinctive about emotions as such, namely their physiological effects and the resulting sensations, be by and large irrelevant to our mental lives. In this way, emotions are relegated to the role of a mental appendix: they were useful, perhaps, in the course of our evolution, but we can get along just as well (or even better) without them. Indeed, this is roughly the explicit conclusion Jerome Shaffer draws from a consideration of emotional cognitivism in general: "It is easy enough to imagine individual lives and even a whole world in which things would be much better if there were no emotion."[10] However, I submit, any theory that cannot recognize what is distinctive of emotions as being a meaningful and essential part of our lives must be deficient as a theory of emotions.

2.3.2 *The problem of rational conflict*

A second major problem for emotional cognitivism concerns how we are to understand the nature of potential conflicts between emotions and judgments. Consider the following example, provided by Patricia Greenspan.[11] Having recently been bitten by a rabid dog, I come to be afraid of all dogs, including Fido, "A lovable old dog . . . the familiar pet of some friends." Nonetheless, I know that this fear of Fido is groundless, for even if he wanted to attack me (something I even now doubt very much given his calm, friendly disposition), he would be unable to do so given his age, arthritis, and lack of teeth. Thus, although I know that Fido is in no way dangerous to me, I am still, irrationally, afraid. The question Greenspan raises is that of how we are to understand this irrationality; this is the *problem of rational conflict*.

According to emotional cognitivism, my fear of Fido involves as a component the belief or judgment that he is dangerous; this is what I shall call a *judgmentalist* account insofar as the emotion involves assent to this proposition, an assent which, given its mind-to-world direction of

---

[10] "An Assessment of Emotion," *American Philosophical Quarterly*, 20 (1983), pp. 161–73, at p. 169.

[11] "Emotions as Evaluations," *Pacific Philosophical Quarterly*, 62 (1981), pp. 158–69, at pp. 162–63. For elaboration of this example and further examples, see also her "Emotions, Reasons, and 'Self-Involvement,'" *Philosophical Studies*, 38 (1980), pp. 161–68, and her *Emotions and Reasons*, especially pp. 17–20.

fit, apparently must be either a belief or a judgment. As a result of this judgmentalism, cognitivism assimilates the irrationality of the conflict between my knowledge and my fear to incoherence in judgment. This, as Greenspan rightly points out, does not make sense: conflicts between emotions and judgments do not verge on incoherence, for they are readily intelligible and happen all too often. What is needed, she claims, is a way of understanding the cognitive component of emotions without assimilating it to belief.

Greenspan's solution is to understand emotions as feelings of comfort or discomfort at a thought with the appropriate content; thus, my fear of Fido is discomfort at the thought that Fido is dangerous.[12] In appealing to the notion of a thought, Greenspan intends merely some propositional content, whether or not the subject assents to that thought. In the example of Fido, since I do not assent to the thought that Fido is dangerous, we need not understand the resulting irrationality as that of incoherence in judgment. Thus, by denying that emotions involve assents, Greenspan is offering an *anti-judgmentalist* account of emotions.

Robert Roberts provides a similar anti-judgmentalist account of emotions.[13] According to Roberts, emotions are concern-based construals. As construals, they are ways of thinking about their objects, without necessarily involving assent. In cases like that of Fido, Roberts claims, we can understand the emotion as analogous to a perceptual illusion: an appearance that remains even after we repudiate it in judgment. Like Greenspan, then, Roberts is an anti-judgmentalist insofar as he denies that emotions necessarily involve judgments; consequently, he, too, tries to account for the irrationality of repudiated emotions without assimilating it to incoherence in judgment.

Although these anti-judgmentalist accounts clearly avoid the problem of assimilating conflicts between judgments and emotions to incoherence, it is not clear that they are thereby able to provide a proper understanding of the nature of the resulting irrationality. After all, it is

---

[12] Notice that this account can be understood as a solution to the problem of emotionality insofar as comfort and discomfort, as intentional and evaluative, seem to fill the role of evaluative feeling alluded to in §2.3.1. Nonetheless, Greenspan does not offer a clear account of the nature of such comfort and discomfort but relies instead merely on the intuition. As I shall argue in §2.4, such an intuition is inadequate, and an explicit account is needed that can overcome the problem of import.

[13] See in particular his "What an Emotion Is: A Sketch," pp. 183–209. Another account of emotions similar to those offered by Greenspan and Roberts is that of Gerald F. Gaus in *Value and Justification: The Foundations of Liberal Theory* (Cambridge University Press, 1990); I shall discuss Gaus' view explicitly in §2.4.

not at all irrational to have a stick half-submerged in water look bent even after one has judged that it is straight. If, as the anti-judgmentalist claims, the thoughts or construals emotions involve are not assented to, in what sense are they in rational conflict with judgment?

Roberts' response to this difficulty is most explicit.[14] The difference between the perceptual illusion and the repudiated emotion is that although both are ways of construing one's situation, the emotional construal is based in a concern (§1.4.e):

> The fear has a personal depth and life-disrupting motivational power that the illusion lacks. The bent stick is at most puzzling; the fear is personally compelling. This means that when the subject dissociates from his fear by denying its propositional content, it is like denying a part of himself, whereas denying his visual impression is not.

So, Roberts thinks, it is this personal compellingness of the emotion, a kind of motivational power, that makes intelligible its irrationality. For such motivational force runs contrary to our considered judgment and is irrational insofar as in light of our judgment it is something against which we must struggle. The irrationality of such conflicts, then, is not a cognitive irrationality, as the judgmentalist claims, but a practical one.

Nonetheless, this account of the irrationality of conflicts between emotions and judgments ultimately fails. Roberts tries to make sense of conflicts between emotions and judgments by (1) understanding how emotions can persist in the face of a judgment that repudiates them by understanding them as appearances, and (2) understanding the irrationality of persistent repudiated emotions in light of their motivational force. Both of these cannot be maintained simultaneously.

The way in which emotions motivate is not merely by disposing us to behave in a certain way; emotions are not simply brute causes, pushing or pulling us in determinate ways. Rather, emotions motivate by providing reasons for intentional action, reasons that stem from the evaluation of their targets in light of their formal objects. To see this, consider the following example.[15] As I walk down the ramp to board the

---

[14] See his "Shaped Passions: An Essay in Moral Psychology" (manuscript in progress), §1.4.d, "Emotions Without Assent." Although Greenspan's account is not so explicit, her answer seems to be essentially the same, though I shall note some differences below.

[15] I take this example to be representative of the way in which emotions motivate in general, and I shall defend this view in §3.4. Nonetheless, all I need for the purposes of my argument against the anti-judgmentalists is a single case in which understanding how a repudiated emotion motivates requires understanding it as a kind of assent to the view of the world the emotion presents – an assent that cannot simply be traced to belief or judgment.

plane, I feel an intense fear of flying and so am motivated to turn around and not get on the plane. Of course, I may intellectually realize that this fear is unwarranted, that flying is one of the safest modes of transportation around, and so I repudiate my emotion. On the anti-judgmentalist account, this repudiated fear – this phobia – can be irrational only if it persists in providing a reason for action in spite of its repudiation; indeed, my fear does persist and continues to provide a powerful motivation for getting off the plane. However, the persistence of this motivation is unintelligible if we understand my repudiated fear merely in terms of the appearance of danger. For, although a repudiated appearance can persist, to repudiate it just is to undermine whatever reason it might provide for action: to believe that what one sees is a mirage is consistent with continuing to have it appear as a puddle of water but not with being motivated to go over and drink from it. That my fear in this case persists in motivating me, despite the repudiation, indicates that it not merely presents me with the appearance of danger but that I in some sense continue to assent to the presence of that danger; otherwise, I can have no reason, not even a bad one (as the repudiation would suggest), to be motivated in this way. Consequently, cognitive and practical irrationality cannot be separated as neatly as the anti-judgmentalist requires.

Of course, an anti-judgmentalist might try to save the account of motivation by appealing to a notion of desire either as a component of the emotion or as caused by it. Once such a desire is in the picture, we apparently need not worry about whether the rest of the emotion involves an assent or not. Indeed, this appeal to desire seems to be implicit in Greenspan's notions of comfort and discomfort and in Roberts' notion of a concern as the source of the way in which the emotion is personally compelling.[16] Nonetheless, this misses the point. The desire at issue must be not merely, as in the Fido example, a general concern for my well-being, a concern that, according to Roberts, is the basis of my construal of Fido as dangerous, but a specific desire to avoid Fido here and now. If this specific desire is to reflect well or poorly on the emotion's warrant, it must be made rationally intelligible by the

---

[16] See Greenspan's *Emotions and Reasons*, p. 31: "Discomfort is here construed as a state that an agent would naturally want to escape from – not itself a desire, but a source of desires, under appropriate circumstances." See also Roberts' discussion of concern in "What an Emotion Is: A Sketch," p. 202: "I use 'concern' to denote desires and aversions, and the attachments and interests from which many of our desires and aversions derive."

evaluation of my present circumstances implicit in the emotion. That is possible only if I assent to that emotional evaluation.

This criticism does not quite fit Greenspan's account. According to Greenspan, what motivates the desire is not the evaluation but the discomfort: it is rational to want to get rid of such discomfort, whatever its source. Yet on this account we still cannot make sense of the irrationality of conflicts between emotions and judgments. For how one acts on the desire to get rid of the discomfort depends not on the emotion but on other beliefs connected to it via instrumental reason. Consequently, to satisfy the desire to remove the discomfort at the thought that Fido is dangerous, in the face of the knowledge that he is completely harmless, will require not running away but rather something like removing the thought; failure to do this is irrational, but not in a way that is traceable to the emotion. Hence, on such an account, the irrationality does not lie with the emotion itself but arises from the poor way in which one copes with the emotion. So the problem of rational conflict remains unsolved.

This seems to present us with a choice between two unsatisfactory alternatives: either we must be judgmentalists and accept an overly strong conception of rational conflict between emotion and judgment, or we must be anti-judgmentalists and give up hope of accounting for such conflict. The choice, however, is a false one. The judgmentalist, correctly noting that the sort of evaluation emotions involve, as one that rationally motivates action, must involve assent, falsely concludes that emotions are judgments of a certain kind. The anti-judgmentalist, correctly noting that it is possible to have an emotion without making the corresponding judgment, falsely concludes that emotions are not assents. In each case, the conclusion presupposes the implicit premise that all assent is judgmental. The way out is to deny this premise: emotions must be understood as a kind of assent if we are to make sense of rational conflict with judgment at all, but not a kind that can be reduced to judgment if we are to make sense of that conflict as something other than incoherence.[17] The idea of such distinctively emotional assent is implicit in the idea that emotions are evaluative feelings: being pleased or pained by things being

---

[17] Roberts may seem to offer a position something like this: he sometimes talks as if the kind of construal emotions essentially are is a kind of assent, albeit an assent only of a "part of the person" but not the "whole person" (§1.4.e). Yet this does not make sense of the idea that it is the agent – the whole person – who is irrational when the repudiated emotion persists, and not merely the emotion itself.

thus and so is a kind of acceptance that things really are that way, an acceptance that falls short of full-blown judgment. The need to make sense of such distinctively emotional assent, therefore, undermines emotional cognitivism's attempts to reduce emotions to antecedently intelligible mental states of cognition and conation.[18]

2.4 PROBLEM OF IMPORT AND THE COGNITIVE–CONATIVE DIVIDE

If the foregoing is correct, the problems of emotionality and of rational conflict both stem from emotional cognitivism's insistence on providing a reductivist account of emotions, and so cannot be solved by emotional cognitivism thus conceived. Nonetheless, it might seem that emotional cognitivism has a way out of the problems of both emotionality and rational conflict by rejecting reductionism and so providing an account of emotions in terms of a distinctively emotional kind of cognitive or conative state. What I shall now argue is that this way out does not escape the more fundamental problem of import, a problem that cannot be solved if we accept the cognitive–conative divide.

First, let me describe this way out in more detail – one that might seem to be provided by Gerald Gaus' account of emotions.[19] According to Gaus, emotions are affects (likings or dislikings) directed at some content, where these affects are caused and justified by grounding beliefs. The idea of emotions as intentional affects – as intentional feelings – might seem to provide the right sort of account of the emotionality of emotions: such intentional feelings are a kind of state that is distinctively emotional. Moreover, it might seem that Gaus can solve the problem of rational conflict as well: although emotions themselves are not assents, it is a necessary condition of their warrant that they are "grounded in" – caused by – certain beliefs that serve to justify them. Thus, Gaus says (p. 65): "If Betty fears Alf, she must not only must [*sic*] have her fear grounded in beliefs about him, but by certain relevant beliefs, that is, he is threatening or dangerous." If this belief is unjustified, then the emotion is unwarranted and so irrational, thereby explaining the conflict. Finally, Gaus attempts to give a solution to the problem of import, or

---

[18] This notion of distinctively emotional assent, of course, needs to be worked out more fully, and I shall do so beginning in §3.1. My aim here, however, is merely to point out that the persistent problem of rational conflict can be solved if we give up on one of the fundamental tenets of emotional cognitivism.

[19] See his *Value and Justification*; all page references to Gaus in the text refer to this volume.

"intrinsic value" as he calls it: "to value something (intrinsically) is to possess a dispositional emotion towards it" (p. 145; cf. p. 111).

Yet consider more carefully Gaus' solution to the problem of rational conflict. In the case of repudiated fear, Gaus still requires that one believe both that the object of the fear is dangerous (as a cause of the relevant affect) and that it is not dangerous (as the repudiating belief). To believe both these things, however, just is the kind of incoherence in judgment that an account of the irrationality of such emotions must avoid. Of course Gaus might avoid this consequence by claiming that one initially believes that something is dangerous and as a consequence comes to fear it, but only subsequently comes to believe that it is not dangerous. In this case, the subsequent belief might simply replace the initial belief (without incoherence), and yet, insofar as the emotion persists, it is still irrational because it was ill-grounded. Yet although this might be true in some cases, it is not true in all: it is entirely possible to believe from the start that Fido is harmless and feel fear nonetheless.

The real difficulty with Gaus' account, however, lies in his under-standing of affect as a kind of liking or disliking, and this threatens to undermine not only the answer he provides to the problem of emotion-ality but also his solution to the problem of import. Gaus claims that such likings or dislikings are not themselves desires but are more generic pro- or con-attitudes that are the source of desire.[20] Yet this is inadequate as an account of a notion that is intended to solve the problem of import and, as I shall argue shortly, must fail.

Similar problems arise for Michael Stocker's account of emotions.[21] According to Stocker, the difference between the fear of falling on ice and "an intellectual appreciation of those dangers [together with] a pro forma desire to avoid them" is

not given by a change in beliefs, but by a change in the emotional ways the beliefs are taken. When I am afraid, the beliefs are emotionally present, emotionally charged, and feeling-laden; when they are not, I am not afraid.[22]

Such "emotionally charged" beliefs are ones we take "*seriously*": we "really" believe in these dangers, and we "really" want to avoid them (p. 47; cf. p. 36). Moreover, Stocker claims, we can take a thought

---

[20] Such a notion is similar to Greenspan's notion of comfort or discomfort and Roberts' notion of a concern; the criticisms I offer of Gaus here apply equally well to them.

[21] *Valuing Emotions* (Cambridge University Press, 1996).

[22] Ibid., p. 47. Notice that insofar as Stocker thinks emotions require that beliefs are present, albeit emotionally, he fails properly to solve the problem of rational conflict.

seriously – with "emotional seriousness" – without believing it – without taking it with "evidential seriousness";[23] the difference, he insists, should be understood in terms of affect, an irreducible component of emotional thoughts to which we must appeal in making sense of these differences between intellectual and emotional thoughts. Finally, Stocker argues, it is in terms of such distinctively emotional affect that we can make sense of emotions as meaningful constituents of our lives; indeed, this is the central conclusion of his *Valuing Emotions*.

Although I agree with Stocker that we must appeal to some such notion of distinctively emotional feeling in order to account for the emotionality of emotions, I do not think we can make sense of such a feeling in the way he does. For Stocker, what distinguishes emotions from other thoughts is the way in which we attend to the relevant cognitive evaluation: whether with or without emotional seriousness, and so whether affectively or not. However, what is needed, and what Stocker fails to provide, is a clear account of the nature of this affectivity that can justify an appeal to it in order to account for emotionality. Indeed, insofar as Stocker conceives of emotional affect as a way of attending to a cognitive evaluation, he presupposes a kind of solution to the problem of import that cannot be had. For, in the context of the cognitive–conative divide, we must make sense of our evaluations as either constituting evaluations or discovering evaluations. As I shall now argue, neither of these kinds of evaluation can do the trick, thus providing a powerful motivation for rejecting the cognitive–conative divide and so, in chapter 3, to completing the sketch of the account of emotions begun in §2.2.

Nonetheless, the argument presented in this section will not, of course, be conclusive against the assumption of the cognitive–conative divide, for that assumption is too deeply entrenched in current philo-sophical thinking to be dislodged by any single argument. That is why I have claimed only to have motivated its rejection. In chapter 1, I argued that the assumption of the cognitive–conative divide results in a mis-understanding of the motivational and deliberative problems that under-mines any attempt to give a satisfactory solution to these problems. Whether or not that is a reason to reject the cognitive–conative divide depends on whether an intelligible and satisfactory alternative is in the offing, and that is what I aim to provide in the remainder of this book.

---

[23] "Emotional Thoughts," *American Philosophical Quarterly*, 24 (1987), 59–69, at p. 62.

As I described it in §2.1, import is a kind of worthiness imparted by a subject's concern for something. The initial need for a notion of import was motivated by the need to distinguish, within the context of the mind–body problem, genuine desire from mere goal-directedness in terms of the idea that to desire something is to find it worth pursuing. As we have seen subsequently, the notion of import is broader than merely worthiness of pursuit insofar as kinds of emotions are distinguished in large part by the kinds of import implicit in their formal objects. Nonetheless, in each case, the same problem remains: how are we to make sense of import as having a place in a world that, at least as described by modern science, seems entirely devoid of worth? My claim will be that this problem cannot be solved once we make the assumption of the cognitive–conative divide.

One way of thinking about the problem of import, a way encouraged by the cognitive–conative divide, is as a kind of Euthyphro question: do we evaluate things as good or bad because they have import, or do things have import because we evaluate them as good or bad? To answer in terms of the former is to understand the evaluations as discovering evaluations – as cognitions – and so requires locating the source of import outside these evaluations; call this the *"cognitive account"* of import. This answer has some intuitive appeal insofar as our evaluations can be mistaken. Thus, consider again the example given above (p. 34) of my annoyance at my exuberant dog which results from my frustrations at work being displaced onto my dog: my annoyance here is unwarranted precisely because it is not properly responsive to the imports things have for me. This is true not only of emotions but also of desires as well. Thus, I may desire things that I recognize to be not good for me, as when I feel drawn to the pack of cigarettes on the desk even though I recognize that they are injurious to my and my family's health and that money spent on cigarettes really should go toward my daughter's college savings account. Once again, the desire here is unwarranted precisely because its object is not really worth pursuing, even by my own lights. The objectivity of import in each case suggests that import is ontologically prior to our evaluations of it, thus confirming the implicit cognitivism of this first answer.[24]

It might be objected, especially in response to this example of the desire for a cigarette, that this desire is unwarranted not because it is not

---

[24] Notice that on such an account it would be improper to describe import, as I have done, as imparted by a subject's concern.

properly responsive to the import things objectively have, as is suggested by the first answer, but rather because it conflicts with some other, more fundamental constituting evaluation, such as a desire endorsed by judgment. Moreover, import is clearly relative to the individual, insofar as what has import to me need not have import to you. This relativity again seems to suggest that import is constituted by our attitudes rather than some attitude-independent fact about us. On their own, these objections do not establish the falsity of the above cognitivist account, for they merely offer an alternative interpretation of why our evaluations are unwarranted. Nonetheless, they do raise the question of what the source of import is if not some constituting evaluation.

In the face of these objections, perhaps the most promising way for a cognitivist to spell out the source of import is to appeal to an individual's biology. Thus, as a living organism, I have certain functions that must be carried out if I am to continue living. Consequently, a cognitivist might think, particular items like food, water, and shelter have import to me – as worthy of my pursuit – in light of their contribution to my successfully carrying out these functions. Moreover, these items can vary according to the particulars of my situation and so can be appropriately relative to me. Such import therefore provides an independent standard of the warrant of desire, emotion, and judgment, enabling us to say that we make these evaluations because of the import things have for us.

This appeal to attitude-independent facts about us, however, fails as an account of import for several reasons. First, in light of the assumption of the cognitive–conative divide, it changes our understanding of desire in one of two unacceptable ways. Either we understand the responsiveness to import to be a part of desire or external to it. If the former, then desire turns out to be a cognition, not a conation: to be assessed for warrant in light of whether things have objective import just is to have mind-to-world direction of fit. This is counterintuitive, to say the least. If the latter, then we cannot distinguish between desire and mere goal-directedness and so have failed to solve the problem of import. (Of course, we could stipulate that desire is directedness towards a goal that one also simultaneously cognizes as having import, but this stipulation seems merely to be a stretch in order to save the phenomenon rather than a satisfying account of desire.)

Second, although this account may make sense of the idea that import is relative to the individual in some cases, in light of peculiarities of my circumstances, for example, it cannot account for that relativity in every case. For some imports cannot be understood in terms of their contribution to fitness – either of myself or of my genes. After all, what contribution does my Beanie Baby collection, which I care about very much, make to my fitness? Apparently it is my caring about it, my having this attitude, that constitutes its import to me, and it is hard to square this with any cognitive account of import.

Finally, and most important, this appeal to biological fitness presupposes rather than explains import. For food, water, and shelter, as instrumentally necessary for my (or my genes') survival, are worth pursuing only insofar as my life or my genes are worth preserving, and the worth of these has simply been presupposed rather than accounted for. It might be thought that my life is important to me just by virtue of my being alive, so that biology does after all ground import. Yet this suggestion cannot work for paramecia: if we assume their lives have import to them just by virtue of their being alive, we are thereby committed to understanding their goal-directedness in service of the preservation of their lives as full-fledged desire, which is surely too strong a claim. Something must differentiate creatures like the higher mammals from creatures like paramecia in virtue of which our lives matter to us and their lives do not; clearly life itself cannot account for the difference.

This all suggests that we should try to answer the modified Euthyphro question the other way around: things have import to us because we evaluate them as good or bad. This would be to appeal to the other side of the cognitive–conative divide: to conation; call this the *"conative account"* of import.[25] On such an account, the relevant evaluations must be understood as constituting evaluations, laying down standards to which the world ought to conform. In contrast to the previous answer, this one has the advantage of making sense of the relativity of import in terms of the agent's constituting evaluations, which seemingly can be different for different agents. The difficulty, of course, lies in providing an account of such constituting evaluations.

One source of difficulty here lies in the conditions of the warrant of our conations. The above cognitive account interpreted the conditions of the warrant of desire in terms of a responsiveness to attitude-independent import. Having rejected this cognitive account in favor of a conative account, this connection between warranted conations and

---

[25] Such a conative account of import would seem best to fit Gaus', Greenspan's, and Roberts' understandings of their respective notions of liking, comfort, and concern.

import needs to be reinterpreted as follows: only warranted conations are constituting evaluations; unwarranted conations are evaluations that fail to constitute their objects as having import precisely because of their lack of warrant. Consequently, if we are to maintain the conceptual priority of our conations over import implicit in this answer to the Euthyphro question, we must find a way to articulate the conditions of the warrant of the relevant conations without reference to import as an independent object. I shall now argue that this approach fails as well.

One way to articulate such conditions of warrant is in terms of some fundamental conation that is somehow automatically warranted, such that other conations are warranted or not depending on their relation to this fundamental conation. Pleasure and pain are, plausibly, such fundamental conations, automatically constituting their causes as good or bad. There is much that is right about this intuitive appeal to pleasure and pain in an account of import, and in chapter 3 I shall provide an account of import that makes sense of this intuition. Nonetheless, aside from the difficulties of providing an account of pleasure and pain that can do the trick,[26] the very idea of an automatically warranted constituting evaluation is unworkable. Thus, it is common to be led by pleasure or pain to

---

[26] One way to make sense of pleasure and pain is as purely qualitative states of feeling. (See, e.g., Saul Kripke's identification of pain with an "immediate phenomenal quality," *Naming and Necessity* [Cambridge, MA: Harvard University Press, 1980], p. 152; and George Graham's definition of phenomenal qualia in terms of pain as the paradigm case in *Philosophy of Mind: An Introduction* [Oxford: Blackwell, 1993], p. 179.) However, such an account does not seem to get the notion of import into the picture. After all, to specify a quale in terms of its intensity, its character as burning or crushing, etc. is not yet to specify its badness. Rather, to get import into the picture we must say that the feeling itself *hurts*, where such hurting is something in addition to the phenomenal qualities of the feeling. (That hurting is conceptually distinct from the phenomenal feel is clear from the intelligibility of such cases as morphine pain, in which subjects having received morphine report that the pain no longer hurts even though what they feel remains unchanged. See A. Keats and H. Beecher, "Pain Relief with Hypnotic Doses of Barbiturates and a Hypothesis," *Journal of Pharmacology and Experimental Therapeutics*, 100 [1950], pp. 1–13. For similar claims about the way in which lobotomy can relieve pain, see J. B. Dynes and J. L. Poppen, "Lobotomy for Intractable Pain," *Journal of the American Medical Association*, 140 [1949], pp. 15–19; and A. Elithorn, E. Glitherno, and E. Slater, "Leucotomy for Pain," *Journal of Neurology, Neurosurgery, and Psychiatry*, 21 [1958], pp. 249–61.) Faced with this difficulty, we might try to build the evaluation explicitly into the account of pleasure and pain, but doing so requires an account of the relevant sort of evaluation, and no non-question-begging account has been forthcoming. Thus, for example, Richard Hall provides an account of how pains hurt (and so are evaluative) in terms of desire, but without an independent account of desire this simply begs the question raised by the problem of import. (See Hall's "Are Pains Necessarily Unpleasant?," *Philosophy and Phenomenological Research*, 49 [1989], pp. 643–59.)

act contrary to the imports things have for us, and so we need some way of bringing the evaluations implicit in pleasure and pain into alignment with a more general evaluative framework; that is simply to undermine their status as automatically warranted.

The same goes for any other evaluative attitude: the potential for ambivalence is ever present, and such ambivalence will need to be resolved into an all-things-considered evaluation that must depend on the way these ambivalent attitudes fit into a broader holistic framework. To see this, consider again the example of a desire for a cigarette. What makes this desire unwarranted is, apparently, the way it fits into a broader context of other evaluative attitudes I have. Thus, it is because I want to promote my and my family's health as well as to save money for my daughter's college education that I come to see cigarette smoking as bad, and it is the lack of fit between my current desire for a cigarette and these background evaluations that makes it intelligible as unwarranted. The basic idea, then, is that a particular conative attitude must be assessed for warrant only in light of the other evaluations we make based on other conative attitudes.[27] This is a holistic account of the standards of warrant and so of these conations as constituting evaluations, and so it is in terms of the relevant holism that we can distinguish genuine desire, as potentially import constituting, from mere rationally mediated goal-directedness.[28]

Solving the problem of import in this way in terms of constituting evaluations therefore requires articulating the interconnections among conations that define the relevant holism. These interconnections must be rational so as to account for the relevant standards of warrant. Consequently, the coherence of the pattern must be defined at least in part in terms of the content of the relevant conations.

---

[27] Notice that this way of putting the point leaves room for cognition to have a role in evaluation. Thus, it is my beliefs that cigarettes are unhealthy and expensive that make sense of the final evaluation of cigarettes as bad. This is, in effect, the kind of theory of the warrant of import-constituting affects offered by Gaus. According to Gaus, we can criticize these emotional affects, thereby potentially criticizing the import they constitute, by criticizing the cognitive content of the beliefs that ground them. (See §10.4 of his *Value and Justification*.) Nonetheless, given the assumption of the cognitive–conative divide, such beliefs, as cognitions, must be based on antecedent conations in order to make sense of the notion of a constituting evaluation and so of the current way of answering the Euthyphro question.

[28] This means that a creature is intelligible as having the capacity for desire only insofar as the particular occurrent instances of such conations are intelligible as potentially fitting into such a holism. I shall return to this point in more detail in chapter 3.

An appeal to instrumental rationality is helpful in articulating the relevant holism insofar as, for example, desires for ends that are instrumental to attaining other ends already constituted as worthy of pursuit are themselves warranted (other things being equal). Yet instrumental rationality on its own is insufficient, as I argued in §2.1: it simply presupposes the import of the ends and transmits that import to the means. It is similarly insufficient to appeal to a lack of conflict among the relevant conations. Thus, a chess-playing computer may have a lack of conflict within the hierarchy of its ends, and that hierarchy can be defined in part by instrumental rationality; yet none of this argues for the computer having genuine desires as opposed to mere goal-directedness. In part, this is because such a lack of conflict – such *negative coherence* – even in conjunction with instrumental rationality, is possible among even arbitrary sets of conations and so cannot tell us how to resolve cases of conflict by identifying which of the conflicting conations is unwarranted. Although a failure of coherence indicates that at least one conation in the pattern is unwarranted, that does not mean that the absence of that failure is what makes these conations warranted.

Harry Frankfurt has tried to combine the appeal to a fundamental conation with negative coherence to provide an account of import.[29] The basic idea is that *second-order volitions* – desires that some desire to act be our will – that do not conflict with any other second-order (or higher-order) volitions constitute what has import for us. The basic motivation for this view is that a second-order volition is, in effect, a self-conscious endorsement of the action, whereby we identify ourselves with it; the negative coherence is necessary to ensure that we are "wholehearted" in this identification and so of a single mind concerning it. However, this account fails as a general response to the problem of import, for the appeal to second-order volitions is meant by Frankfurt to be what distinguishes persons from mere animals, whereas the problem of import is a problem that arises for the higher mammals, like dogs and monkeys, just as much as for persons. Thus, the point of the appeal to import is to articulate a feature that distinguishes such higher animals from things like paramecia and chess-playing computers, which are capable merely of goal-directedness. Frankfurt's aim, therefore, is to provide an account not of import in general but of a kind of import

---

[29] See his *The Importance of What We Care About* (Cambridge University Press, 1988), and his "The Faintest Passion," *Proceedings and Addresses of the APA*, 66 (1992), pp. 5–16.

distinctive of persons, and his account therefore presupposes a solution to this general problem.[30]

In order to articulate the relevant holism so as to make clear how it can ground the conditions of the warrant of conation, therefore, we need to appeal instead to a *positive coherence:* a principle that holds these conations together non-arbitrarily. Yet how else can we make sense of such a principle if not by appeal to instrumental rationality, negative coherence, or self-conscious endorsement? If this account of import in terms of conation is to succeed, we must be able to articulate such a principle without reference to import; otherwise, we give up on the world-to-mind direction of fit required by the assumption of the cognitive–conative divide. Here we seem to be caught in a bind, however. On the one hand, with such a restriction in place, the resources we are left with seem inadequate to account for the kind of positive coherence necessary for an account of the standards of warrant. On the other hand, if we give up on the restriction, we have a natural candidate for such positive coherence, namely import itself. That is, these conations can be understood to be warranted quite simply in terms of the prior import of their common object, and it is in this way that these conations form a broader pattern that is non-arbitrary. Yet such an appeal to import seems to return us, unhappily, to the apparently failed cognitivist account of import.

In the context of the assumption of the cognitive–conative divide, these two choices offered by the modified Euthyphro question seem mutually exclusive and exhaustive. In particular, it seems, we cannot have it both ways: true both that evaluations are warranted because their objects have import and that an object has import because we evaluate it as good or bad. To a proponent of the cognitive–conative divide, this sounds viciously circular, for, if import is what grounds the warrant of our conations, then import must have a kind of priority that is inconsistent with its also being constituted by these conations. This inconsistency might be traced to differing conceptions, implicit in the choices offered by the modified Euthyphro question, of the ontological status of import as objective or subjective. Thus, if we allow that our evaluations

---

[30] The same basic criticism applies as well to other attempts to leverage the moral psychology of persons to provide meta-ethical accounts of value; see, e.g., Allan Gibbard's *Wise Choices, Apt Feelings,* Simon Blackburn's *Ruling Passions,* and Christine Korsgaard's "The Sources of Normativity," in Grethe Peterson, ed., *The Tanner Lectures on Human Values,* vol. 15 (Salt Lake City: University of Utah Press, 1994). There are other problems with Frankfurt's account, which I shall discuss in chapters 5, 6 and 8.

are warranted because their objects have import, that requires that import have an objective status as an independent standard that is ontologically and conceptually prior to these evaluations. Conversely, if we allow that our evaluations constitute import, that requires that import have a subjective status as projected by, and so ontologically and conceptually posterior to, these evaluations. So, it seems that we have two and only two options for solving the problem of import, and neither is satisfactory; hence the bind.

Nonetheless, we can find a way out of this bind if we reject the assumption of the cognitive–conative divide. What makes this possible is an alternative conception of the objectivity and subjectivity of import that allows us to have our cake and eat it too.

To see this, consider three different kinds of ontological status something might have as more or less objective or subjective. First is the objectivity of primary qualities, which is independent of possible experiences of subjects. Second is the status of secondary qualities, which are *perspectivally subjective* in the sense that their existence is intelligible only in terms of their being the objects of a certain sort of awareness, a certain perspective on the world.[31] For example, for something to be red is for it to be such that people generally ought to see it as red, and what it is to be red is not intelligible apart from such visual experiences. Thus, in contrast to primary qualities, there is a sense in which we might say that secondary qualities do not "really" exist, for if we were to transcend the perspective afforded by our experiences we would be unable to make sense of their existence. Nonetheless, this would be misleading insofar as, given the possibility of the relevant experiences, secondary qualities are objects we might discover, or mistakenly seem to discover, in the world.

Finally, at the most subjective end of the scale (where it scarcely makes sense to speak of an object at all), something may be *projected* onto the world in the sense that its existence depends entirely on particular mental states of the subject. This kind of subjectivity applies most straightforwardly to those properties reflective of one's preferences. Chocolate ice-cream is (now, for me) better than vanilla ice-cream, because that is what I currently prefer; if in the future I instead have a craving for vanilla, then vanilla would (then) be better than chocolate. Here the claim that one is better than the other is simply a matter of my

---

[31] This account of perspectival subjectivity and its relevance to understanding the ontological status of import owes much to McDowell's "Values and Secondary Qualities."

projecting my present preferences onto the world. In contrast to this kind of subjectivity, secondary qualities are clearly more objective because they are not relative to persons or occasions. We cannot make sense of something's being red to me here and now apart from its being red *simpliciter*, for the standards in terms of which we evaluate color experience hold intersubjectively irrespective of circumstances. Consequently, the colors things in fact have are conceptually prior to particular color experiences: seeing it as red does not make it red. This priority is what makes intelligible the kind of objectivity that secondary qualities have (in contrast to projected qualities), even though secondary qualities are not intelligible as conceptually prior to such experiences generally.

How, then, does import fit into these kinds of objectivity and subjectivity? Roughly, the idea is this. First, we can accommodate what is right about the idea that things have import because we evaluate them as good or bad by understanding import to be perspectivally subjective: something's having import is intelligible only in light of a subject's evaluative perspective. Of course, in contrast to secondary qualities, import can be relative to the individual, and is in this way more subjective than secondary qualities. This might lead one to suspect that import must be merely projected and so not perspectivally subjective. Nonetheless, all that is required to make sense of the relativity of import is that we understand the relevant evaluative perspective to be that of the individual subject. Such a perspective is constituted not by particular evaluations (such as, according to the conative account of import, constituting evaluations) but rather by a broader pattern in our evaluative attitudes.[32] This is to reject the idea, implicit in the cognitive account of import, that import is ontologically and rationally prior to our (discovering) evaluations.

What is interesting about this appeal to the pattern as a whole that constitutes the evaluative perspective is that patterns can continue to exist even in the presence of gaps or anomalies in the pattern. Thus, a performance of Beethoven's Fifth Symphony is still Beethoven's Fifth even if the horn player miscounts and misses her solo entirely or the bassoonist mischievously plays his entire part in the wrong key. Indeed,

---

[32] Note the shift in vocabulary away from "cognition" and "conation" that marks my rejection of the cognitive–conative divide: by "evaluative attitudes" I intend not only our desires and emotions but also our evaluative judgments, and I shall argue in subsequent chapters for a conception of all of these for which the notion of a direction of fit, with its assumption of rational and ontological priority, does not apply.

no single note is sacrosanct, such that in its absence the piece would no longer be Beethoven's Fifth; rather, each note, taken one by one, is expendable without destroying the overall pattern, so long as not too many notes are missing or out of place. Analogously, each particular evaluative attitude that is an element of the pattern constitutive of the relevant evaluative perspective, taken one by one, is expendable without destroying the pattern (or the import it constitutes), so long as not too many such evaluative attitudes are missing or misdirected. This means, second, we can accommodate what is right about the idea that our evaluations are warranted because their objects have import: insofar as import is constituted by the whole pattern, and insofar as each evaluative attitude that is an element of that pattern is expendable, import is rationally prior to the warrant of each particular evaluative attitude and so can serve as a standard of warrant for each. In this way, we can understand import as objective in the sense of being not projected by particular conations, thus rejecting the idea, implicit in the conative account of import, that particular (constituting) evaluations are ontologically and rationally prior to import.

In short, if we are to provide an adequate solution to the problem of import, we must appeal to a kind of holism that rejects both the assumption that the world is ontologically prior to our cognitions and the assumption that our conations are ontologically prior to the world, assumptions built into the cognitive–conative divide.

2.5 CONCLUSION

It should be clear that the discussion in the last few paragraphs has been largely schematic, and the argument against the assumption of the cognitive–conative divide is so far inconclusive, relying as it does on contestable intuitions at various points about the inadequacy of purely cognitive or purely conative accounts. Nonetheless, the argument is highly suggestive, and it clearly motivates the attempt to find an alternative account of emotions and so of import. The success of this argument rejecting the cognitive–conative divide therefore depends ultimately on the success of this alternative – not just as a solution to the problem of import, but also as a solution to the motivational and deliberative problems discussed in chapter 1.

Part of what falls with the cognitive–conative divide is the appeal of emotional cognitivism and its attempt to provide an account of emotions as compound states of cognition, conation, and bodily sensation. More-over, with the rejection of the cognitive–conative divide goes as well one of the most powerful objections against the account of emotions I outlined in §2.2. My claim there was that emotions are evaluative feelings in the sense that they are a distinctive kind of passive assent to their targets as having the import defined by their formal objects, and I have described such passive assents as feelings of pleasure and pain: to be afraid is to be pained by danger, to feel hope is to be pleased by the prospects for success, to feel frustration is to be pained by repeated failure to attain some good, etc. This appeal to pleasure and pain is intended to make three points: first concerning the way in which emotions, as passive assents to import, are evaluations of a kind that differs from evaluative judgment; second concerning the way in which emotions motivate subsequent action; and third concerning how emotions feel – their phenomenology. Implicit in this appeal to pleasure and pain is the idea that emotions are unitary and not compound states of evaluative feeling, states involving elements of both cognition and conation simul-taneously.

My aim in chapter 3, therefore, will be to fill in and provide further arguments for this outline of theories both of emotions as evaluative feelings and of import in terms of holistic patterns of evaluative attitudes. In part, the strategy will be to articulate a kind of rational commitment that defines a broader pattern among our evaluative attitudes, in par-ticular our emotions. Such rational commitments, I shall argue, provide the sort of positive coherence necessary for the resulting pattern of evaluative attitudes to constitute import. Moreover, I shall argue that these evaluative attitudes become intelligible as the evaluative attitudes they are – as emotions, desires, etc. – only because of the possibility of their fitting into such patterns constitutive of import. In this way, our evaluative attitudes and import emerge together as a part of a conceptual package, neither of which is prior to the other.

3

Constituting import

In chapter 2, I offered a brief sketch of a theory of emotions as evaluative feelings: to feel an emotion is to feel the target of that emotion as having a certain kind of import – that is, to be pleased by things going well or pained by things going poorly. To describe emotions as feelings of this sort implies that emotions are passive with respect to import: in feeling an emotion, the import of one's situation impresses itself upon one, pleasing or paining one, and this implies that import has a kind of objectivity. Such a theory, I suggested, can overcome two of the major problems for cognitivist theories of emotions and provides hopes for overcoming the third. Thus, first, we can understand the emotionality of emotions in terms of the distinctive kind of evaluative feeling emotions are, as a way of being pleased or pained by the import of one's situation. Second, we can understand the kind of rational conflict that is possible between emotions and judgments in terms of a distinctively emotional kind of assent (being pleased or pained by things being thus and so) that falls short of full-blown judgment. Finally, insofar as this theory rejects the assumption of the cognitive–conative divide by understanding emotions, as pleasures and pains, to be unitary states of assent and motivation, it holds out promise for solving the problem of import by making sense of the dual objectivity and subjectivity of import.

This, of course, is a tall order for such a brief sketch of a theory. My aim in this chapter is to fill in the details so as to make good on these promises. Indeed, part of the problem here is that several of the strands of my argument in chapter 2 might seem disconnected or even incompatible. In particular, two problems carry over concerning the intelligibility of a theory founded on the rejection of the cognitive–conative divide. First is the problem discussed in §2.3 of how we can understand pleasure and pain to be both responses (even assents) to how things are and sources of motivation without understanding them to be constituted by separable mental states of cognition and conation. My claim, defended largely in §3.4, will be that it is only because pleasures and pains are feelings of import that they are intelligible as motivating, and it is only as motivating that they can constitute import and so make it intelligible as an object of feeling. Consequently, we must understand pleasure and pain to be inseparable states of assent and motivation.

Second is a problem that arises concerning the dual objectivity and subjectivity of import. How can it be true both that import (as objective) is able to make sense of our emotions as a kind of receptivity and that import (as subjective) is constituted by our emotions? If import is intelligible as impressing itself on us in our having emotions, then it seems that import is ontologically prior to these emotions; how then can we make sense of these very same emotions as constituting (and so being ontologically prior to) import? My answer, provided initially in §§3.2–3.3 and expanded in §§3.4–3.5, will be to articulate more fully the kind of positive coherence of the relevant pattern constitutive of import in terms of a notion of emotional commitment. Such commitments, I shall claim, enable us to make sense of an attunement of our emotional sensibilities to situations of a certain kind: namely, those involving import. Thus, particular emotions must be understood as (potentially defective) exercises of that attunement to situations of that kind – as, that is, a receptivity to import. Import, therefore, can impress itself upon us in the sense that we are receptive to situations of this kind, and that is consistent with import's being simultaneously constituted by the broader pattern of emotions defined positively by such emotional commitments. As I indicated in §2.4, such an account involves dropping claims of ontological priority between import and our emotions and so rejecting the assumption of the cognitive–conative divide.

My strategy in this chapter, therefore, will be first, in §3.1, to provide an initial account of emotions as evaluative feelings and, in particular, of the kind of emotional assent such feelings involve in contrast to judgmental assent. In §3.2, I begin to fill in this account of distinctively emotional assent in terms of an account of emotional commitment and how such commitment can be the positive principle of coherence for a broader pattern of emotions, a pattern that, as I argue in §3.3, is at least part of what constitutes import. In §3.4, I provide an account of the way in which emotions as commitments of this sort motivate intentional action, arguing in part that a proper account of such motivation requires giving up the assumption of the cognitive–conative divide. This will provide an account of emotions as

61

"felt evaluations," an account I shall extend in §§3.5–3.6 to include desires and bodily pleasures and pains.

3.1 EVALUATIVE FEELINGS AND EMOTIONAL ASSENT

Emotions, I have claimed, are evaluative feelings in the sense that to feel an emotion is to be pleased or pained by the import of one's situation. This language of "evaluative feelings" is meant to capture the idea that emotions have a distinct phenomenology, that they are passions, and that they involve evaluative content. (I shall discuss the phenomenology of emotions in more detail in §3.4; for now I shall concentrate on their passivity and evaluative content.) Moreover, the way in which emotions "involve" evaluative content, I have claimed, is twofold: both as responsive to and as constitutive of import. In this section and the next, I shall discuss the passivity of emotions in terms of their responsiveness to import, arguing for an understanding of that responsiveness as a distinctly emotional assent.

To say that emotions are (potentially defective) responses to import can be misleading insofar as it might seem to imply that import is a single object – goodness or badness – to which all emotions respond equally; indeed, this understanding can seem to be encouraged by my promises of an account of import as constituted by patterns of emotions, each responsive to the import they jointly constitute. As I shall argue in §3.2, this is right – in a sense; nonetheless, it should be clear that different emotions are, in a different sense, responsive to different kinds of import. Thus, fear is intelligible only as a response to danger, whereas anger is intelligible only as a response to an offense. In this way we can define an emotion's *formal object* as the kind of import the responsiveness to which makes each emotion intelligible as the emotion it is: danger and offensiveness are the formal objects of fear and anger, respectively. (Notice the subtle shift in the account of formal object here from that provided in §2.2 [p. 34]. There I defined the formal object of an emotion in terms of a kind of evaluation implicit in the emotion, whereas here I define it in terms of responsiveness to a kind of import. The point of the shift is to register my current understanding of import as having a kind of objective status, as able to impress itself on one in feeling an emotion that is nonetheless consistent with the idea that import is also constituted by patterns of emotions; again, this understanding will be vindicated in §3.3.)

Of course, it is easy to identify the formal objects of fear and anger; it is less clear, however, that we can do this for every emotion type, as is required by the notion of a formal object. What, after all, is the formal object of embarrassment or joy? To say that their formal objects are the embarrassing and the joyful can seem to be viciously circular in a way that undermines the very notion of a formal object. Indeed, this circularity can even be found in the notion of danger, as Robert Gordon notes:

The concept of danger . . . seems tied to the notion of what is *worthy of being feared*. To use the concept in the analysis of fearing would be circular.[1]

This thought gets echoed in Gordon's review of Ronald de Sousa's *The Rationality of Emotion*:

de Sousa suggests [that] the formal object of a given emotion type . . . is *definitive* of the emotion type. (But if being frightening is understood as the axiological property of being worthy of fright, can it also be definitive of fright? Is fright, then, simply whatever the frightening is worthy of?)[2]

Thus, Gordon claims, on de Sousa's account of the notion of a formal object, we can state criteria for what it is to have a particular emotion only in terms of the formal object of that emotion (so that fear is whatever the frightening is worthy of), and we can state criteria for what it is to have the formal object of an emotion only in terms of that emotion (so that the frightening is whatever is worthy of fear); this, he claims, is clearly viciously circular.

Although there is circularity here, it is not a vicious circularity. The objection succeeds only if in providing such an analysis we must understand the formal object of an emotion to be conceptually prior to the emotion, or vice versa. However, such priority is clearly false: one cannot have a prior understanding of what it is to be afraid (or embarrassed) and only subsequently come to understand what it is for something to be dangerous (or embarrassing); conversely one cannot have a prior understanding of what it is for something to be dangerous (or embarrassing) and only subsequently come to understand what it is to be afraid (or embarrassed). Rather, an understanding of the formal object and the emotion can only come simultaneously if either is possible. Such a circularity is not vicious but is rather a feature of the kind of

---

[1] *The Structure of Emotions: Investigations in Cognitive Psychology* (Cambridge University Press, 1987), p. 70.

[2] "Review of *The Rationality of Emotion* by Ronald de Sousa," *The Philosophical Review*, 100 (1991), pp. 284–88, at p. 286.

perspectival subjectivity import, and so the formal object of an emotion, have.[3]

The notion of a formal object is important insofar as it is in terms of the kind of import defined by the formal object that we assess the warrant of emotions: an emotion is *warranted* just in case the target of the emotion has, or intelligibly seems to have, the import defined by the emotion's formal object. The standard of warrant the formal object provides is part of what makes intelligible the intentionality of emotions (and vice versa): the idea that emotions are not merely responses to import but have that import as a part of their content. For, roughly, an emotion is unwarranted just in case it has gotten the world wrong, and so an emotion is warranted just in case it has gotten the world right. (This is actually too strong, for unwarranted emotions, like unjustified beliefs, can present a view of the world that is right, although merely by chance; likewise, warranted emotions, like justified beliefs, can present a view of the world that is wrong, although through no fault of the subject's. Nonetheless, such cases are clearly parasitic on the standard cases of warranted and unwarranted emotions, and so in no way undermine the conceptual connection between intentionality and the standards of emotional warrant.)

Of course, there is a sense in which the mere appearance of a puddle of water on the pavement can also get the world right or wrong: it presents a view of the world that does or does not correspond to how things are. In this respect, mere appearances are intentional as well. Nonetheless, mere appearances are not subject to assessment as warranted or not precisely because they are "mere" appearances: they are ways in which the world presents itself that we do not endorse as how things really are. By contrast, the warrant of emotions is intelligible only because the emotion implicitly endorses or assents to the view of the world the emotion presents, for it is that assent, and not the mere appearance, that is evaluated as warranted or not. Consequently, the

---

[3] The same is true of the perspectival subjectivity of color: what it is to be red cannot be disentangled from what it is to experience things as red, nor can what it is to experience things as red be disentangled from things being red. Such circularity does not mean there is no objective fact about what things are red, nor does it mean that we cannot have mistaken experiences of (only apparently) red things.

Notice also the inference in the text from the perspectival relativity of import in general to the perspectival relativity of the special kind of import involved in an emotion's formal object. The connection between the two will be discussed further in §3.2.

warrant of an emotion is a standard of the rational defensibility of such an assent as accurately reflecting the imports things have.[4]

This notion of the kind of assent implicit in emotions needs to be clarified. As I argued in §2.3.2, this idea that emotions essentially involve a kind of assent to the presence of import is required to make sense of both how emotions motivate intentional action and the possibility of rational conflict (or accord) between emotions and judgment; in this way, I argued against both anti-judgmentalism and judgmentalism about emotions. Recall that, according to a judgmentalist theory of emotions, we should understand the kind of assent implicit in an emotion in terms of belief or judgment, which is thereby understood to be a component of the emotion. Anti-judgmentalists correctly criticize such an account by noting that it understands the kind of rational conflict between emotions and the judgments that repudiate them to be, implausibly, that of incoherence in judgment. The conclusion anti-judgmentalists draw from this is that emotions are merely ways in which the world appears to us, without our necessarily having to assent to that appearance. However, I argued, the anti-judgmentalist's attempt to make sense of such irrational conflicts in terms of the way in which emotions motivate us to act fails unless we understand emotions themselves to be assents, contrary to the anti-judgmentalist position. However, I suggested, this does not mean we have to be judgmentalists; the way out is to understand emotions to be a kind of assent – distinctively emotional assent – that falls short of judging or believing in the appearance. Nonetheless, two lacunae in that argument, raised in notes 15 and 18 of chapter 2, need to be filled in for the argument to be convincing: both the distinctive kind of emotional assent and the connection between such assent and motivation need to be articulated more fully. I shall now discuss emotional assent, leaving the account of motivation until §3.4.

To begin to understand distinctively emotional assent so as to solve the problem of rational conflict between emotion and judgment, note that judgments are active whereas emotions are passive. To make a judgment is to do something *actively*, consciously, and (for the most part) freely, and it is in large part for this reason that incoherence in judgment is unintelligible. That judgments are active, conscious, and free in this

---

[4] As will become clear in §4.3, there are other ways in which emotions can be rationally defensible or not – in terms, for example, of their propriety in a given social situation.

way is part of what makes them so central to our cognitive lives.[5] By contrast, emotions are *passive:* they are states of consciousness that for the most part come over us in a way very much like that of perception, without our having to do anything more than (passively) be receptive to them. Indeed, this is the point of my claim that emotions are evaluative feelings: in feeling an emotion we are pleased or pained by the import of our situation impressing itself on us.

Although this distinction is still hazy, it nonetheless enables us to understand judgments as being prior to emotions in two senses. First, judgments, as free, conscious, and active assents, normally have a kind of priority over emotions as articulations of our understanding of how things are. Second, given this priority, judgments normally have a kind of rational priority over emotions insofar as in cases of conflict between emotion and judgment it is emotion, as passive, that usually seems to thrust a vision of the world upon us contrary to what we in some sense really think. The conflict is therefore irrational, but, given the passivity of emotional assent and the corresponding rational priority of judgment, it is not incoherent.[6]

I do not mean to suggest that just any instance of passively taking in evaluative content counts as emotional. Perceptual belief is passive as well, and it might seem that an emotional cognitivist could appeal to the passivity of such beliefs in giving an account of the sort of passive assent characteristic of emotions. One problem with this suggestion, however, is that, although our initial acquisition of perceptual beliefs involves a process in which we are passive, the assent implicit in the belief thus acquired is potentially one with respect to which we are active: as further evidence comes to light, we may actively revise or confirm such beliefs. Although we can have a kind of control over our emotions and so can be responsible for them (see §6.4 for an explicit account), exercising this control for the most part involves training and habituation. Consequently, the kind of control we can exercise over such a belief is very

---

[5] In understanding judgment as active and free in this way, I do not mean to presuppose a kind of belief voluntarism – the view that we have complete control over what we believe and judge. I shall discuss explicitly how to make sense of the relevant kind of activity and freedom in more detail in Part II, especially §§6.3–6.4 and §7.4.

[6] Notice the qualifications explicit in these two kinds of priority of judgment over emotion: judgment is *normally* prior to emotion both as an articulation of our understanding of the world and rationally. Nonetheless, as I shall argue in chapter 5, such priority is not absolute, for emotions can in a way correct our judgments as well as vice versa; indeed, it is in part this fact about judgment that provides some limits on the kind of active control we can exercise over what judgments we make (cf. note 5).

different with respect to the activity of assenting than that which we can exercise over our emotions.

Yet the distinction between emotional assent and the kind of assent involved in judgment and belief involves more than this distinction between passivity and activity. For import, as an object of emotional assent, is not intelligible as independent of the subject's perspective on it; indeed, it is precisely for this reason that the language of cognition, as distinct from conation, does not apply to emotional assent in the way it does for ordinary judgmental assent. Rather, as I shall argue in §3.3, import itself is constituted by the patterns of our emotional assents insofar as such assent involves a commitment to continue to feel and act in the appropriate ways; for this reason, I shall distinguish *cognitive assent*, as the kind inherent in ordinary judgment and belief, from *disclosive assent*, as the kind inherent in emotions and the other evaluative attitudes that are simultaneously responsive to and constitutive of import.[7] The structure of this commitment must now be examined carefully.

3.2 EMOTIONAL COMMITMENTS

It is important to understand emotions not as isolated mental states, but rather in terms of their rational connections to other mental states, including other emotions. My aim in this section is to discuss the structure of the rational interconnections among emotions by initially articulating two kinds of commitments among emotions, namely transitional and tonal commitments, eventually arguing that these two kinds of commitments are special instances of a more general kind of emotional commitment. As I shall argue in §3.3, these emotional commitments are what provide the positive principle of coherence that makes the resulting pattern intelligible as constituting import, thereby providing a more complete account of disclosive assent. I shall subsequently expand this understanding of emotional commitments to include the interconnections among emotions and desires (in §3.5) and evaluative judgment (in chapter 5), thereby coming to understand both desire and evaluative judgment as involving disclosive assent as well.

Consider first transitional commitments. One way of dividing emotions into kinds is in terms of whether they are forward-looking or backward-looking. *Forward-looking emotions*, such as hope and fear,

---

[7] Notice the qualification here: it is "ordinary" judgment and belief that involve cognitive assent. As I shall argue in chapter 5, evaluative judgment involves disclosive assent as well.

anticipate good or bad things that are currently happening or might well happen, whereas *backward-looking emotions*, such as relief and disappointment, are responses to something good or bad that has already happened. Consequently, as the relevant things happen in the world, forward-looking emotions rationally ought to become the corresponding backward-looking emotions: there is something rationally unwarranted, other things being equal, about feeling fear that one's prize Ming vase is about to be destroyed, but feeling neither relief when it miraculously escapes unscathed nor sadness or anger when one's fear is borne out. To say that one rationally ought to have the corresponding backwards-looking emotion given that one experiences the forward-looking emotion is to articulate the *transitional commitments* involved in these emotions – commitments concerning the temporal transitions from one emotion to another.

Second, consider tonal commitments. Here we need to make a distinction in kinds of emotions in terms of their evaluative tone as positive or negative; this distinction is orthogonal to that between forward- and backward-looking emotions. *Positive emotions*, like satisfaction and hope, are emotions directed at good things that have happened or might well happen, whereas *negative emotions*, like disappointment and fear, are emotions directed at the corresponding bad things. To say that emotions involve *tonal commitments* is to say that if one experiences a positive emotion in response to something good that has happened or might happen, then, other things being equal, one rationally ought to have experienced the corresponding negative emotion if instead what happened (or conspicuously might happen) were something bad; not to experience this emotion would be unwarranted. Thus, to feel satisfaction is normally to be committed to feel some corresponding negative emotion in the relevant counterfactual situations: disappointment were it the case that you did not get what you wanted, or anger if you did not get what you wanted because someone else maliciously prevented you from getting it. (The same goes, *mutatis mutandis*, for negative emotions imposing tonal commitments on the corresponding positive emotions.)

Notice that in these descriptions of transitional and tonal commitments I have only vaguely identified the "corresponding" emotions one is committed to. In part this is because which emotions are the "corresponding" emotions depends on how we imagine the details of the counterfactual situation, as the examples given above illustrate. Nonetheless, what defines the range of emotions to which a particular emotion commits one no matter what the counterfactual situation is that emotion's *focus:* the background object having import to the subject that makes intelligible the evaluation implicit in the emotion. Thus, my fear of earthquakes and my anger at you for throwing the baseball in the house are both made intelligible in light of the import my prize Ming vase has for me, for it is this vase that the earthquake threatens and it is in virtue of your callous disregard for the vase that you offend me. It is only because the forward- and backward-looking emotions in this example share a common focus that we can understand them as imposing transitional commitments on each other. The same goes for positive and negative emotions imposing tonal commitments on each other: we can understand my satisfaction now imposing a tonal commitment on my feeling anger in certain counterfactual situations only because the satisfaction and anger share a common focus.

This notion of an emotion's focus enables us to refine our understanding of an emotion's formal object. In §3.1, I defined the formal object as the kind of import the responsiveness to which makes each emotion intelligible as the emotion it is. Now we can understand the specific kind of import at issue in each emotion's formal object in terms of a relation between its target and focus. Thus, we can understand danger, the formal object of fear, in terms of the target being a threat to the focus of the emotion such that it is the import of the focus that makes intelligible the resulting import of the target. Of course, as I acknowledged in §3.1, it is not always so easy to articulate the formal objects of other emotions except in a way that involves a (non-vicious) kind of circularity, and so it will not always be so easy to articulate the precise relation between the target and the focus at issue. Nonetheless, my point is that we can understand the import of the target as deriving from the import of the focus together with the details of the particular circumstances.

This has two fundamentally important implications. First, because import is in this way central to the formal object of any emotion, to have an emotion is to be committed to the import of that emotion's focus; call this the emotion's *focal commitment*. We can now see that focal commitments are a more general kind of commitment of which transitional and tonal commitments are species, for emotions impose transitional and tonal commitments on each other only by virtue of sharing a common focus. Moreover, this notion of a focal commitment helps us understand rational connections among emotions that do not neatly fit into this categorization of transitional and tonal commitments, such as the connection between relief that the vase was not destroyed in the earthquake and the appropriateness of anger if, counterfactually, it were destroyed by the baseball you threw.

Second, precisely because of the commitment to the import of its focus each emotion involves, each emotion in general imposes rational commitments on one to display a broader pattern of emotions with the same focus in the relevant (actual and counterfactual) situations. For a failure to have this pattern of other emotions in the relevant circumstances is to undermine this commitment to import. For example, my fear for the vase as the baseball hurls towards it would be unwarranted unless I would also, other things being equal, feel relief if the vase were to emerge unscathed, disappointment, sadness, or grief if it were destroyed, anger at the neighbor kid for his casual disregard for the vase, etc. Or, again, somewhat more generally, if you are hopeful that some end can be achieved, then it would be unwarranted (other things being equal) not also to be afraid when its accomplishment is threatened, to be relieved when the threat does not in fact materialize, to be angry at those who impede one's progress, or to be satisfied when one finally attains the end (or disappointed when one ultimately fails). This means that the broader pattern of other emotions with a common focus defined by these focal commitments is *rational* in that belonging to the pattern is a necessary condition of the warrant of particular emotions. In saying that the patterns are rational, I am not claiming that emotions belonging to the pattern are merely permitted by the import of their common focus. Rather, part of the point of talking about such rational interconnections as commitments is that, other things being equal, the failure to experience emotions that fit into the pattern when otherwise appropriate is a rational failure. (So far, I have justified the idea that these patterns of emotions are rational only intuitively; deeper reasons for the rationality of these focal commitments will emerge in my discussion of import, as that to which one is thereby committed, in §3.3.)

That these patterns of emotions are rational in this way implies that they are in general *projectible* as well. For, given that rationality is the constitutive ideal of the mental, to have the capacity for emotions at all requires that one's exercise of this capacity be by and large rational. Having the capacity for emotions therefore requires that one be disposed both actually and counterfactually to experience these emotions when rationally required and not when rationally prohibited; this just is to require that these patterns of emotions, as necessary conditions of the warrant of their constituents, be projectible. This is not to say that one must feel emotions every time they are warranted in order for the overall pattern to persist. Isolated failures to feel particular emotions, though unwarranted, do not undermine the rational coherence of the broader pattern so long as these failures remain isolated. In this way, the pattern of emotions, given their mutual commitments, exerts *rational pressure* on one to have subsequent emotions that conform to it in the relevant circumstances.

Consequently, by virtue of the projectibility and rationality of the patterns instituted by the focal commitments among emotions, we can see how such commitments provide a positive principle of coherence for the resulting pattern: it is not merely that these emotions form a pattern by virtue of their lack of conflict; rather, particular emotions are *beholden* to the broader pattern insofar as (a) belonging to the pattern is partly constitutive of the emotion's warrant, (b) failure to feel the emotion in the relevant circumstances is, other things being equal, rationally inappropriate, and (c) the broader pattern exerts rational pressure on one to feel these emotions in the relevant circumstances.

3.3 FELT EVALUATIONS: CONSTITUTING IMPORT

As I have said, my claim will be that import is constituted by a pattern of evaluative attitudes with the right sort of principle of positive coherence. Why, then, should we think these focal commitments among emotions provide a principle of the right sort? To answer this, we first need to consider import itself.

Intuitively, at least part of what it is to have *import* is to be a worthy object of attention and action: insofar as something has import for one, one ought to pay attention to what happens to it and so be prepared to act on its behalf when otherwise appropriate. Consequently, that something is worthy of attention and action means not merely that it is permissible or a good thing to pay attention to it and act on its behalf; rather, it means that attention and action are, by and large, required on pain of giving up or at least undermining the idea that it really has import to one. After all, it is hard (though perhaps not impossible) to credit someone with caring about, say, having a clean house even though he never or rarely notices when it gets dirty, or never or rarely does anything about it even when he does notice. Of course, this is not to deny that someone who genuinely cares may in some cases be distracted by other things that are more important, and so occasionally may not notice that his house is getting dirty or act so as to clean it up. What is required is a consistent pattern of attending to and acting on behalf of the object in question.

Consider first how to make sense of something's having import as, in part, being worthy of attention.[8] Insofar as the attention of the subject is by and large required by such worthiness, the subject must therefore be vigilant for what happens or might well happen to it. The kind of vigilance that is required here is not merely *active vigilance*, in which one consciously directs one's attention towards it, as when waiting impatiently for the traffic light to change. Given the range of things that have import to us, such active vigilance on its own would rapidly overwhelm our abilities to attend to the relevant objects. Rather, the kind of vigilance primarily at issue is *passive vigilance:* an attunement of one's sensibilities such that one's attention is naturally drawn to the appropriate kinds of situations involving import.

At this point we can see that there is a two-way conceptual connection between import and the pattern of emotions defined by their mutual commitments to a common focus. First, the kind of passive vigilance normally required for import is largely an attunement of one's emotions of a sort made possible by the projectibility of the relevant pattern of emotions: to display the pattern is to be disposed to respond to the focus of that pattern when and because it is affected favorably or adversely. Moreover, the rationality of this pattern means that a failure to feel an emotion one is rationally committed to feeling by virtue of the overall pattern is a failure to respond as one ought to the focus of the pattern. That focus, therefore, is intelligible as worthy of attention precisely because of the focal commitments that define the overall pattern. In this way, the kind of positive coherence provided by emotional commitments, by instituting an attunement of one's sensibilities, is of the right kind: the pattern of emotions is partially constitutive of import. This is what is behind the intuition, expressed in §2.2, that it is hard to make sense of something having import to someone if she does not respond emotionally, no matter what, when it is affected favorably or adversely.[9]

---

[8] I shall return to the idea that to have import is to be worthy of action only later in §3.4 and §3.5 in discussing how emotions and desires motivate.

[9] I say that it is "hard to make sense of" such import in the absence of the broader pattern of emotions because there are other elements that go into constituting something's

This may make it look as if the pattern of emotions is conceptually prior to import, but that would be to ignore the second conceptual connection between the two. In my discussion of the focal commitments that define these broader patterns of emotions, I appealed merely to intuition in claiming that the pattern of such commitments imposes a rational requirement on one to have subsequent emotions with the same focus. Now, in light of this understanding of import as worthiness of attention and action, we can see why this is a rational requirement. For, insofar as particular emotions are feelings of import, to feel a particular emotion is to feel its focus as having import and so as calling for those other emotional responses in the appropriate circumstances. It is for this reason that the failure to feel these other emotions is a rational failure: a failure to attend as one ought to this import. Moreover, which circumstances are the "appropriate" circumstances is intelligible only in terms of this import: those circumstances that are such as rationally to engage one's emotional sensibilities – one's passive vigilance. In other words, the pattern of emotions is essentially a pattern of responsiveness to import, and the rationality of the pattern, as that which makes intelligible one's having the capacity for emotions at all, is an essential feature of this responsiveness. In this way, import is necessary to make sense of the rationality and projectibility of the relevant pattern of emotions.

This means that import and such a projectible, rational pattern of emotions come together as a conceptual package, each partially constitutive of the other. This explains how import can be simultaneously both subjective and objective. Thus, first, I claimed that import is *perspectivally subjective* insofar as something is intelligible as having import only from a particular point of view, which is, moreover, relative to the individual. Such a point of view and its relativity to the subject are intelligible in terms of these patterns of emotions: it is the pattern in a particular subject's emotions that provides the relevant point of view, the relevant attunement of one's sensibilities to a common focus. (To emphasize this subjectivity we might speak not of the object's having import but rather

---

having import to one, such as one's desires and judgments, and these may constitute import even in the face of a general failure of emotional response. Doing so, however, requires a special story about why the pattern of emotions is absent so as to explain away that absence (and its irrationality) while preserving the coherence of the overall pattern. (I will describe such a case, in which the import defined largely by one's emotions and that defined largely by one's judgments pull apart, in §5.2.)

of our *caring* about or *valuing* it.) Nonetheless, second, import is *objective* in the sense that it is a standard in terms of which the warrant of particular emotions is to be assessed and so is conceptually prior to particular emotions. In light of this objectivity, then, we can make sense of the intuition that import *impresses* itself upon us in our feeling particular emotions. For the projectible, rational pattern of emotions is a kind of receptivity to or passive vigilance for situations of a certain kind: namely situations involving import. Consequently, particular emotions, as exercises of this receptivity to the import of such situations, are, conversely, feelings engendered by import impressing itself on us.

Emotions, I have claimed, are evaluative feelings: feelings of evaluative content, whereby import impresses itself upon us. Yet, to emphasize the role emotions have in constituting import, we might also say that emotions are *felt evaluations:* evaluations that we make by feeling them, and my account of the projectible, rational patterns instituted by commitments to import is, in effect, a theory of such felt evaluations.

By articulating these projectible rational patterns of emotions and their two-way conceptual connections with import, I have begun to fill in the sketch of an account of import provided in §2.4, thus vindicating to some extent the rejection of the assumption of the cognitive–conative divide at least with respect to the emotions. For, insofar as import and our emotional evaluations come as a conceptual package with neither prior to the other, we must reject the idea that emotions have either mind-to-world or world-to-mind direction of fit: emotions are both responsive to and constitutive of import. Moreover, we can make sense of the positive principle of coherence of the pattern in terms of the idea that each emotion that is an element of the pattern is a commitment to import and, thereby, to having other emotions with that common focus in the relevant circumstances.

Nonetheless, the account is so far incomplete in two respects. First, I have only dealt with the idea that to have import is to be worthy of attention and not with the idea that it is also to be worthy of action. I shall redress this deficiency, thereby filling in as well the account of felt evaluations, in providing an account of emotions and motivation (in §3.4) and in providing an account of desire (in §3.5). Second, it is clear that emotions on their own are not the only things that constitute import; this has been implicit in my qualifications, at various points, concerning the necessity and sufficiency of emotional response for the intelligibility of import. Thus, I have claimed that it is "hard" – but not impossible – to make sense of import in the absence of emotional response, and that the relevant pattern of emotions is only "partially" constitutive of import. In particular, desire and evaluative judgment must have a place in any account of import, and I shall argue in §3.5 and in chapter 5 that this is intelligible only if they are elements of the pattern of emotions just described.

3.4 PLEASURE, PAIN, AND MOTIVATION

My aim in this section is to understand the way in which emotions, as pleasures and pains, motivate action and so make intelligible the sense in which to have import is to be a worthy object of action.

One kind of behavioral effect emotions can have is non-intentional behavior: trembling from fear, hanging one's head in shame (even when alone), shaking one's fist at someone in anger, etc. These are non-intentional behaviors because they do not have a point or end in terms of which notions of success or failure are intelligible: although you can tremble from fear or hang your head in shame at otherwise inopportune moments, there is nothing that would count as trembling or hanging one's head correctly or incorrectly. Because such behaviors are without a point, there is nothing in the content of the emotion that makes them intelligible by saying something in favor of behaving in these ways. Rather, we might say, such behaviors are *arational expressions* of these emotions insofar as particular emotion kinds typically cause such characteristic behaviors. Nonetheless, there is nothing about these behaviors that makes them an essential part of the emotions they express, for it is entirely possible to experience fear or anger without ever expressing them in these ways. For this reason, and because such behaviors are disconnected from rationality, my main focus in this book, I shall have little more to say about them.

A second kind of behavioral effect of emotions is intentional action aimed at some end to be achieved. Thus, fear might cause us to try to escape the relevant danger, and anger or jealousy might cause us to seek revenge. Because this is intentional action, there is the possibility of success or failure. Consequently, in this case the emotion explains the action not merely by causing it but by motivating it, thereby making it intelligible within a broader context of rationality: the evaluation implicit in the emotion's formal object justifies the action by revealing its end to be worth pursuing in the present circumstances, other things being equal.[10] For to feel the target of an emotion to have the import specified by the emotion's formal object is in part to feel it to be a worthy object of action. Thus, we should not specify the formal object of fear or anger merely as danger or offense, but, rather, to make explicit the way in which it can justify action, as danger worth avoiding (or mitigating) or offense worth punishing. Consequently, to specify the ways in which emotions can justify intentional action is, in effect, to provide a clearer specification of the kind of evaluation implicit in their formal objects.

It is important, however, not to overintellectualize the way in which emotions motivate intentional action by understanding in every case the kind of rational intelligibility such motivation provides in terms of an end the action seeks to achieve, so that the explanation of action proceeds in light of the familiar belief–desire model. Thus, in the example given above of fear motivating escape, it might be tempting to think that we already had a desire to avoid injury; the emotion would then merely provide us with cognitive access to the presence of a current danger, so that what explains our attempt to escape are this desire and this cognition. Yet, even if this is true in some cases, it is clearly not true of all cases. In her "Arational Actions,"[11] Rosalind Hursthouse provides a series of examples of intentional actions expressive of emotions that nonetheless cannot be explained by "reasons in the sense that there is a true description of the action of the form 'X did it (in order) to . . .'" (p. 59). Such examples include rumpling the hair of or kissing someone out of (occurrent) love, kicking out of frustration a door that refuses to shut or a car that refuses to start, jumping for joy, and crying out of sadness. Thus, she rightly argues, it is not plausible to think of the explanation of the agent's kicking the door in terms of the desire to injure it and the belief that kicking it is the means to accomplish this.

---

[10] This is, of course, a controversial claim, and not one that I am able to defend in detail here. (For a clear defense, see William Dray's *Laws and Explanation in History*, especially chapter 5.) The alternative (which Dray is in part concerned with refuting) is a view of intentional action as explicable in much the same way that we explain any event occurring in nature: in terms of universal laws. Paul Churchland, a recent proponent of this covering-law model, argues that, because psychological explanation depends on empirical universal laws, we might discover that these laws are fundamentally mistaken and need to be replaced with other laws that do not make reference to the theoretical terms of psychology, such as "belief," "desire," and "emotion"; this view is known as *eliminative materialism*. (See Churchland's *A Neurocomputational Perspective: The Nature of Mind and the Structure of Science* [Cambridge, MA: MIT Press, 1989].) I take the cogency of Churchland's arguments for eliminative materialism given the covering-law model to be a reductio of that model.

[11] *Journal of Philosophy*, 88 (1991), pp. 57–68.

Nonetheless, Hursthouse concludes from this that such intentional actions are *arational* – are "done without reason" (p. 66). This conclusion is too hasty. Hursthouse mistakenly thinks that all rational explanation of action proceeds in light of the familiar belief–desire model in which one desires some end and believes that acting in this way is a means to that end: that all reasons for intentional action are instrumental. Yet all that is needed for a rational explanation of action is that the action have a point that the explanation reveals as worthwhile. In many cases the point can be an end to be achieved, but it need not be. Thus, I may play the piano simply for the sake of playing the piano and not because doing so accomplishes anything; nonetheless, playing piano does have a point. (Of course, one might say that I play the piano because I enjoy it, and this may seem to indicate that my enjoyment is the end for the sake of which I play the piano. Although this may be true in some cases, it cannot be true of all cases on pain of collapsing the important distinction between activity engaged in for its own sake and activity engaged in for the sake of something else. Indeed, this is part of what Hursthouse gets right in her article.) Similarly, I may jump for joy or cry out of sadness, where my engaging in such an activity also has a point: celebration or mourning. The idea here is that jumping for joy is not a means to celebrating; it is celebrating. The joy I feel provides a rational explanation of my jumping because feeling joy is in part to feel the target to be worthy of celebration. The same goes for crying out of sadness, rumpling someone's hair out of love, and kicking the door out of frustration: in each case, the emotion provides a reason for the action by saying something in favor of that action, revealing its point as worthwhile, even if that point is not an end to be achieved and so even if the reason for it is not instrumental. Such non-goal-directed intentional action can properly be understood to be an expression of the emotion – this time a *rational expression*: activity engaged in because, in light of the evaluation of the target implicit in the emotion's formal object, such activity is here and now revealed to be worth engaging in for its own sake.

In short, emotions explain intentional action by providing reasons for that action in light of their responsiveness not only to the import of their foci, but also, in light of their implicit sense of the situation, to the consequent import of their targets. However, this is clearly not sufficient for an account of emotional motivation, for the connection between the reasons emotions provide and our being moved to action is still unclear. After all, judgment could just as well provide the same reasons for action, as when I judge someone to have offended me and so to be worthy of punishment. Yet the connection between emotions and motivation is somehow much more direct than that between evaluative judgment and motivation, and this "directness" needs to be accounted for.

One way to account for such directness, already addressed in my discussion of anti-judgmentalism in §2.3.2, is to appeal to a desire that is somehow directly associated with the emotion but not with the judgment. As I argued there, this misses the point, for the desire itself, as not merely a general desire but one that is specific to the occasion, must be motivated by the evaluation implicit in the emotion. Consequently, the appeal to desire merely backs us up one step without solving the underlying problem: why should my emotional evaluation somehow more directly engage such a desire than judgmental evaluation does? (Moreover, as I shall argue in §3.5, desires themselves must be understood as a kind of felt evaluation and so as motivating action in much the same way emotions do.)

The solution depends on understanding the way in which emotions, as felt evaluations, are connected to import. As I argued in §3.3, there is a two-way conceptual connection between import and the relevant pattern of emotions, a conceptual connection grounded in the idea that to have import is to be worthy of attention. The same conceptual connection holds, I shall now argue, when we consider the idea that to have import is to be worthy of action.

Consider this conceptual connection first from the perspective of import as subjective – of our caring about something as the focus of a projectible, rational pattern of emotions. The focal commitments that define this pattern are commitments to the import of their common focus. As such, they are commitments not merely to attend to that focus by feeling the relevant emotions when otherwise appropriate, but also to act appropriately on behalf of that focus. Just as a failure to attend in the relevant circumstances is, other things being equal, inappropriate, so, too, a failure to act is, other things being equal, inappropriate given the import to which one is committed in feeling these emotions. Likewise, just as gaps or abnormalities in the pattern of emotional attention focused on a particular object can, if they are widespread enough, undermine the coherence of that pattern and so the import of its focus, so, too, gaps or abnormalities in the pattern of emotional action focused on that object can, if sufficiently widespread, undermine the coherence of that same pattern. In this way, the connection between emotions and motivation is conceptual: it is a condition of the possibility of import and so also of one's having the capacity for emotions at all that these emotions, as commitments to that import, normally motivate one to act appropriately.

This same point can be made from the perspective of import as objective – as impressing itself on us in our having particular emotions. To say that we are motivated by import is not merely to say that we acquire an additional premise to be used in practical reasoning, as we do with perceptual belief or with active evaluative judgment. Rather, just as import, as worthy of attention, impresses itself on us, holding our attention, so, too, import, as worthy of action, *enthralls* us by moving us to act. Of course, in having our motivation "gripped" by import in this way, we are not automatically led to act accordingly. Reasons other than that provided by such import may also provide motivation to act in conflicting ways. Nonetheless, in being enthralled by import in this way, we feel some pull to act accordingly, even if we are able to overcome that pull to some degree. (I say "to some degree" here because in some cases we can overcome the motivational pull of an emotion only by channeling its motivation from an intentional action into a non-intentional expression. Thus, in response to someone's insult that angers me, I may feel the pull to retaliate by lashing out at her, but control this impulse by getting myself merely to shake my fist in her direction.)

This idea that import can enthrall us in this way may sound mysterious, but it is not. For, just as import's impressing itself on us presupposes that we are already attuned to that import, so, too, import's enthralling us presupposes that we are already prepared to act on its behalf in being receptive emotionally to that import. In each case, the attunement and the preparedness is made possible by the focal commitments defining the pattern constitutive of import. Yet we should not think that all the work here is being done by the commitment, for that commitment is essentially a commitment to import. Hence, the attunement and preparedness this commitment makes possible are essentially an attunement to, and preparedness to act on behalf of, that import, and are not intelligible otherwise: emotions and import are a conceptual package, with neither prior to the other.

Consequently, given the dual objectivity and subjectivity of import made possible by the way in which import and the emotions are a conceptual package, it is true both that emotions motivate only because they are evaluative – because import impresses itself on us in having the emotion – and that emotions evaluate (i.e., constitute import) only because they motivate. Moreover, the connection between the evaluation and the motivation is established not between conceptually separable states of cognition and conation, as emotional cognitivism and the assumption of the cognitive–conative divide would have it. Rather, the very receptivity to evaluative content whereby import impresses itself on us, as an enthrallment by that import, is itself essentially motivating. This means that emotions are conceptually indivisible states of felt evaluations that both evaluate and motivate in a way that undermines the assumption of the cognitive–conative divide.

In short, emotions are *felt evaluations* in the sense that (a) by virtue of their mutual focal commitments they form projectible, rational patterns that constitute import, and (b) they are nonetheless individually responsive to that import impressing itself on us in such a way that (c) we are enthralled by its practical import and so motivated to act.

Two final loose threads need to be tied up before I complete this initial account of emotions and import. First, it is because emotions are felt evaluations that we can make sense of them as pleasures and pains. As I argued in §2.2, emotions are pleasures and pains not in the sense that they involve bodily sensations but rather because they are a distinctive kind of intentional feeling of import: to feel fear is to be pained by danger, and to feel satisfaction is to be pleased by success. This kind of intentional feeling of import is now revealed to be that of felt evaluations. Thus, to feel good (be pleased) or feel bad (be pained) is to have the import of one's situation, as good or bad, impress itself on one. Such an account of emotional pleasure and pain as felt evaluations can, therefore, account for both the way in which pleasures and pains intrinsically motivate and the intuition that pleasure and pain have a special connection to what it is for something to be good or bad.

Of course, no account of pleasure and pain worth the name is complete without saying something about the phenomenology of such states; how, then, can we understand the phenomenology of emotional pleasures and pains? The answer lies in the kind of feeling emotions are as felt evaluations. Emotions come over us in the sense that the evaluation impresses itself on us and enthralls us by holding both our attention and our motivation in its grip. This gripping of our attention and motivation by the import that impresses itself on and enthralls us just is how the emotion feels – its phenomenology, its "qualitative feel," if you like. Thus, emotions please or pain us – they feel good or bad – in that they are responses of this kind to import. This is not, of course, an account of emotional qualia understood as conceptually separable components of emotions: apart from the import impressing itself on one and enthralling one, apart from this intentional, motivating, evaluative content that thrusts itself upon one, there is no way that emotions feel that is essential to and definitive of emotions as such.

This is not to deny that in feeling an emotion we may also feel certain bodily sensations that both accompany it and contribute to our overall phenomenal experience. Indeed, such accompanying sensations are commonplace: people very often feel queasy when afraid or flushed when angry, and these sensations themselves may be uncomfortable or even painful. Nonetheless, such sensations must be understood as something we feel in addition to fear or anger and not as an essential part of these emotions; it is perfectly intelligible to feel fear or anger with different accompanying bodily sensations or with none at all. That is why a proper understanding of the phenomenology of emotions need have nothing to say about such bodily sensations as a separable component.

The second loose thread concerns the emotionality of emotions – what is distinctive of emotions as the kind of mental state they are. In §2.3.1, this was raised as a problem for emotional cognitivism given its strategy of reducing emotions to antecedently intelligible states of belief, desire, and bodily sensation. The intuitive suggestion I made at the time was that we should understand the emotionality of emotions in terms of the kind of pleasures and pains emotions essentially are. It should now be clear how the account of emotional pleasures and pains, as felt evaluations, vindicates this suggestion.

3.5 DESIRES AS FELT EVALUATIONS

I have argued that import is partly constituted by the projectible, rational patterns in one's emotions defined by their mutual commitments – that is, that these patterns of emotions are only a part of a larger package that constitutes import. What else needs to be added to this picture in order to have a complete account of import? One obvious candidate is desire.

Desires, I have claimed, must be carefully distinguished from mere goal-directedness: to have a desire is not merely to have a disposition to pursue a goal insofar as desires find their objects to be worth pursuing or avoiding – to have import – where such import provides a reason for acting; indeed, we might say, worthiness of pursuit is the formal object of desire. So desires differ from goal-directedness by motivating in light of an implicit evaluation, in light of an essential connection with import. Nonetheless, as was the case for emotions in §3.4, the kind of evaluation implicit in desire must be distinguished from the evaluations we make in judgment, for evaluative judgment can be disconnected from motivation in ways in which desire cannot. How, then, are we to distinguish the special sort of evaluation implicit in desire (as essentially motivating) from those explicit in evaluative judgment (which need not motivate)? The answer, I shall argue, is that desires like emotions are a kind of felt evaluation.

Before fleshing out this answer in more detail, I need to consider an objection to this conception of desire as essentially for the good, forcefully articulated by David Velleman.[12] According to Velleman, that desire does not aim at what is good is manifest when we consider *perverse desires* – desires whose

propositional object implies that it is inappropriate. That is, the perverse subject desires that something undesirable occur, and its being undesirable is part of the description under which he desires it. (p. 18)

If desire essentially aims at the good, Velleman argues, then it would be "impossible" to desire what is bad because it is bad. Consequently, the very existence of perverse desires shows that desire does not aim at the good.

Velleman diagnoses the mistake involved in saying that desire is for the good in light of a mistaken conception of the way desires, as conations, are distinguished from cognitions in terms of their direction of fit. Thus, Velleman says (p. 13):

Direction of fit has traditionally been defined in terms of the *locus* of responsibility for correspondence between an attitude and the world. Whether an attitude has one direction of fit or the other is said to depend on whether the attitude is responsible for conforming itself to the world or makes the world responsible for conforming itself to the attitude.

However, he argues, this is a mistake, for we understand assumptions to have mind-to-world direction of fit and yet not be something we hold responsible for failing to fit the world: "fit between such an assumption and the world is of no importance and is therefore neither party's

---

[12] See his "The Guise of the Good," *Noûs*, 26 (1992), pp. 3–26; page references in the text are to this article. See also his "The Possibility of Practical Reason," *Ethics*, 106 (1996), pp. 694–726; and *Practical Reflection* (Princeton University Press, 1989), especially chapter 7.

responsibility" (p. 13). Rather, Velleman claims, the notion of direction of fit should be understood as follows: "in cognitive attitudes, a proposition is grasped as patterned after the world; whereas in conative attitudes, a proposition is grasped as a pattern for the world to follow" (p. 8). Hence, cognitions regard their propositions as true, whereas conations regard their propositions as to be made true.

In light of this way of making sense of the notion of direction of fit, Velleman argues that there is a sense in which desires regard their objects as good: namely, as expressing the desire's world-to-mind direction of fit, as to be made true. It would be a mistake, however, to understand this notion of goodness as evaluative, for in evaluations the idea that something is good is a part of the content of the proposition, whereas in desire its goodness is a part of the attitude towards that proposition (p. 8). Desire, therefore, is not an evaluation; we are mistakenly led to understand it as such because we confuse a characterization of the attitude with a characterization of the content. So, Velleman concludes, the formal object of desire is not worthiness of pursuit, as I have claimed, but the "attainable" (p. 17).

There is much that is right about this understanding of the notion of direction of fit; indeed, Velleman's argument against understanding desire as either a discovering (cognitive) evaluation or a constituting (non-cognitive) evaluation is similar to the argument I provided in chapter 2 about the impossibility of solving the problem of import in light of the cognitive–conative divide. Nonetheless, I do not think this means desire should not be understood as an evaluation at all.

Consider again the notion of a perverse desire. Velleman's argument that perverse desires are a decisive counterexample to the idea that desires are for the good requires that we understand the formal object of a kind of mental state to impose a requirement on each instance of that kind: namely the requirement that, in the face of evidence that the target of that mental state does not have the property defined by the formal object, the mental state must change. Thus, as Velleman says about belief, with its formal object of truth, a person

is not a potential believer with respect to a proposition – and hence not subject to reasons for believing it – in the absence of an inclination that would cause him to be swayed by indicators of its truth.[13]

To accept a proposition that is manifestly false is to accept it irrespective

---

[13] "Possibility of Practical Reason," p. 712.

of its truth, and such an acceptance cannot amount to belief.[14] Likewise, Velleman says, if we assume that the formal object of desire is the good (or worthiness of pursuit), to regard as to be made true a prospect that presents itself as bad (or worth avoiding) is to have a conation concerning it irrespective of its goodness, and such a conation cannot, given the assumption, be desire. That is why the existence of even a single perverse desire tells against the conception of desire as having goodness as its formal object.

However, it is perfectly consistent with understanding the formal object of desire or belief to be the good or the true, and so with understanding goodness and truth to be a part of our concepts of desire and belief, that particular desires or beliefs may not be swayed by indicators of goodness or truth. For goodness or truth as a formal object is a condition of the intelligibility not of particular desires or beliefs but rather of the subject's capacity for desire or belief. Thus, the subject must normally be swayed by such indicators in her desiring or believing in order to be intelligible as having the capacity, even though in exceptional cases a desire or belief may be intelligible as a defective exercise of that capacity, without her being responsive to such indicators. Perverse desires and beliefs, therefore, must be the exception: a subject that displayed mostly perverse desires or perverse beliefs would not be intelligible as having the capacity for desire or belief in the first place. Indeed, this is precisely the point of calling them perverse.

Ironically, Velleman himself implicitly acknowledges this point in his argument that perverse desires are a counterexample to the idea that goodness is the formal object of desire: if, as Velleman says, a perverse desire is one whose object is "inappropriate" or "unworthy" of desire, in what sense is that object "inappropriate"? If we understand desire, as Velleman does, as a matter of regarding the attainable as to be made true, there would be nothing inappropriate or unworthy from the perspective of desire about desiring bad things. The only way to make sense of the bad as an inappropriate object of desire, or the good as an appropriate object of desire, is to understand the good as at least part of the formal object of desire: inappropriate desires are inappropriate precisely because their objects are not good. In this way, perverse desires are analogous to phobias: fear of objects the subject knows to be not dangerous. I

---

[14] Cf. "The Guise of the Good," p. 18.

conclude, therefore, that desires are evaluative, and it is precisely in this way that they are to be distinguished from mere goal-directedness.

How, then, are the evaluations implicit in desire, as essentially motivating, to be distinguished from those explicit in evaluative judgment? As I indicated above, the rough answer is that desire, like emotion, is a kind of felt evaluation. This answer, however, is complicated by an important distinction between occurrent desires and long-term desires, which I shall consider in turn.

The most straightforward kind of desire is occurrent desire, which fits my model of felt evaluations quite naturally: to feel an *occurrent desire* is to have the import of its object impress itself on one and enthrall one, such that this import grips one's attention and motivation. Thus, as it nears lunch time and my hunger increases, the sandwich stashed in my desk "calls out my name," consistently grabbing my attention, distracting me from my work, and drawing me to it as worth pursuing. In this way, I feel the desire as the import of its object impresses itself on me and enthralls me, so that the desire is, in part, a response to that import.

As with emotional responses to import, we can assess the warrant of the desire in terms of whether its object actually has, or intelligibly seems to have, import. Given the role of emotions in constituting import, this means that these emotions impose rational constraints on what occurrent desires it is warranted to feel: if something is to be worth pursuing for one, it must also be a suitable focus of one's emotions, so that consistently exhibiting (or failing to exhibit) the relevant emotions in the appropriate circumstances supports (or undermines) the warrant of occurrent desire. Thus, for example, my desire to howl at the moon can be unwarranted because howling at the moon has no import for me. Of course, it might have that import: I might care about howling at the moon insofar as I feel excitement as the time for the full moon approaches, fear that the clouds may obscure the moon (and feel subsequent disappointment or relief depending on whether they do or not), get angry at my parents for imposing a curfew on me, etc. Indeed, given this pattern of emotions it would be inappropriate not to feel the desire, other things being equal, for this is a pattern of commitments to the import of its focus and so to act on its behalf when appropriate. However, in the absence of that pattern and the import it constitutes, the desire cannot be understood as a response to import and is for this reason unwarranted.

Occurrent desires are not merely responses to the import constituted by such a pattern of emotions, but are as well a central part of that pattern. For occurrent desires themselves must be understood as commitments to their objects as having import insofar as they are worth pursuing, and such a commitment to import is *ipso facto* a commitment to these objects as worthy of attention and action, including emotional attention and action. In this way, occurrent desires impose rational constraints on emotions as well. Thus, these emotions focused on the moon are hard to make sense of in the absence of a pattern of occurrent desires to howl at it when appropriate, with the resulting motivational pull those desires involve. Consequently, the kind of commitment to import that is implicit in both desires and emotions and that defines the projectible, rational pattern constitutive of that import must be a commitment to have other emotions and desires when these are appropriate.

One might object that this understanding of occurrent desires as felt evaluations cannot make sense of those occurrent desires we feel as an attraction to an object on our first encounter with it, such as my desire to listen carefully to some music (which turns out to be a Mozart symphony) even though I have never heard it or even anything like it before. For, the objection goes, before we have encountered it, we cannot have established the requisite pattern of emotions and desires constitutive of its import and so cannot make sense of that import as impressing itself on us in our having this initial occurrent desire. Indeed, such initial experiences of desire might be thought to have a central role in practical reasoning as a kind of fundamental conviction of desirability, much like perceptual experience can provide us with a fundamental conviction as to how things are.[15]

In reply, we might understand this response to the Mozart symphony as arising from a susceptibility to its having import for me: I am so constituted as to come to care about Mozart even after being exposed to it only once.[16] This means that along with the desire to hear more, my

---

[15] For a detailed account along these lines, see Elijah Millgram's *Practical Induction* (Cambridge, MA: Harvard University Press, 1997). Millgram understands such convictions of desirability to be experiences of pleasure, which he assimilates to judgments of desirability. However, this assimilation of pleasure to judgment does not make sense of its phenomenology or its passivity as a kind of assent. Moreover, as is clear from Millgram's understanding of pleasure as a sign or indication of desirability, he conceives of pleasure as merely a cognition, with mind-to-world direction of fit. This raises the question of what it is for something to be desirable and, consequently, the problem of import, which Millgram has not adequately confronted.

[16] There are other ways in which one might come to care about something. Thus, some cares (such as my caring about coffee) might be developed because we pursue their objects for other reasons (its having caffeine), a pursuit that leads us gradually to develop

initial experience instills in me as well a broader attunement of my emotional sensibilities – in short, the whole projectible, rational pattern of emotions and desires constitutive of its import. Of course, it is entirely possible for an occurrent desire to be unwarranted, and so to be merely as if the (non-existent) import of its object enthralls one; mere whims can be like this. In such a case, the illusion of import impressing itself on one is in principle no harder to make sense of than false perceptual beliefs, where it is merely as if some object impresses itself on one's senses. Moreover, it is entirely possible in a particular case that it is not determinate whether the object of one's desire has import to one or not, so that it is only later, in retrospect, as one's felt evaluations gradually become (or fail to become) attuned to that object, that we can make sense of this desire as warranted or not in light of the way it fits into this evolving pattern. The objection therefore fails.

The upshot is that occurrent desire is a felt evaluation. To feel an occurrent desire is for its object to impress itself on one as worth pursuing or avoiding: it feels good or bad in this way and consequently draws one to it or repels one, and occurrent desires thus are a kind of pleasure or pain. This kind of pleasure or pain should not be confused with either the expectation of the pleasure that achieving one's end will bring about or with the pain of not currently having the object of one's desire, a pain we might understand to be that of yearning rather than desire. Rather, the pleasure or pain of desire just is the felt evaluation of its object as worth pursuing or avoiding. It is in this way that the evaluation implicit in desires differs from that explicit in evaluative judgment.

Now consider *long-term desires*, such as the desire to graduate from Ohio State with a master's degree in architecture. Long-term desires differ from occurrent desires insofar as they are not felt all the time we have them. As such, they require, first, a kind of vigilance for or attunement to opportunities to make progress towards satisfying one's desire and, consequently (other things being equal), feeling the relevant occurrent desires (and the broader pattern of emotions of which these occurrent desires are a part) in those situations. Moreover, second, they typically require instrumental deliberation so as to provide content to the kinds of situations one must be vigilant for. Consequently, long-term

---

a taste for the object itself; or, we can come to care about other objects (such as Shostakovich symphonies) only because, through initial painful exposure to them, we come to learn enough so that their beauty, their import, can become apparent.

desires can be understood as a mode of caring about their objects, where such caring is to be understood as our being committed, by virtue of a projectible, rational pattern of emotions and desires, to the import of the focus of that pattern.[17]

The example just given is of a long-term desire with a definite object. However, long-term desires are typically desires for indefinite objects, such as the desire to buy a house, but not any particular house, and here there may seem to be problems for my account. For if there is no definite object of my desire, how can I be attuned to "it"? Indeed, a similar problem arises for occurrent desires with indefinite objects, such as a desire to eat something: how is it possible for such an indefinite object to impress itself on me and enthrall me so as to motivate me to act?

In reply, we should not conceive of such attunement or enthrallment, as the objection presupposes, in terms of an independent object causing us to have the response, in a way analogous to that of perceptual belief. More precisely, what we are attuned to or enthralled by is import, which is not the sort of independent object that can exert such a causal influence. What makes intelligible such attunement and enthrallment is the way in which import is constituted by the projectible, rational patterns of emotions and desires. Thus, it is entirely possible for the focus of the pattern to be a vaguely defined, intentional object such as a good house. In searching for a good house, I can be hopeful that the next house I see will be a good one, disappointed when it is not (or, if it is, dismayed by its exorbitant cost), frustrated by the lack of good houses around, etc. Such a pattern of emotions therefore involves being vigilant for specific opportunities for pursuing my long-term desire, as articulated in part by instrumental reasoning,[18] and in part such vigilance involves feeling occurrent desires for such opportunities. All of these emotions and occurrent desires are focused on the ideal of a good house, however well specified that ideal may be, and the pattern of such emotions and occurrent desires constitutes the import of that ideal in exactly the same

---

[17] I shall have more to say both about caring in §4.1, and about the way in which instrumental reason enters into determining the subsequent shape of the requisite pattern of emotions and desires in §4.4.

[18] Of course, for an end as vaguely specified as "a good house," instrumental reasoning on its own will be insufficient, for it will often be necessary first to specify the end more precisely before instrumental reasoning will be possible. I shall discuss such "constitutive reasoning," as it is sometimes called, in chapter 7 by way of articulating more fully the rational interconnections between emotions and judgments.

way they constitute the import of ordinary objects. So there is no special problem about the attunement to or enthrallment by such import.

One important consequence of this account of desire is that it understands desires as essentially located within the same projectible, rational pattern that emotions form and that is partly constitutive of import. This means that the capacity for desire is not possible for a creature without the capacity for emotions, and vice versa: emotions, desires, and import form a conceptual package neither part of which is intelligible without the other. This explains why the chess-playing computer of §2.1 does not have genuine desires: lacking the projectible, rational pattern of emotions and desires partly constitutive of import, the chess-playing computer can only display mere rationally mediated goal-directedness.

3.6 BODILY PLEASURES AND PAINS AS FELT EVALUATIONS

I argued in §3.4 that emotional pleasures and pains are to be understood as felt evaluations, for the notion of a felt evaluation makes intelligible both the connections between pleasure or pain and evaluation and motivation, and the phenomenology of pleasure and pain. Nonetheless, this account of emotional pleasure and pain can seem disconnected from our ordinary understanding of pleasure and pain, especially as it is implicated in bodily sensation. Consequently, I shall now discuss these other kinds of pleasures and pains, arguing that what makes bodily sensations intelligible as pleasant or painful is that they, too, are felt evaluations, and this provides me with a unified account.

As my torturer straps my arm down and holds a burning match to it, I feel pain; as my lover caresses my arm, I feel pleasure. How are we to understand the pain and pleasure in such cases?[19] It is tempting in each of these cases to understand the feeling simply in terms of *qualia*: phenomenal properties that a feeling has irrespective of its relations to anything else. Although it is surely right that pleasures and pains have a certain phenomenological feel to them in virtue of which they are pleasures and pains, such an understanding of pleasures and pains does not commit us to the qualia view.

One problem for the qualia view is that of understanding how pleasures and pains can motivate us to act. Given that, according to this view, pleasure and pain are intrinsic properties of sensations, it seems we

---

[19] To avoid tedium, throughout this section I shall use "pleasure" and "pain" to denote bodily pleasures and pains, unless explicitly noted otherwise.

can understand how they motivate subsequent behavior only in terms of their having usual (but not necessary) causal effects. (These causal effects cannot be necessary to the qualia that are pleasures and pains for at least two reasons. First, qualia are defined non-relationally, and so without reference to causes or effects, and, second, in unusual cases motivation can be dissociated from the pain: patients on morphine, for example, sometimes report feeling pain without having any impulse to do anything about it.[20] Indeed, cases of morphine pain might seem to provide evidence in favor of the qualia view.) As George Graham, a proponent of the qualia view, argues:

Painful qualia (feelings) naturally trigger psychological mechanisms or overt actions to eliminate the qualia or their causes. I avoid the flame because it hurts.[21]

One difficulty for this view is that pains do not simply cause us to behave in certain ways; they rationally motivate such behavior. That is, the appeal to pain as an explanation of what I do makes intelligible my subsequent behavior as (at least prima facie) rationally appropriate action: in the face of pain, it is rational for me to do what I can to prevent or mitigate it. Moreover, pain motivates not merely a single stereotyped action, such as jerking my arm away from the flame; when my arm is strapped down by my torturer so that I cannot move away from the flame, I am motivated to try other things to remove the cause of my pain, such as attempting to blow the match out.

On the face of it, Graham's account of how pain motivates action can seem to handle such cases. After all, according to Graham pain can cause not merely "overt action" but also other "psychological mechanisms." So, Graham might reply, all we need to do in order to handle both the idea that pain rationally motivates action and the variety of actions pain might cause is to postulate an intervening desire that is caused by the pain, such that this desire, together with one's beliefs, rationally motivates our attempts to stop or mitigate the pain. However, this reply merely pushes the problem back one step: even if the desire rationally motivates the action, still, the desire itself is an appropriate response to the pain. In virtue of what is the desire appropriate? Intuitively, the

---

[20] For more on morphine pain, see J. B. Dynes & J. L. Poppen, "Lobotomy for Intractable Pain"; A. Keats & H. Beecher, "Pain Relief with Hypnotic Doses of Barbiturates and a Hypothesis"; and A. Elithorn, E. Glitherno, & E. Slater, "Leucotomy for Pain." I shall discuss morphine cases in a bit more detail below.

[21] *Philosophy of Mind*, p. 185.

answer is that pains are intrinsically bad (or pleasures intrinsically good), and this rationally motivates the desire to avoid pains and seek out pleasures. Yet in what sense is a quale intelligible as intrinsically good or bad? To specify a quale, for example, in terms of its intensity – as intensely burning, say – is not yet to specify its badness (or goodness). What is needed instead is an understanding of pleasure and pain as likable or as dislikable, but, insofar as this specifies the goodness or badness of pain in terms of its connection to desire and other attitudes, it is not a purely qualitative account.

Richard Hall tries to understand our dislike of painful qualia as the result of their association with "nociceptual reports of bodily damage," which itself is bad: our disliking pains "is like the ruler who slew the messenger who brought the bad news."[22] Yet this fails to give the right sort of account of the connection between the pain and the desire insofar as it makes that connection out to be irrational: as Hall goes on to say, providing what one might think a reductio of his view, "pain sensations are no more inherently bad than that messenger" (p. 647), which is patently false of the pains themselves.

These problems with the qualia view might lead one to adopt a *perceptual view* of pain: pains are perceptions of bodily damage or potentially damaging occurrences – of "disordered states" of the body.[23] Nonetheless, such an account of the badness of pain fails for much the same reason an appeal to biology fails as a general account of import (cf. §2.4): apart from the subject's antecedently caring about the state of his body, the mere fact that he perceives some disordered state of his body does not by itself provide even a prima facie reason to stop it. Indeed, George Pitcher essentially concedes this point in talking about a "spontaneous inclination" to want pain perceptions to stop as what is needed to explain how pains can motivate, and he argues that the perceptual view is therefore no worse off on this count than the qualia view (p. 380). No worse off, surely, but no better off either: in each case the underlying evaluation stands in need of explanation.

---

[22] "Are Pains Necessarily Unpleasant?," p. 647.

[23] George Pitcher, "Pain Perception," *Philosophical Review*, 79 (1970), pp. 368–93, at p. 371. For further perceptual accounts of pain, see D. M. Armstrong, *The Nature of Mind and Other Essays* (Ithaca: Cornell University Press, 1981), and Natika Newton, "On Viewing Pain as a Secondary Quality," *Noûs*, 23 (1989), pp. 569–98. Notice, however, that it is hard to know how to generalize a perceptual view of pain to include pleasure as well.

Understanding the way in which pleasure and pain rationally motivate subsequent action or other mental states therefore requires understanding them as involving an implicit evaluation. Thus, my headache rationally motivates me to take some aspirin, to be grateful to you for giving me a neck rub, to be annoyed at the teenager next door as he practices his drums, etc., only because of the badness of the headache – only because, that is, in having the sensation I feel it to be bad. According to Norton Nelkin, we should understand the evaluation that is a part of pain in terms of evaluative judgment:

> Pains are *bad*, but no phenomenal state *in and of itself* wears that evaluation . . . [Rather,] pain involves both a phenomenal state . . . and a spontaneous, non-inferential evaluation of that state as representing a harm to the body . . . ([T]he evaluation *is* a kind of judgment.)[24]

In understanding pain to involve spontaneous, non-inferential evaluative judgments, Nelkin tries to forestall the objection that, if pains were to consist in part in judgment, then we could simply control when we feel pain by controlling our judgments. Thus, if you judge that the sensations you feel while having a root canal seem to represent not a harm but a repair of the body, your pain would, according to this objection, be non-existent. Of course, pains do not work this way, and that is the point of requiring that the judgments be spontaneous and non-inferential: the evaluations are (somehow) thrust upon us so that we find ourselves saddled with them. In this way, the evaluation implicit in pain (and pleasure) is objective insofar as it impresses itself on one, in something like the way I have argued that import impresses itself on one in emotion and desire.

Nonetheless, it is a mistake to understand the evaluation implicit in pleasure and pain in terms of judgment, as Nelkin does, once again because of the way in which pains motivate action. For the connection between pleasure or pain and action is much tighter or more direct than that between judgment and action. Indeed, it is commonplace for

---

[24] "Reconsidering Pain," *Philosophical Psychology*, 7 (1994), pp. 325–43, at p. 332 (Nelkin's emphasis throughout). Presumably Nelkin means by "harm" not merely that there has been some damage to the functional mechanism of the body, but that this is a bad thing. For alternative versions of the evaluative view, see G. Lynn Stephens & George Graham, "Minding Your P's and Q's: Pain and Sensible Qualities," *Noûs*, 21 (1987), pp. 395–405, and Michael Tye, *Ten Problems of Consciousness: A Representational Theory of the Phenomenal Mind* (Cambridge, MA: MIT Press, 1995) and "A Representational Theory of Pains," *Philosophical Perspectives 9: AI, Connectionism, and Philosophical Psychology* (1995), pp. 223–39.

someone to make an evaluative judgment but not be motivated to act on it, even if there is no real cost to following through. Yet the idea of a pleasure or pain that is disconnected in this way from motivation is almost unintelligible. (Nelkin formulates his theory so as intentionally to sever any conceptual connection between pain and motivation in order to accommodate cases of morphine pain, in which patients claim to feel pain without minding it. However, Nelkin accommodates morphine cases too easily: they become readily intelligible, whereas in reality these cases are troubling in that they threaten to undermine our sense that we have a clear concept of pain.[25] Conceptual revision may be appropriate, but too much conceptual revision so as readily to accommodate rare and bizarre cases is not.) Consequently, the kind of evaluation implicit in pleasure and pain must be distinguished from ordinary judgments somehow other than by simply being spontaneous and non-inferential, and the problem is to find a non-question-begging way to articulate the difference.

A further problem for this understanding of pleasure or pain as involving evaluative judgment arises from the dual objectivity and subjectivity of the relevant evaluation. I have already indicated that such an evaluation must be objective insofar as it imposes itself on one in feeling the pleasure or pain; this is an essential part of the phenomenology of pleasure and pain, and it is part of what Nelkin acknowledges in requiring the evaluation to be spontaneous and non-inferential. Nonetheless, such an evaluation must also be subjective insofar as it is intelligible only in light of some background concern of the subject. To see this, consider the case of a caress. At first blush, it may seem that a caress is an inherently pleasant stimulus not dependent on any background concern. This impression, however, depends on an incomplete specification of the circumstances surrounding the caress, circumstances necessary to make sense of that background concern. Thus, the caress of a lover as an expression of that love is pleasurable, but the caress of a rapist, even if given with identical gentleness, is painful, and the similar bodily stimulation when one accidentally brushes by the velvet drapes is neither pleasant nor painful. In these cases it is the background concern, for one's lover in the first example and for one's safety and integrity in the second, that accounts for the difference between them as pleasant or painful, and it is the absence of

---

[25] Cf. Daniel Dennett's "Why You Can't Make a Computer that Feels Pain," *Synthese*, 38 (1978), pp. 415–49.

this concern that accounts for the neutrality of the third example. (In the case of pain, the background concern is typically concern for one's physical well-being; bodily pleasures have background concerns that are typically more varied.) Consequently, the evaluation implicit in the feeling of pleasure or pain is subjective as well by implicitly bringing to bear that background concern in one's feeling of the sensation. Indeed, we might think, that one feels pleasure or pain in such circumstances is partly constitutive of the evaluation at issue. Thus, taking pleasure in the rapist's caress cannot simply be dismissed as a mistaken evaluation, for such a mistake would be, in the context of this assault on one's integrity, virtually unintelligible.

In short, pleasures and pains are sensations whereby an evaluation impresses itself on one, such that the sensation both motivates action in light of that evaluation and is partly constitutive of that evaluation. In all these respects, pleasures and pains are like felt evaluations, and my claim is that we can therefore make best sense of bodily pleasures and pains by understanding them to be felt evaluations: particular bodily sensations are pleasant or painful because they are feelings of the goodness or badness of what is going on (or intelligibly seems to be going on) in the relevant body part, where such goodness or badness impresses itself on and enthralls us by grabbing and holding our attention and motivation. To make sense of the way in which import impresses itself on and enthralls us in feeling bodily pleasures and pains, we must understand them normally to be a part of the projectible, rational pattern of emotions and desires partially constitutive of this import. In fact, this is precisely what we find, for to feel a bodily pleasure or pain is to be committed to feeling the relevant emotions and desires in the sense that it would be rationally inappropriate to fail to experience fear in the face of anticipated pain, anger at someone who intentionally inflicts pain on you, frustration at the lack of physical contact with a lover, etc. To fail to feel these emotions and desires is to call into question the intelligibility of that sensation's being a pleasure or pain.

Indeed, this is precisely the difficulty we face in making sense of morphine pain. How can some patients while under the influence of morphine claim that they are in pain that is just as intense as it was before they received the morphine, though they do not mind it and have no particular desire to do anything to get rid of it? Such sensations are intelligible as pains because of their historical connection with sensations that did hurt, though we can understand them as abnormal, defective pains insofar as they are now disconnected from the normal pattern of emotions and desires constituting their import. Morphine pains, therefore, are intelligible only as parasitic on this normal pattern of felt evaluations.

That bodily pleasures and pains fit into this broader pattern of emotional and desiderative rationality, therefore, is not an incidental consequence of their being pleasures and pains, but rather is constitutive of them as such. Bodily pleasures and pains just are felt evaluations.

Of course, bodily pleasures and pains are essentially phenomenal states. Once again we can understand the phenomenology of bodily pleasures and pains in terms of the kind of feeling they are as felt evaluations. Thus, the delight or the hurt of bodily pleasure or pain is a feeling of the import, the goodness or badness, of what is going on in one's body impressing itself on one, enthralling one, and so holding both one's attention and one's motivation in its grip; it is precisely in this way that bodily pleasures and pains feel good or bad. Of course, what we feel when we have bodily pleasures or pains are sensations, and these sensations will have qualities other than their delighting or hurting us. Thus, we experience bodily pleasures not only as delighting us but also as smooth, gentle, warm, etc., and we experience bodily pains not only as hurting but also as burning, aching, stabbing, or even tickling – that is, we feel these sensations along the various dimensions of touch, including temperature, pressure, and texture, and as located in particular parts of our bodies. Consequently, the experiences we undergo when we feel bodily pleasure or pain will be richer than I have just indicated, with the delight or hurt being itself a part of the sensation: as the torturer brings the lit match up to my arm, I feel what is happening to my arm both as burning and as impressing itself on me as bad and to be avoided, and it is this single feeling that is the painful burning sensation. Nonetheless, the normal core of these experiences of bodily pleasure and pain as such is the felt evaluation, where this felt evaluation is itself a part of the sensation.

One might object to this account of bodily pleasure and pain that, as felt evaluations, such sensations get analyzed as a kind of assent to intentional evaluative content. After all, bodily pleasures and pains are not intelligible as true or false, correct or incorrect, nor do we ordinarily hold people responsible for mistaken pleasures and pains. Consequently, such an account seems overly intellectual. Surely, it might be thought, bodily pleasures and pains are merely ways in which a sensation feels, which is something we can understand without all this cognitive baggage.

What motivates this objection seems in part to be the thought that bodily pleasures and pains are mere qualia, and I have already argued against that view: we need to understand even bodily pleasures and pains as evaluations in order to make sense of their rational connections to motivation and to other mental states like emotion and desire. Consequently, bodily pleasures and pains must have intentional content: what is happening to or in one's body is evaluated as good or bad in light of some background concern, and here we find bodily pleasures and pains subject to illusions, such as phantom limb pain.

Even if bodily pleasures and pains involve such evaluative content, it may still seem odd to understand them as a kind of assent to that content. However, it is important not to mischaracterize the kind of assent at issue. After all, the kind of assent at issue in felt evaluations is not cognitive assent but disclosive assent. As disclosive, such assent is partly constitutive of the very object to which it is a passive response, and so cannot be said to be true or false, correct or incorrect, in the straightforward cognitive sense of those terms, as involving mind-to-world direction of fit. Moreover, such assent is passive not only in that it is responsive to import impressing itself on us, but also in that it is not susceptible to direct control by revising our active judgmental evaluations. The point of calling felt evaluations "assents" is to make sense of the structure of their rational commitments both to other felt evaluations with the same focus and to action, where it is the structure of such commitments that, by constituting import, makes intelligible the standards of warrant for particular felt evaluations. This means that even bodily pleasures and pains are intelligible as warranted or not, depending on whether their objects (what is going on in one's body) can intelligibly seem to have the relevant import. Thus, for example, we criticize children for feeling pain too readily ("That doesn't hurt! Don't be a sissy!"), and we criticize each other for taking pleasure in inappropriate objects (such as deviant sexual pleasures). Of course, with bodily pleasure and pain we find intelligible an extremely broad range of evaluations, and so for the most part have little room to criticize others for feeling pleasure or pain without warrant. But to say that there is little room is not to say that there is no room at all.

I conclude, therefore, that bodily pleasures and pains, like emotions and desires, are felt evaluations.

3.7 CONCLUSION

In this chapter I have argued that import is partly constituted by projectible, rational patterns of emotions, desires, and bodily pleasures and pains – of felt evaluations – and I have articulated the kind of focal commitments among the felt evaluations that define this pattern and make intelligible its projectibility and rationality. Import, therefore, is not conceptually prior to these patterns of felt evaluations. Nonetheless, this does not imply that the felt evaluations that make up the pattern are conceptually prior to the import that pattern constitutes – a priority that would suggest a conative account of import such that these felt evaluations have merely world-to-mind direction of fit. For, although these patterns of felt evaluations partly constitute import, that import is itself what impresses itself on us in our having particular felt evaluations and so is that to which these felt evaluations must be properly responsive as a condition of their warrant. Consequently, neither import nor felt evaluations are conceptually prior to the other; rather, they must come as a conceptual package. It is therefore improper to understand emotions, desires, or bodily pleasures and pains as either cognitions or conations: the distinction between cognition and conation, with its implicit assumption of conceptual priority, simply does not apply to these mental states. In this way, I have solved the problem of import by rejecting the cognitive–conative divide.

The account I have given of emotions, desires, and bodily pleasures and pains understands them as essentially a part of a broader pattern constitutive of import. The account, therefore, is holistic and non-reductive: emotions, desires, and bodily pleasures and pains are all distinctive species of the genus of felt evaluation. In this way, I have accounted for the conditions of their warrant, the way in which they motivate both action and other mental states, and their phenomenology as pleasures and pains. Consequently, pleasure and pain are not separable constituents of emotions, desires, and some bodily sensations, but rather are part of how these are all felt evaluations.

Nonetheless, this account of the kind of rational commitments characteristic of felt evaluations and definitive of the projectible pattern constitutive of import is incomplete – as is signaled by my qualifying the pattern as articulated thus far as only "partly" constitutive of import. In particular, it is clear that evaluative judgment is also relevant to constituting import, and I shall argue in chapter 5 that evaluative judgments must likewise be understood as elements of these projectible rational patterns of felt evaluations, although they are not themselves felt evaluations. Moreover, although in §1.4 I alluded to a distinction between caring and valuing as kinds of import differentiated in terms of their relative "depth," I have not yet had anything to say about how this distinction is to be fleshed out, nor have I had anything to say about the sense in which one thing can have greater import to one than another; this will be my task in chapter 4.

Finally, it should also be clear that, although I claim to have solved the problem of import and so to have made sense of import as having a kind of objectivity as that to which particular felt evaluations are properly responsive, this kind of objectivity is very limited. In particular, it is not sufficient to make intelligible the idea that something should or should not have import to you – an idea that is central to an adequate solution of the deliberative problem. Making sense of this more robust kind of objectivity will be a large part of my aim in the account of practical reason in Part II, especially chapter 7.

4

Varieties of import: cares, values, and preferences

In chapter 3, I presented an account of import as constituted by projectible, rational patterns in one's felt evaluations. In doing so, I implicitly made two simplifying assumptions: that import is a single, homogeneous kind of thing, and that the interconnections among elements within such patterns are all we need in order to make sense of import. It is now time to complicate matters by lifting the veil these simplifying assumptions provide. Thus, first, we need to make a distinction between two kinds of import, caring and valuing, in terms of their depth, for this distinction will prove to be central in understanding the difference between persons and mere animals and so to making sense of how deliberation about value is possible for us persons. Second, in order to provide an account of practical reason in Part II, I need to make sense of relations among the various things that have import, including means–end relations and relations of relative degree of import.

My aim in this chapter, therefore, is to provide a richer, more complicated account of import by shedding these oversimplifications so as to come to a clearer understanding of the kinds of rationality that make that import possible. Consequently, to a large extent my concern in this chapter will be with the conditions of the warrant of the felt evaluations that are elements of the patterns constitutive of import. By filling out the rational interconnections at issue in defining individual patterns and their relations to each other, the accounts of both import and felt evaluations will be strengthened and enriched. My strategy will be to examine first in §§4.1–4.2 the kinds of rational connections supporting the depth and degree of import that occur within particular patterns of felt evaluations, and then in §4.3 to enrich this account by examining the rational connections among these patterns so as to make sense of preferences. Finally, in §4.4, I shall consider the way in which instrumental rationality is to be understood in terms of this framework, thereby clearing up some puzzles left over from the account of desire in §3.5.1.

4.1 CARING AND VALUING

I provided an account of import in chapter 3 that understands it to be constituted by the projectible, rational patterns of a subject's felt evaluations. In part, this account of import provides us with a way of understanding how we can invest ourselves in something in virtue of the import it has for us. For example, insofar as the local opera company has import to him, Albert devotes countless hours as a volunteer to ensure its success, and he does so in such a way as to "make himself vulnerable to losses and susceptible to benefits depending on whether [it] is diminished or enhanced."[1] Indeed, given the account of import presented so far, this vulnerability or susceptibility is evident in the kinds of pleasures or pains – the kinds of felt evaluations – he feels in response to what happens to it. By making ourselves vulnerable to what happens to something in this way, Frankfurt says, we are in a sense identifying ourselves with it.

Nonetheless, we might intuitively distinguish two senses in which we can identify with something based on their relative depth: caring and valuing. (Recall that we can talk about import as objective, insofar as it is the standard of warrant for our felt evaluations, or as subjective, insofar as it is constituted by the projectible, rational patterns of felt evaluations with a common focus. This language of "caring about" [and, later, "valuing"] something reflects the subjective side of import, and it should be clear that our caring about [or valuing] something is nothing other than its having import for us.) Consider caring first. The account of import I have given so far understands our responsiveness to import to be wholly unreflective and unselfconscious, as simply a matter of having that import impress itself on us in our feeling the relevant emotions and desires. Thus, Albert might identify himself with the local opera company in the sense that it has become a project that is truly his: he takes pleasure (such as joy or satisfaction) in its successes or feels pain

---

[1] Harry Frankfurt, *The Importance of What We Care About*, p. 83.

(such as frustration or disappointment) in its failures. Yet, although this project is important to him, it is not fundamental to his sense of himself: what is at stake in its success or failure is not his own worth. Such a responsiveness to import therefore lacks any real depth: it is a matter merely of *caring* about that thing.

There is, however, a difference between those things one cares about and those things that have import to one at least in part because of an understanding of the kind of person one finds worth being. Insofar as the import of something bears in this way on one's self-worth, the kind of vulnerability one has to how it fares takes on a kind of depth lacking in the sort of caring just described. For here, one makes who one is depend on the object by finding in it value and meaning in terms of which one can understand not only what one does but also the kind of person one is. Values are, therefore, deeper than cares insofar as they provide a framework of meaning in terms of which one can understand who one is, a framework that can provide direction to one's life as a whole. If Albert values the opera company, then a bad year for the company might therefore result in his having a diminished sense of self-worth, or, more seriously, the opera company's going under might leave Albert open to a crisis of not knowing who he is or what he stands for any more – a crisis of identity.[2]

Given this intuitive distinction, which stands in need of clarification, I shall reserve the word, "identification," for valuing, because of its depth by virtue of its involvement of one's self. To *value* something or *identify* oneself with it, then, is to find one's own worth in terms of it and how one conducts oneself with respect to it. It should be clear, however, that this is an extremely limited sense of identification; what one is identified with in this sense (i.e., one's *identity*) is only a limited aspect of who one is. Other aspects, which I shall largely ignore here, include one's physical attributes and abilities; past history and accomplishments (or failures); character traits such as moodiness, courage, and strength of will; and ideology – that is, roughly, the characteristic ways in which one tends to interpret one's own motives, actions, and responses, as well as objects and events in the world. Of course, there will be complex relations between one's identity and these other aspects of who one is. One's physical attributes and abilities will set limits on what one can successfully

---

[2] This basic understanding of valuing owes much to Charles Taylor's "What Is Human Agency?" in *Human Agency and Language*, pp. 15–44.

identify with; one's past history, especially one's upbringing as a child, will influence if not partially constitute one's identity; various character traits will impact on one's ability to change one's identity; and one's ideology might seem to go hand in hand with one's identity in providing meaning to one's life. Nonetheless, I shall here largely ignore these interesting and important (though to some extent empirical) topics in order to try to understand more clearly the very notion of valuing or identification and, ultimately, how it is possible for us to deliberate about and so take responsibility for what we value.

In order to make this distinction between caring and valuing more precise, I need to examine more carefully the sense in which valuing something involves finding one's own worth in it. Because of this focus on oneself, to have values is in effect to be concerned with the kind of person one finds worth being and the motives for action that, as constituents of this kind of person, are most truly one's own; such a concern, therefore, must include at least a partial self-understanding. It is natural to make sense of this by appealing to explicit, self-conscious deliberation and judgment. For to have the relevant sort of self-understanding is in part to have standards in terms of which to evaluate oneself, standards one endorses and is therefore willing to use in understanding one's success in becoming the kind of person one finds worth being. What else could such an endorsement amount to if not an evaluative judgment about one's identity?

Although I think the role of self-conscious deliberation and judgment in valuing is fundamentally important, and although I shall return to it in Part II, it would be a mistake to understand the distinction between caring and valuing wholly in terms of that role or even to require explicit and self-conscious choice as a necessary condition of valuing. For our values, like our cares, can be instilled in us as the result of our upbringing and without self-conscious choice and deliberation.

To see this, consider the case of Betty. Betty was brought up in the 1950s in a conservative family with what were then traditional values. She naturally came to adopt a subservient role in the family, catering to others and, just as naturally, came to find self–esteem in anticipating and fulfilling their desires and supporting their aspirations. To say that she finds self-esteem here is to say in part that she takes pride in her fulfillment of this role and, conversely, becomes disappointed in herself for undertaking more selfish pursuits instead of catering to the needs and aspirations of others. Such disappointment can easily turn to shame and loss of faith in herself as a good person, a faith that can be restored only by subordinating her desires even more completely to those of others. When she marries and has her own children, she again, quite naturally, adopts this role with respect to her husband and children, taking great pride in silencing any aspirations of her own in order to devote herself completely to those of her family. In caring so deeply about fulfilling this subservient role as to find her self–esteem in it, she is identifying herself with that role: she finds her worth in it. For Betty, not to be the kind of person who subordinates herself in this way to the needs of others, and so not to be the kind of person who finds things valuable only insofar as they promote the welfare of others, is to be shamefully selfish. Consequently, any aspirations of her own are simply stifled as not being a part of the kind of person she finds worth being.

In such a case, it would seem unnecessary to require that Betty has explicitly thought the matter through and self-consciously endorsed this subservient role as a part of her identity in order for her to value it. Rather, given the way I have described the case, it might seem that we can make sense of the self-understanding, the concern with herself and her motives for action, to be implicit in her felt evaluations.

To make persuasive this intuition and so this way of distinguishing between caring and valuing, it will be necessary to distinguish reflexive from non-reflexive felt evaluations. *Non-reflexive* felt evaluations are those emotions and desires whose targets are things in the world; non-reflexive felt evaluations include fear, relief, disappointment, joy, anger, frustration, satisfaction, and the like, as well as what Frankfurt has called *first-order desires*.[3] By contrast, *reflexive* felt evaluations are those emotions and desires that focus on one's being a certain kind of person; such reflexive felt evaluations include pride, self-approbation, shame, mortification, remorse, anxiety, and self-assurance, as well as what Frankfurt has called second-order volitions. As Frankfurt understands it, a *second-order volition* is a desire that one be moved to act by a first-order desire, and, as such, it involves finding having that motive to act to be itself worth pursuing. In this way, second-order volitions are reflexive insofar as to feel the worth of having a certain motive is in part to feel the worth of being a certain kind of person. Similarly, *pride*, in the sense I intend it here, is a positive evaluation of oneself or one's character in light of one's

[3] See his "Freedom of the Will and the Concept of a Person," in *The Importance of What We Care About*, pp. 11–25.

sense of the kind of person one ought to be.[4] *Shame*[5] or, more strongly, *mortification*, is a negative evaluation of oneself for not living up to one's sense of who one ought to be. *Anxiety* (again, in the sense I intend it here) is a kind of anticipation of one's failure to act in accordance with one's sense of the kind of person one ought to be, and it can thus turn into shame or a kind of *self–affirming relief* when confirmed or not. Likewise, *self–assurance* is an emotion anticipating one's meeting one's standards for the kind of person one ought to be, and it, in turn, can become pride when confirmed or guilt, shame, or remorse when not.[6]

Like non-reflexive felt evaluations, these reflexive felt evaluations form projectible, rational patterns by virtue of their mutual commitments and their structure as forward- or backward-looking and as positive or negative. Yet, because reflexive felt evaluations are focused on one's being a certain kind of person, the patterns they form will be distinct from those formed by non-reflexive felt evaluations. Thus, for it to be warranted to be proud of being courageous on particular occasions, such pride must be a part of a more general pattern of reflexive felt evaluations such that one also, other things being equal, feels ashamed when one fails to be courageous when courage is called for, feels self-assured or anxious

---

[4] This account of pride as reflexive coheres well with Gabriele Taylor's understanding of pride (*Pride, Shame, and Guilt: Emotions of Self-Assessment* [Oxford University Press, 1985]). Taylor, however, understands pride in terms of beliefs, in line with a vaguely cognitivist account of emotions. Thus, she says (p. 41), "a person who experiences pride believes that she stands in a relation of belonging to [something] . . . which she thinks desirable in some respect [and because of this] believes her worth to be increased." My aim here is to show, in line with my general criticism of emotional cognitivism in chapter 2, that we should not understand this kind of reflexive evaluation in terms of cognitive states like belief because of the role such emotions play as simultaneously both discovering and constituting evaluations.

[5] Gabriele Taylor claims that shame, unlike pride, "is connected with the thought that eyes are upon one" – that others are negatively evaluating the kind of person one is (p. 53). This is, I think, a mistake: we can feel shame for things we do in complete privacy, confident that no one else is watching. The reflexive emotion Taylor seems to be analyzing might better be called "disgrace."

[6] There are, of course, other kinds of pride, shame, anxiety, and self–assurance than the kinds I am articulating here. Thus, one can be anxious in many ways – about whether one can pay the bills, say – that are not anticipations of one's failure to live well. (It should be clear, however, that the kind of anxiety I have in mind is not that of Heidegger, for Heidegger's notion of anxiety involves coming face to face with there being no external source of the meaningfulness of one's life, whereas mine simply presupposes meaningfulness without prejudging its source.) Moreover, self–assurance can simply be a character trait that is not necessarily rationally responsive to the import of one's situation, rather than an emotion. With these caveats in place, however, my aim is to isolate and define a certain family of emotions that, although they are common to our human experience, have not been so clearly delineated in at least English.

over situations in which one's courage will be tested, a self-assurance or anxiety that ought to become pride or shame after one has acted, and so on. Consequently, having these reflexive felt evaluations requires that one consistently respond when one is motivated to act in ways that are for one worthy or base and not otherwise. The resulting projectible, rational pattern of felt evaluations therefore constitutes the import being a courageous person has for one.

To value something, I have said, is to make who one is depend on it by finding one's own worth in it. We can now see how the import constituted by a projectible, rational pattern of reflexive felt evaluations just is this kind of value. For what has such import is being a certain kind of person, and such import is therefore a standard in terms of which one's own worth is to be evaluated. Valuing something and so identifying with it just means finding it to be central to the kind of person it is worth one's being. In this way, we can make sense of the self-understanding that is a part of valuing to be implicit in the projectible, rational patterns of reflexive felt evaluations constitutive of one's values. For to display such a pattern is to be attuned to the way in which such a kind of person serves as a standard for who one is to be, and so to opportunities for acting in accordance with that standard as well as to occasions on which one succeeds or fails to live up to it.

Consequently, the sort of self-understanding essential to valuing need not be explicitly articulated in advance of having those values: values do not require self-conscious deliberation and judgment. Something having import to one does not in general presuppose that one has engaged in self-conscious deliberation about its worth, and there is no reason to think that the import constituted by reflexive felt evaluations is any different. Indeed, we generally undergo such deliberation mostly when conflicts arise among the various things we value and not when we come to have these values in the first place. Of course, one might come to have particular values because one has explicitly thought about the kind of person one wants to be, but this need not always be the case. Although self-conscious deliberation about one's values and the kind of person it is worth one's being surely has an important role in articulating, refining, and criticizing oneself and one's values, such deliberation should not be thought essential to one's having values in every case.

The distinction between caring and valuing, therefore, is made intelligible in terms of a distinction between non-reflexive and reflexive felt evaluations and the projectible, rational patterns they make up.

Nonetheless, in articulating the distinction in this way, I do not want to minimize the role evaluative judgment properly has in constituting both one's cares and one's values. As I hinted above, I shall argue in chapter 5 that evaluative judgment itself must have a place in these projectible, rational patterns of felt evaluations – including both non-reflexive and reflexive felt evaluations. This will further enrich the account of both caring and valuing in a way that I shall leverage in chapters 6–7 in providing an account of practical reason that solves the motivational and deliberative problems.

4.2 DEGREES OF IMPORT

As I indicated above, the account of import presented in chapter 3 involved the simplifying assumption that all import is homogeneous. The distinction just made between caring and valuing serves to complicate this oversimplified picture of import in one way. I now want to complicate the picture in another way, in light of the notion of *degrees of import*: a measure of how much we care about or value something. How is this notion to be captured in terms of patterns of felt evaluations?

One obvious place to begin is with the notion of strength of desire or preference: we can desire some things more than (or prefer them to) others, and this might provide a basis for thinking that the former have more import to us.[7] Whether this tack succeeds depends in part on how the notion of strength of desire gets cashed out, and here there are two obvious ways to go. First, we might understand it in terms of the perceived relative worth of the options: a person more strongly desires one thing than another if she finds it to be more worthy of desire for her. In the present context, however, this is viciously circular, for something being found more worthy of desire just is its having a greater degree of import.

A second way to articulate the notion of strength of desire is in terms of relative motivational strength: a person desires one thing more strongly than another just in case he would be more strongly motivated to pursue it if offered a choice between the two. However, this seems

---

[7] One might think that we ought to capture it instead in terms of the evaluative judgment that one thing is more important than another. One difficulty for such a suggestion is that it would not make sense of the idea that animals like dogs and cats, incapable of engaging in evaluative judgments, can nonetheless care about things to a greater or lesser degree. Other problems for this view run parallel to those raised for the strength of desire view; see note 8, below.

inadequate as an account of relative degree of import. For import serves as a reason for pursuit, and degree of import should likewise be understood as the strength of that reason: if something has more import than something else, then, other things being equal, one has reason to pursue the former more strenuously than the latter. The mere fact that a person is more strongly motivated to pursue it cannot on its own constitute the reason for that motivation, for that would undermine the normative force of reasons and so make unintelligible the possibility of succumbing to the temptation of a lesser good.

The problem with these two ways of making sense of degree of import in terms of strength of desire lies in an inadequate conception of desire in terms of the cognitive–conative divide. Thus, on the one hand, the first attempt implicitly understands strength of desire as a kind of discovering evaluation (or cognition) of degree of import, and it therefore presupposes rather than provides an account of degree of import. On the other hand, the second attempt implicitly understands strength of desire as a constituting evaluation (or conation), and it fails therefore to make sense of its objectivity as a reason for action. Both of these ideas are partially right, but each fails to capture the whole truth.[8] Instead, what is needed, as was the case for the account of import itself, is to reject the cognitive–conative divide: because desire is a felt evaluation, the notion of strength of desire can both help constitute degree of import and be rationally assessed in terms of the degree of import to which it is properly responsive. This is possible, I shall argue, only because desire is one element of a broader rational pattern of other felt evaluations, each with its own intensity normally attuned to degree of import, that as a whole constitutes import and degree of import. Articulating this idea will require consideration not only of strength of desire but also of the intensity of emotion.

As I argued in chapter 3, neither felt evaluation nor import is conceptually prior to the other: they each come as part of a larger conceptual package, all of which is required for any of it to be intelligible. This means, in part, that the rational pattern of felt evalua-

---

[8] The same moral holds for an account of degree of import in terms of evaluative judgment. If we understand evaluative judgment as a discovering evaluation, we presuppose rather than explain degree of import, whereas if we understand it as a constituting evaluation, we cannot make sense of its objectivity as a reason. As I shall argue in chapter 5 (especially §§5.3–5.4), insofar as evaluative judgment has a role in constituting import and degree of import, that is because it is another element in the projectible, rational pattern I have been describing in terms of felt evaluations.

tions constitutive of import can always be described from two perspectives: that of the felt evaluations that constitute import by imposing rational commitments on each other (the subjectivity of import), and that of import as impressing itself on us in our having felt evaluations and so as that in terms of which the warrant of these felt evaluations is to be assessed (the objectivity of import). In complicating the account of this pattern so as to include both the intensity of felt evaluation and the degree of import, we must therefore consider both perspectives in order to achieve a complete description of the relevant pattern.

Consider first the perspective of the subjectivity of import, starting with the emotions. The rational commitments emotions impose on each other are commitments not simply to feel these other emotions, whatever their intensity, as I tacitly assumed in §3.2. Other things being equal,[9] to feel an emotion with a particular intensity in one situation is to be committed to feel with similar intensity other emotions having the same focus when otherwise appropriate. Emotions that are too intense or too weak relative to the resulting pattern of emotional commitments are, to that extent, out of proportion in a way that reflects poorly on their warrant. To say this is, in part, to expand our conception of warrant as not merely something that an emotion either has or fails to have but rather as something that can come in degrees. Thus, anger that is too intense or grief that is too weak both involve a kind of rational failing in light of their failure to live up to this pattern of commitments.[10] The same can be said for desires, as another kind of felt evaluation: desires must normally, other things being equal, have strength proportional to emotional intensity, and having a desire with a particular strength imposes a rational commitment to feel emotions having the same focus with proportionate intensity; desires that are too weak or too strong relative to that broader pattern are, to that extent, out of proportion and unwarranted. Consequently, particular felt evaluations are beholden to the broader pattern of other felt evaluations with the same focus in a way that regulates their intensity as well as whether they are had at all.

So far, these assertions about mutual commitments among felt evaluations applying also to the intensity of those felt evaluations may look

---

[9] In general, other things are not equal, and I shall discuss below some complications for this still-all-too-simple understanding of emotional intensity.

[10] From the perspective of the objectivity of import, we might put the rational failure this way: emotions whose intensities are out of proportion are not properly responsive to degree of import. I shall return to this point shortly.

108

ad hoc: why should we think that the degree of warrant of an emotion or desire depends in this way on such mutual commitments? After all, it might be thought, the intensity of an emotion is simply a matter of its phenomenology and has nothing to do with the conditions of its warrant.

The answer requires considering this projectible, rational pattern from the other perspective: that of the objectivity of import as that which impresses itself on us and so is a standard of warrant for these emotions. As I argued in §3.3, what makes such a pattern of felt evaluations intelligible as rational and so partly constitutive of the warrant of its elements is that such a pattern is constitutive of import, as that to which particular felt evaluations must be properly responsive. Thus, the projectibility of the pattern of felt evaluations instituted by their mutual commitments is in effect an attunement of one's sensibilities to the import of the focus of that pattern, such that we can make sense of that import as impressing itself on us in having particular felt evaluations. Now we can see this as applying to degree of import as well. For what we are attuned to as the result of the projectibility of the pattern is not just the presence or absence of import in a situation but also its degree: import impresses itself on us and enthralls us to a greater or lesser degree. It is precisely this fact that enables us to make sense of particular felt evaluations as having greater or lesser intensity not simply as a matter of their phenomenology, but rather as a kind of responsiveness to degree of import. (Of course, it is a matter of phenomenology as well. As I argued in §3.4, we should understand the phenomenology of emotions in terms of the way in which import impresses itself on us and enthralls us by grabbing both our attention and our motivation: the import impressing itself on us in this way feels good or bad, pleasant or painful. Consequently, import of greater or lesser degree as it impresses itself on us feels more or less good or bad, more or less pleasant or painful. Nonetheless, this account of their phenomenology falls out of the root phenomenon of the mutual commitments among felt evaluations constituting their attunement to degree of import.) Thus, degree of import, as having a kind of objectivity as constituted by the overall pattern, can serve as a standard of warrant for the intensity of felt evaluations because it is that to which particular felt evaluations must be properly responsive by being more or less intense.

It is important not to forget that felt evaluation is not merely a mode of attention to import; it is also a source of motivation. As I argued in

§3.4, we can understand such motivation in light of the subjectivity of import by focusing on the idea that the commitment implicit in a felt evaluation is not merely a commitment to attend to import by having other such felt evaluations in the appropriate circumstances; it is also a commitment to act appropriately. From the perspective of the objectivity of import, we can put the same point as follows: import impresses itself on us, enthralling us and motivating us to act in virtue of the practical reason that import provides. Now we can see that the strength of this motivation depends on the degree of import that impresses itself on us – on, that is, the intensity of the mutual commitments among felt evaluations to which particular felt evaluations are beholden. Of course, such "dependence" is not such that strength of motivation will automatically correspond to degree of import. Rather, it should be understood as a rational dependence insofar as motivational strength rationally ought to correspond to degree of import, in light of the broader pattern of mutual commitments among felt evaluations. Nonetheless, isolated gaps or inconsistencies within the pattern, such as a failure of motivation in a particular case, are possible so long as they remain isolated and do not undermine the pattern as a whole.

This account of the intensity of felt evaluations, however, is still overly simplistic, for it ignores a complication hinted at above (cf. note 9). The intensity of felt evaluations varies not merely with degree of import but also with what we might call the "severity" of the situation.[11] For example, my fear in one situation might be properly more intense than my fear in another situation focused on the same object, having the same degree of import, because the threat in the former case is more severe. Likewise, the intensity of anger varies properly with the severity of the offensiveness of its target, the intensity of frustration varies properly with the severity of the obstacles one confronts, etc. Thus, we might say, *severity* is a measure of the degree to which the evaluation implicit in the formal object of an emotion applies to its target, irrespective of the degree of import of that emotion's focus. Emotions track severity, in much the same way they track degree of import, in the sense that their warrant depends on the extent to which their intensity correlates with it.

---

[11] Intensity of felt evaluation also varies with the way in which one's preferences enter into the current situations as well as the "distance" of a sub-goal from the final end. I shall discuss these complications and the implications they have for our understanding of degree of import in §4.3 and §4.4. respectively.

The language of "severity" seems to fit negative emotions better than positive emotions, for we would not ordinarily say that hope, for example, tracks the "severity" of the likelihood of success. Nonetheless, the phenomenon of severity is a condition of the warrant of these positive emotions as well, in part by virtue of their tonal commitments with negative emotions. The point this language of severity is meant to convey is that the intensity of emotions is situation-sensitive. Indeed, put this way we can see the point as applying to desire as well: the degree to which an end is worth pursuing here and now depends not only on the degree of import of that end but also on the broader features of one's situation, such as the timing and ordering of one's actions in pursuit of various ends.

The upshot is that the kind of consistency of intensity that is rationally required within the pattern of felt evaluations by virtue of their mutual commitments is consistency modulo severity; such consistency in the projectible, rational pattern of felt evaluations therefore partly constitutes degree of import. The dual objectivity and subjectivity of degree of import means that degree of import and intensity of felt evaluation are part of a conceptual package, neither part of which is intelligible apart from the other. Of course, it is possible to have the general pattern of felt evaluations constitutive of import without that consistency in intensity, though such a pattern must be considered to be abnormal and unstable. This would result in the focus of that pattern having import without any determinate degree and would require that the pattern otherwise be robust – for otherwise the inconsistency in intensity might mean that there is no determinate fact of the matter about whether the pattern is there at all, and so whether the focus has import or not.

So far, this account of the degree of import has concentrated on the rational connections simply within a projectible, rational pattern of felt evaluations constitutive of import and degree of import; indeed, the way I have defined the notion of degree of import, as a measure of how much we care about or value something, encourages this concentration. Yet this account is still incomplete – hence the claim in the last paragraph that such internal rational commitments only partly constitute degree of import. For solving the motivational and deliberative problems requires making intelligible direct comparisons of the relative import things have, and this notion of degree of import provides the grounds for making only indirect comparisons. In order to fill out the account so as to have a better understanding both of degree of import and of the intensity of felt evaluation, therefore, we must consider as well rational connections between patterns with different foci and the ways in which such connections affect the appropriateness of felt evaluations in particular situations. This will be my aim in §§4.3–4.4.

4.3 PREFERENCES AND THE DAMPENING EFFECT

Consider the following example. On a recent trip to Washington D.C., Karl finds himself with some time to see an exhibition. Two strike him as particularly interesting: a photography exhibition at the National Archives and a portrait exhibition at the National Gallery. Although he wants to see both of them, he only has time for one, and so he chooses the photography exhibition. Such a choice reveals his *preferences*: the relative degree of import these options have for him – and such preferences affect the felt evaluations it is appropriate for him to have. Thus, Karl's desire to see the portrait exhibition has been frustrated by his going to the National Archives instead, and so, given the account of felt evaluations presented so far, it would seem warranted that he feel disappointment of an intensity proportionate to both the intensity of his desire and the severity of the import in these circumstances. (Indeed, as we might expect, such severity is fairly high: if he misses it now, he will likely never be able to see it.) Yet this is wrong: although it would be appropriate for Karl to have felt such disappointment if he had chosen to see the portrait exhibition but for some other reason was prevented from doing so, in a context in which he prefers to see the other exhibition there would be something wrong with feeling disappointed, at least with this much intensity. That is, the intensity of disappointment that is warranted in these circumstances is properly dampened because of the way in which preferences are involved in defining the circumstances; I shall call this the *dampening effect*.[12]

This dampening effect is pervasive in contexts involving preferences, and not simply in those cases involving antecedent choice. Thus, Theresa's annoyance at her pizza's being delivered late is properly dampened by her joy that her team has just won the championship. Again, this

---

[12] The dampening effect can be either partial, as in Karl's case, or total: when offered a choice between my wife's life or a large sum of money, the import of my wife in effect *silences* any desire I may have for money, such that in the circumstances the money offers no reason at all for sacrificing my wife. (Cf. John McDowell's "Are Moral Requirements Hypothetical Imperatives?" *Proceedings of the Aristotelian Society*, Supplement, 52 [1978], pp. 13–29.)

dampening effect is made intelligible in light of her preferences: the fate of her team has a greater degree of import to her relative to whether her pizza arrives on time or not.

How, then, are we to understand preferences? In effect this requires an expansion of the account of degree of import and so requires that we consider both the objectivity and subjectivity of degree of import. Consider first the subjectivity of import: the way in which degree of import, and so preferences, depend on the patterns in our felt evaluations. To make sense of the dampening effect requires that we understand felt evaluations to be commitments not only to have other felt evaluations with the same focus and the same intensity in the relevant circumstances, other things being equal; in addition such a commitment must be to dampen felt evaluations, the import of whose foci is of lesser degree, as well as to be dampened by imports of other foci of still greater degree, other things being equal. Once again, to be intelligible as such, these commitments must impose rational pressure on subsequent felt evaluations with various foci to conform in a way that is generally transitive and asymmetric. When one's felt evaluations generally do conform to these mutual commitments, the result is a pattern of responsiveness not merely to the import of a particular focus but to the broader circumstances in a way that defines the dampening relations among various foci. Moreover, this pattern of responsiveness will be projectible and rational in virtue of the kind of pressure such commitments impose: given this pattern of commitments, it is rational, other things being equal, for a felt evaluation with one focus to be dampened in the face of relevant circumstances involving another focus. Our preferences, therefore, emerge out of precisely this sort of projectible, rational pattern among felt evaluations with different foci: to prefer one thing to another, for the former to have greater degree of import relative to the latter, just is to be committed to such transitive and asymmetrical dampening relations, other things being equal.

Notice that throughout I have used the caveat, "other things being equal," in describing the relevant patterns of commitments constitutive of preferences. One obvious case in which other things may not be equal is when there is a disparity in the severity of the relevant imports. Thus, if Theresa's team loses as the result of a strategic decision to rest their key players after having clinched a playoff berth, the degree of import of the loss in these circumstances of such minor severity may well be less than that of the lateness of her pizza. Consequently, the conditions of the appropriateness of the dampening effect are modulo severity. Other cases in which other things are not equal include those in which Freudian mechanisms of transference, repression, or displacement are at issue, as when, in the face of her team's loss, Theresa becomes (without warrant) still even more annoyed at the lateness of her pizza. In such cases we can, in light of these Freudian mechanisms, explain away particular responses as isolated lapses of rationality, and so as mere noise rather than as evidence of a change in the pattern itself (and so in her preferences). Nonetheless, it is crucial that such lapses of rationality be intelligible as isolated, for too many such cases undermines the pattern of mutual commitments constitutive of preferences at all.

As with import and degree of import themselves, we must not understand preferences to be merely subjective and so conceptually posterior to such felt evaluations. For we can make sense of the rationality of the relevant commitments implicit in these felt evaluations only if we understand the commitments as to certain preferences. Consequently, the pattern of responsiveness these commitments define is in effect an attunement to preferences, and we can therefore criticize as warranted or not particular felt evaluations, as well as the way in which they motivate us to act, for being out of place in the general pattern precisely because they run contrary to one's preferences. In this way, preferences stand as an object to which a subject ought to be properly responsive on pain of irrationality; indeed, in this way we can understand the dampening effect to be not merely a psychological phenomenon, whereby my sensitivity to the import of something is diminished, but rather a fact about the degree of import that impresses itself on me in the circumstances.

This account of the dampening effect provides more substance to the heretofore somewhat vague notion of the intensity of felt evaluation. For, to have a felt evaluation of high intensity is to be highly intent on the import it involves and so unlikely to be distracted from that import by other imports of lesser degree, in accordance with the dampening effect. In addition it is to be motivated more strongly by that import in the sense that one is unlikely to be swayed from such a course of action by other imports of lesser degree. Although these things are unlikely, they can happen, as in cases of weakness of will. Nonetheless, such cases are rational failures, and it is a condition of the possibility of both preferences and one's being committed to preferences that they generally do not.

114

The upshot is that we cannot, as my account in chapter 3 may seem to have suggested, understand a subject's receptivity to import, her evaluative perspective, as divided into independent modules each defined simply by a pattern of felt evaluations with a common focus. Rather, given the sensitivity to relative import required by the dampening effect, we must understand these distinct cares and values to be unified into a single evaluative perspective – as both a commitment and receptivity to import in general.

It should be clear, however, that the kind of consistency demanded within this pattern of commitment to preferences need not be so rigorous as to enable us to locate everything that has import to us on a single scale defined by degree of import, a scale that defines a neat hierarchy of preferences. For, first, one may simply have no preference in a particular case, perhaps because of simple indeterminacy. Thus, we might imagine, Karl might never have encountered a situation in which the imports of photographs and paintings simultaneously impressed themselves on him, and so the relative import of these may never have been established. Or, perhaps, they have simultaneously impressed themselves on him in the past, but his felt evaluations in response to such circumstances were not asymmetric. Such an inconsistency in his commitments is surely possible, but only as parasitic on standard cases in which his commitments are in general consistent, on pain of giving up the idea that what he is committed to is preferences – to relative degree of import – at all.

A second and more important reason for there being no neat hierarchy of preferences is that the imports of some things may be *incommensurable* in the sense that they cannot be located on a single scale of degree of import (modulo severity), even setting indeterminacy aside. Thus, we might think, the import of my work may be incommensurable with that of my family insofar as there is no way of saying in advance of particular situations which has greater import. Sometimes work and sometimes family are more important, and we may not be able to articulate which cases are which in any neat and systematic way by appealing to such factors as severity.

How is such incommensurability to be differentiated from mere indeterminacy given that in each case there is no straightforward pattern of commitments among the relevant felt evaluations constitutive of a preference? The answer comes through a distinction between preferences and priorities: one thing takes *priority* over another just in case one not only has a preference for it but also values having that preference. Priorities can be *general*, in that one values in every case the one over the other, other things being equal; or they can be *particular*, such that one might value preferring the one over the other in one circumstance, but value the opposite preference in other circumstances. Thus, for example, I may find that to choose my job over my family in one circumstance is selfish and, because of my value of unselfishness, does not enter into the kind of person I find worth being, yet, in other circumstances, I might find that choice to be courageous, something else I value. Insofar as there need not be any systematic relationship between the concepts of unselfishness and courage that define my values, there may be no value-neutral way of specifying which has a general priority over the other. Hence, the imports of work and of family are incommensurable even though it is not simply indeterminate which ought to take priority over the other in particular circumstances. (This will be discussed in greater detail in §7.4.2.)

This account of preferences in terms of patterns of commitments in felt evaluations both to have other felt evaluations having the same focus with the same intensity and to have certain transitive and asymmetric dampening relations with felt evaluations having different foci, other things being equal, is nonetheless incomplete. For we can undertake such commitments to preferences not only passively in felt evaluations but also actively in evaluative judgment. Indeed, it might be thought, these patterns of felt evaluations in the end are irrelevant to constituting our preferences, for all that matters is evaluative judgment. Thus, Sarah Buss argues that "the normative character of an agent's preferences is tied to the impossibility of regarding them as something forced upon her against her will"; but because, she thinks, it is judgment and judgment alone that can prevent such alienation from our preferences, an "all-things-considered [evaluative] judgment is a *sufficient*, as well as a *necessary*, condition of preference."[13] This is, I think, too quick, though adequately responding to the objection requires providing a detailed account of the rational interconnections among evaluative judgments and felt evaluations. I shall undertake this in chapter 5, thereby supplementing my account of preferences in light of an understanding of the role evaluative judgment plays in the same rational pattern of felt evaluations constitutive of preferences.

[13] "Weakness of Will," *Pacific Philosophical Quarterly*, 78 (1997), pp. 13–44, at p. 21 and p. 20, respectively.

4.4 INSTRUMENTAL RATIONALITY

Thus far in this chapter, I have complicated our understanding of import in two ways: by accommodating the distinction between caring and valuing, and by offering an account of preferences and priorities. The way in which these complications were accommodated within my account was by articulating the relevant rational connections both within the patterns of felt evaluations with a common focus and among various such patterns with different foci. I shall now examine one further complication concerning these connections: instrumental rationality. My aim is not to offer a complete account of instrumental rationality, but only to suggest ways in which it can be accommodated within my broader account.

The nature of instrumental rationality is commonly captured by the following principle: if you want an end, then you ought to want to take what you believe to be the necessary means to that end, other things being equal. It should be clear, however, that the importance of instrumental rationality lies not simply with desire or with motivation but more generally with import: if buying a house has import to me and I believe I need to get a loan in order to buy a house, then getting a loan ought to have import to me. Put this way, we can see how instrumental rationality imposes rational requirements on one's felt evaluations quite generally. Thus, as the opportunity arises, I ought not only to feel the occurrent desire to get a loan and so be motivated to act appropriately, but also to feel frustration, hope, disappointment, anger, satisfaction, etc. depending on how my attempts to secure a loan proceed. In general, therefore, we might adopt the following *instrumental principle:* if an end has import to you, then what you believe to be the necessary means to that end ought also to have import to you, other things being equal.

There is, however, an ambiguity in this instrumental principle concerning the nature of the import of the means. We can clarify the kind of import at issue here by considering an apparent counterexample to my account of desire. If buying a house has import for me, then the instrumental principle requires not only that securing a loan have import for me, but also that gathering up the necessary financial records does as well. Clearly, therefore, there is a sense in which I ought to desire to gather up these financial records. However, it may seem, such a desire does not fit my account of desires as felt evaluations, for the import of gathering up financial records does not impress itself upon me, both

117

enthralling me and motivating me to act. Rather, doing this strikes me as a hassle, something in which I in no way take pleasure but only do because I must in order to achieve the end I care about, namely buying a house. The sense in which I want to do this, therefore, seems not to be a sense that fits my account of desire, and, insofar as it is a straightforward instance of desire, it seems to be a counterexample to the account I have provided of desire as a felt evaluation.

This is too quick, however, for we need to make a distinction, hitherto missing in my account of import, between something's having import for its own sake and its having import merely for the sake of something else. For it is clear that the sense in which gathering my financial records has import to me is only the latter sense, and it does not have import on its own; indeed, instrumental rationality imposes requirements on what ought to have import for one only in this latter sense. The account of something's having import I have provided in terms of its being the focus of the relevant projectible, rational pattern in one's felt evaluations, however, is intended to be an account of something's having import for its own sake. Clearly, however, something's having import for the sake of something else does not require that it be the focus of such a pattern of felt evaluations. Indeed, this is demonstrated in the alleged counterexample to my account of desire: the import of gathering financial records does not impress itself on and enthrall me, precisely because gathering those records is not the focus of my felt evaluations.

How, then, are we to make sense of something's having import merely for the sake of something else? When I am frustrated at not being able to find my financial records, when I am hopeful of finding them buried under a stack of other papers, when I get angry at my wife for hiding them from me, etc., the focus of my felt evaluations is not these records but rather my buying a house. Similarly, when I want to gather up these records, what impresses itself on me as worth pursuing, as having import, is buying the house, the focus (but not the target) of my desire. The felt evaluations clustered around gathering my financial records are simply a part of the projectible, rational pattern of felt evaluations focused on buying a house and constituting its import.[14] Consequently, something's having import only for the sake of something else is constituted by its figuring in this way as a part of the pattern of felt

[14] Here, and in what follows, by "import" I intend import for its own sake, unless explicitly noted otherwise.

evaluations focused on that for the sake of which it has that import, and it is instrumental rationality that defines precisely the way it must figure in this broader pattern.

The alleged counterexample to my account of desire is not, therefore, a counterexample. We should not expect the import of the necessary means (i.e., import merely for the sake of some end) to impress itself on and cause in one a desire to act accordingly, for such a means is not on its own the focus of the relevant pattern of felt evaluations. Rather, we should expect that one be enthralled to act in the relevant way by the import of that end. Of course, one may have a (perhaps misguided) overall evaluative perspective on how one's preferences bear on the current situation, and so the import of the end may not be as salient to one as it perhaps should be, thus accounting for one's sense that taking the means is merely a hassle; or one may fail to recognize (or to recognize fully) that this means is necessary to achieving the end, in which case one may need to remind oneself explicitly of the necessity of these means for achieving the end so as to exercise some control over one's motivations.[15] Nonetheless, the account of desire I have presented is able to accommodate such cases.

The important point is that instrumental rationality has emerged as a general requirement on the coherence of the projectible, rational patterns of felt evaluations constitutive of import. Other things being equal, to fail to have felt evaluations "clustered" around necessary means to an end undermines the coherence of the pattern focused on that end. The instrumental principle, therefore, is not a one-way directive, imposing a requirement merely on the necessary means having import for the sake of that end, such that a failure here does not at all reflect badly on the import of the end. Rather, a failure of the means to have this merely instrumental import is a failure of the coherence of the broader pattern constitutive of the import of the end, and such a failure itself may begin to undermine the import of that end.

Of course, the "other things being equal" clause here is important, for the instrumental principle provides only some-things-considered reasons, which are potentially undercut by other considerations. For example, if securing a loan in order to buy a house requires that I put down such a large down payment and accept such a high interest rate that I would no longer be able to afford to put my children through college, this fact

---

[15] I shall discuss this latter kind of case more fully in chapter 6 in the context of a general discussion of how we can exercise control over our actions.

alone may undercut the reason buying a house provides for securing this loan; nonetheless, it need not undermine the import buying a house has for me, and I may continue to economize in order eventually to afford a house. Here, therefore, we can see how instrumental rationality plays a role as well in defining the rational interconnections among felt evaluations with different foci constitutive of preferences. This reveals, therefore, an additional requirement on the pattern of the dampening effect constitutive of preferences. For our felt evaluations must be regulated not only in accordance with the transitivity and asymmetry of preferences and with the degree of import things have, but also in accordance with instrumental rationality. For it is the greater relative import of my children's college education that ought to dampen my desire to accept this loan at the expense of my children's education.

Instrumental rationality, therefore, is a requirement both within particular patterns of felt evaluations and among these patterns, and so it is fundamental to constituting both what has import to us and what our preferences are.

4.5 CONCLUSION

My aim in Part I has been to provide an account of import that is free from illegitimate presuppositions about the nature of desires and emotions. I argued in chapter 2 that standard accounts of belief and desire in the context of the mind–body problem simply ignore the way in which desire presupposes import as that which it is worth pursuing, and so are unable to make a distinction between the rationally mediated goal-directedness of chess-playing computers and creatures like dogs and persons to whom things matter. Yet it is precisely this more robust notion of desire that is presupposed by any serious moral psychology. The resulting mismatch between these two forces us, therefore, to confront the problem of import head-on.

What is important about the problem of import, I argued, is that it forces us to reconceive our understanding of our evaluative attitudes like desires and the emotions in terms other than the standard categories of cognition and conation. For import, I argued, has elements both of objectivity, as a standard for the warrant of emotions and desires, and of subjectivity, as nonetheless constituted by these very same emotions and desires. Thus, I argued, it is true both that we desire things because they have import and that things have import because we desire them.

120

Making sense of import as having this dual objectivity and subjectivity therefore requires understanding import and our evaluative attitudes as a single conceptual package, neither part of which is prior to the other.

In chapter 3, I developed my initial account of this conceptual package in terms of the notion of a felt evaluation. What characterizes a felt evaluation is, first, that it is a kind of responsiveness to import impressing itself on one and enthralling one; in this way, I argued, we can best account for the phenomenology of emotions, desires, and bodily pleasures and pains, as well as the way in which they motivate us to act. Second, felt evaluations are also a kind of commitment to import and thereby impose rational constraints on one's other felt evaluations with the same focus. These mutual focal commitments, I argued, establish a projectible pattern in one's felt evaluations that both is a condition of the warrant of the elements of that pattern and constitutes the import of the pattern's focus. In this way, felt evaluations exhibit elements of both mind-to-world and world-to-mind direction of fit simultaneously, which implies that they are neither cognitions nor conations. Moreover, this account solves the problem of import in a way consistent with the best approaches to the mind–body problem, for it articulates the relevant kinds of rationality that serve as the condition of the possibility of one's having the capacity for these mental states at all.

In this chapter, I have refined the account of felt evaluation and of import in several ways. First, in §4.1, I distinguished two kinds of import, our cares and our values: values, unlike cares, have greater depth insofar as they involve an implicit understanding of the kind of person we each find worth being and so are evaluations not only of things in the world but also of ourselves. I then presented an account of values in terms of reflexive emotions and second-order desires, arguing that the requisite self-understanding is implicit in these patterns of reflexive felt evaluations. Second, in §§4.2–4.3, I presented an account of relative degree of import – of preferences – by complicating our understanding of the rationality of felt evaluations in two ways: (a) in terms of the pattern of intensities of our felt evaluations having a single focus, and (b) in terms of the rational interconnections among the patterns of felt evaluations with different foci that result in the dampening effect. This account of preferences and of the rational interconnections among patterns of felt evaluations with different foci, therefore, requires that we understand our receptivity to import not as divisible into separate modules defined by the patterns of commitments among felt evaluations with a common focus, but rather as the result of a more general evaluative perspective. Third, in §4.4, I again complicated the patterns of felt evaluations in terms of instrumental rationality, thereby making sense of a distinction between something's having import for its own sake and its having import for the sake of something else.

Nonetheless, it should be clear that this account of import is still incomplete, for nothing has been said so far about evaluative judgment, which surely has an important role in constituting both import and preferences. Indeed, the two fundamental problems of practical reason I aim to solve, the motivational and deliberative problems, are problems that arise in part out of the potential for conflicts among desire, emotion, and evaluative judgment. Consequently, my aim in Part II will be to understand the rational interconnections among felt evaluations and evaluative judgments so as to reformulate and solve these fundamental problems.

PART II

Practical reason

5

Single evaluative perspective

My overall goal in this book is to understand the nature of the sort of practical rationality that is distinctive of persons. In chapter 1, I briefly characterized this sort of rationality as linguistically informed, articulate, self-conscious, critical, and reflexive, and I then went on to describe two persistent problems facing any account of such practical reason: the motivational problem and the deliberative problem.

The motivational problem, recall, is roughly that of how to understand the connection between deliberate choice and our being moved to act. The problem is that, in order for us to have rational control over what we do, it seems that we have to postulate an essential connection between our evaluative judgments and our desires, for anything less would seem to make that connection be merely contingent and fortuitous in a way that undermines the thought that we have control. However, it also seems as though there cannot be any such essential connection between evaluation and motivation given the persistent possibility of weakness of will, of our being motivated to act contrary to what we judge best. How, then, is our having rational control over our actions, when we have it, consistent with the simultaneous possibility of weakness of will?

The deliberative problem is roughly that of how it is possible to deliberate about and so choose our cares and values, thereby making intelligible how we can have a say in, and so be responsible for, our identities as persons. However, our having a say in what has import to us seems like a matter of autonomous invention, involving a kind of freedom that is distinctively human. Yet our choice of what has import to us is not merely arbitrary, for such choice can be the outcome of deliberation and so is constrained by reason; anything less would appear arbitrary and so undermine the idea that life can be meaningful. Hence, we must be able to choose correctly or incorrectly, and in this sense our deliberation is a matter of discovery. Thus, it seems essential to our understanding ourselves as persons that what has import to us is a matter both of invention and discovery, and this seems paradoxical: nothing can be simultaneously both invented and discovered, for the concept of discovery implies that the object of discovery is there in advance, whereas the concept of invention implies that it is not. How, then, can we make sense of our being both free and constrained by reason in our choice of our cares and values, and so how can we make sense of ourselves as responsible for who we are?

As I argued in chapter 1, what underlies both these problems as thus conceived is the traditional divide between cognition and conation. For, according to that divide, cognition and conation are distinct existences insofar as (a) they have opposite directions of fit, (b) it is possible to remove one's cognitions but leave one's motivations intact, and (c) it is possible to remove one's conations but leave one's cognitions and their rational basis intact. Consequently, in light of this divide, the motivational problem gets conceived as a problem of figuring out how to bridge the inevitable gap between our evaluative judgments, as cognitions, and our desires, as conations – between these distinct existences – and thereby to achieve rational control. Given this conception of the problem, I argued, no solution is possible, for nothing that bridges the gap could provide the basis for rational control. Whatever bridges the gap must be intentional, for otherwise we could have no rational control over its operation. Yet, if it is intentional, it must, according to the cognitive–conative divide, be either a cognition or a conation. If it is a cognition, then we cannot make sense of its providing a bridge to motivation, and if it is a conation then we cannot make sense of its being properly responsive to reasons. So rational control seems impossible. Likewise, the assumption of the cognitive–conative divide forces us to conceive the deliberative problem in a way that makes it unsolvable. For if any mental state must be either a cognition or a conation, with either mind-to-world or world-to-mind direction of fit, import must either be an object discovered by cognition or invented by conation, but not both simultaneously. So the deliberative problem is conceived in terms of a genuine paradox of invention and discovery, and any solution to it must involve giving up part of our ordinary conception of persons as able both freely and non-arbitrarily to have a say in what has import to us. Such a "solution," I argued, is more a capitulation in the face of the problem than a satisfying resolution of it.

If what underlies both the motivational and deliberative problems, preventing any satisfying solution of them, is the cognitive–conative divide, then it seems the best strategy to solve these problems is to reject that divide. Indeed, the notion of a felt evaluation developed in Part I has enabled me to provide an account of desires, emotions, and bodily pleasures and pains as neither cognitions nor conations, but as states simultaneously both responsive to and constitutive of import. Consequently, it might seem, we are now in a good position to address the motivational and deliberative problems head-on. For this conception of felt evaluations helps solve the motivational problem insofar as it provides an avenue for understanding how evaluation and motivation can be conceptually linked by virtue of the projectible, rational patterns of felt evaluations, while nonetheless allowing for the possibility that one may fail to be motivated by those evaluations in particular cases because of isolated gaps in the pattern. Moreover, this conception of felt evaluations helps solve the deliberative problem insofar as we have seen that there need be no paradox of simultaneous invention and discovery in the case of import, for import, as I have understood it, is constituted by patterns of disclosive rather than cognitive assent.

Nonetheless, this is not yet a solution to either problem. For what is puzzling in both the motivational and deliberative problems lies in part in the nature of evaluative judgment and its connection either to motivation or to import. So it is our judgments, specifically those judgments that are the outcome of rational deliberation, that are at the root of these problems. Yet so far I have said very little about evaluative judgment beyond hinting at its importance and therefore have done little to articulate the kind of practical rationality distinctive of persons.

My aim in this chapter, therefore, is to develop an explicit account of that importance by articulating the rational interconnections among felt evaluations and evaluative judgments. My claim will be that evaluative judgment itself is an element in, and is not in general intelligible apart from, the projectible, rational patterns of felt evaluations, and as such can both correct and be corrected by these other elements in light of that broader pattern. When things go right, our felt evaluations and evaluative judgments present us with a single evaluative perspective that constitutes both the imports things have for us and our preferences; when things go wrong, there is a rational failing, potentially a fragmentation of our evaluative perspective, that can be remedied only by revising some of our felt evaluations or evaluative judgments so as to restore the normal rational coherence among them. Nonetheless, I shall argue, evaluative judgment has a special place in this pattern because it involves active as opposed to passive assent. I will then, in chapters 6 and 7 use this account of these rational interconnections to reformulate and solve both the motivational and deliberative problems.

5.1 PRIMACY OF JUDGMENT: AN OBJECTION

The account of import presented in chapters 3–4 has so far understood it in terms of projectible, rational patterns of felt evaluations. One might object that any account of import – of our caring about or valuing something – cannot be sustained without giving evaluative judgment a prominent, indeed a fundamental role. Here is why.

To care about something or value it is to make it be central to our lives as a worthy object of our attention and action and therefore to be the proper source of desires and emotions that are genuinely one's own.[1] Nonetheless, it does not follow that we care about or value the foci of all desires and emotions, for some desires and emotions can come over us as if alien forces are assailing us from outside, and their foci are for that reason not objects of our cares or values. Thus, consider Harry Frankfurt's example of an unwilling addict:[2] someone may be addicted to cigarettes and so frequently feel a desire to smoke, even though he has committed himself to quitting and so rejects that desire. This desire to smoke, Frankfurt claims quite plausibly, is such an alien force precisely because the addict has self-consciously rejected it.

This can seem problematic for my account of caring and valuing, of import, for it seems that a desire can be alien in this way even though it is a part of the kind of projectible, rational pattern of other felt evaluations I have argued is constitutive of import. Thus, even though the addict has decided to stop smoking and so self-consciously rejects his desires to smoke as alien, he may still consistently desire to smoke, take satisfaction in doing so, get frustrated when he cannot find his cigarettes or angry at those who hide them, etc. By deciding to quit smoking, he is therefore rejecting this whole pattern of emotions and desires as alien. Consequently, one might think, smoking cannot be something he cares

---

[1] Of course, as I argued in §4.1, there is an important distinction between the ways in which cares and values are central to our lives: values, by finding one's own worth in the object of value, therefore involve a kind of depth that is missing from one's cares. This distinction does not matter for present purposes.

[2] "Freedom of the Will and the Concept of a Person," in *The Importance of What We Care About*, pp. 11–25.

about, and my account of caring in terms of projectible, rational patterns of felt evaluations is inadequate. It might therefore seem that a deliberate, self-conscious endorsement in judgment is a necessary or even sufficient condition for caring about or valuing something, for it might seem to be judgment and judgment alone that determines what we really think.[3] Judgment is, therefore, fundamental to any account of import as that to which our felt evaluations must conform if they are to be a proper part of ourselves.

Of course, Frankfurt himself flirts with an account of caring or valuing solely in terms of desire, and we can support the intuition about the centrality of evaluative judgment to such an account by considering why he is led to give judgment a fundamental role. To see this, it is necessary first to establish some of Frankfurt's vocabulary. A *first-order desire* is a desire to do something; it contrasts with a *second-order desire*, which is a desire to have a first-order desire. Thus, my desire to smoke is a first-order desire, whereas my desire that I have the desire to quit is a second-order desire. One's *will*, Frankfurt says, consists in one's effective desires – that is, desires "that move (or will or would move) a person all the way to action," though one need not be successful in achieving one's end.[4] Finally, a second-order volition is a desire that some first-order desire be one's will and so move one to act.[5] To have the capacity for *second-order volition* is to have the possibility of *freedom of the will* – the possibility of success in one's attempts to have the will one wants to have; this possibility, Frankfurt argues, is fundamental to being a person.

According to Frankfurt's initial account, merely to have a second-order volition is to identify oneself with the relevant first-order desire in the sense that it thereby becomes a central part of one's life and so not an alien force; moreover, to have such a second-order volition is to *withdraw* oneself from other first-order desires that conflict with this one, such that these conflicting desires become forces operating contrary to one's volition. Such identification and withdrawal can seem therefore to provide an account of what it is to care about something in roughly the

---

[3] This is roughly the view advocated by Sarah Buss; see her "Weakness of Will," and her "Autonomy Reconsidered," in *Midwest Studies in Philosophy*, 19 (1994), pp. 95–121. A similar view, addressed below, is advocated by Gary Watson.

[4] "Freedom of the Will and the Concept of a Person," p. 14.

[5] Frankfurt thinks that one might have a second-order desire without thereby desiring that one be moved to act by the relevant first-order desire: a desire, say, merely to feel the motivational pull of a desire but not actually to act on it. So the notion of a second-order volition is stronger and more interesting than that of a second-order desire.

way I have understood it: of its being worthy of attention and action. Indeed, Frankfurt himself often uses this language of caring, in his descriptions of what it is to have a second-order volition as, roughly, to "care which of his conflicting first-order desires wins out";[6] similarly, Frankfurt elsewhere characterizes the relevant sense of identification as a matter of

car[ing] about [something] in the sense that he makes himself vulnerable to losses and susceptible to benefits depending upon whether what he cares about is diminished or enhanced. Thus, he concerns himself with what concerns it, giving particular attention to such things and directing his behavior accordingly.[7]

One problem for the account as it stands, as Frankfurt himself notes, is the possibility of an infinite regress.[8] For, just as someone can have a conflict among her first-order desires, so, too, she can have a conflict among her second-order volitions, a conflict that undermines the idea that she has thereby identified herself with anything. Resolving such conflicts seems to require appeal to third-order volitions; similarly, conflicts at the level of third-order volitions require appeal to volitions of still higher orders, and so on. In the face of such a regress, it can seem arbitrary merely to decide that one's third-order volitions, say, are all that matter for identifying oneself with a course of action, and such arbitrariness undermines the account of caring, of something's being worthy of attention and action.

Frankfurt claims to solve this problem of arbitrariness as follows:

it is possible . . . to terminate such a series of acts without cutting it off arbitrarily. When a person identifies himself *decisively* with one of his first-order desires, this commitment "resounds" throughout the potentially endless array of higher orders.[9]

In subsequent works, he elaborates such decisive identification in terms of a wholehearted decision. The *decision* is a judgment that endorses the first-order desire in the strong sense that by making this judgment one in effect cuts off any further deliberation about the matter:

a commitment is *decisive* if and only if . . . the person who makes it does so in the belief that no further accurate inquiry would require him to change his mind.[10]

---

[6] "Freedom of the Will and the Concept of a Person," p. 18.
[7] "The Importance of What We Care About," in *The Importance of What We Care About*, pp. 80–94, at p. 83.
[8] Cf. "Freedom of the Will and the Concept of a Person," pp. 21–22.
[9] Ibid., p. 21.
[10] "Identification and Wholeheartedness," in *The Importance of What We Care About*, pp. 159–76, at pp. 168–69, emphasis added.

Moreover, the decision is *wholehearted* in the sense that one arrives at it "without reservation"[11] and in "an absence of restlessness or resistance."[12] Frankfurt claims that such wholeheartedness (or "*self-satisfaction*," as he also calls it) cannot consist in any particular "deliberate attitude or belief or feeling or intention," for if that were so then that further attitude itself would have to be one with which one is identified by virtue of a still further attitude, thus resulting once again in an infinite regress.[13] Rather, Frankfurt claims:

> Satisfaction with one's self requires . . . no adoption of any cognitive, attitudinal, affective, or intentional stance. It does not require the performance of a particular act; and it also does not require any deliberate abstention. Satisfaction is a state of the entire psychic system – a state constituted just by the absence of any tendency or inclination to alter its condition.[14]

Consequently, according to Frankfurt, to identify with a particular desire or to care about its object is to have a second-order volition concerning it that one endorses decisively in judgment, so that further conflict simply does not arise. In this way he understands evaluative judgment to be a necessary part of caring.

This general conception of caring, and so of the problem of distinguishing those desires that are fully one's own from those that are alien forces, is sustained in Frankfurt's most recent treatment of these issues, though his language has, once again, shifted a bit.[15] Caring still is that in virtue of which a desire becomes most truly one's own, and caring still "consist[s] in [one's] having and identifying with a higher-order desire of this kind" – namely a higher-order desire not to extinguish or abandon a first-order desire.[16] Yet such identification now gets characterized in terms of a special kind of commitment Frankfurt identifies as love. To *love* something, Frankfurt claims, is both to have an interest in it for its own sake and to have it "*captivate*" us in that "we cannot help loving what we love."[17] To be captivated in this way is to be unwilling to give up the object of one's love, where such unwillingness is the result of a "deliberate [and] guiding intent" on our part, in effect a kind of

---

[11] Ibid., p. 168.
[12] "The Faintest Passion," p. 12.
[13] Ibid., p. 13.   [14] Ibid.
[15] See his *Necessity, Volition, and Love* (Cambridge University Press, 1999), especially "On the Necessity of Ideals," "Autonomy, Necessity, and Love," and "On Caring."
[16] "On Caring," p. 161.
[17] "On the Necessity of Ideals," p. 114; see also "Autonomy, Necessity, and Love," p. 135.

deliberate endorsement of such a higher-order desire.[18] This talk of "deliberate endorsement," in line with his earlier talk of "decisive commitment," suggests that it is a matter, at least in part, of making a judgment, albeit, perhaps, an essentially practical judgment in virtue of which one guides one's attention and action; indeed, this is precisely how I shall understand him here. Such captivation, Frankfurt claims, makes this caring "a defining element of [one's] volitional nature," as having a kind of volitional necessity, and so is deeply personal, a matter of one's identity.[19] So, on Frankfurt's account, to care about something is to love it: to endorse a second-order volition for it by judging that one ought to attend to and act in the world in a particular way, such that one actively guides oneself by this judgment and is unwilling to change it or the underlying volition.

Gary Watson thinks even this appeal to evaluative judgment does not go far enough.[20] Watson objects to any appeal to desire, of whatever order, in providing an account of caring, or "valuing," as Watson calls it. (Notice that Watson does not make the distinction between caring and valuing that I have made in §4.1; rather, for him to value something is for it to have import of whatever depth.) Part of Watson's complaint is that what we identify with or commit ourselves to are not desires of

---

[18] "On Caring," pp. 161–62; see also "On the Necessity of Ideals," pp. 111–12. This notion of "guiding" oneself by what one cares about requires, Frankfurt thinks, that one "purposefully direct [one's] attention, attitudes, and behavior in response to circumstances germane to the fortunes of the object about which [one] cares" (p. 111). This sounds very much like the kind of vigilance I have argued is essential to something's having import to one. Yet Frankfurt's appeal to a notion of guidance here suggests that what he has in mind is a kind of active vigilance, a suggestion that is borne out by his insistence that a person's caring must be a person's "*own doing* [and] cannot be simply a matter of inadvertence or passivity on his part" ("On Caring," p. 160). As I claimed in §3.3, however, such active vigilance cannot in general be sustained, for our capacities to attend to those aspects of our circumstances that are potentially relevant to things we care about would quickly be overwhelmed; consequently, I argued, we must be able to make sense of a kind of passive vigilance, an attunement of our sensibilities in which our attention is naturally drawn to what has import to us. Such an account of passive vigilance is not available to Frankfurt insofar as he understands caring to be fundamentally conative, with world-to-mind direction of fit:

> It is not fundamentally because I recognize how valuable or important to me my children are that I love them. My love for them is not derivative from their value or their importance to me. On the contrary, the relationship goes essentially the other way. My children are so valuable and important to me just because I do in fact love them. ("On Caring," pp. 172–73)

[19] "Necessity, Volition, and Love," p. 132.
[20] "Free Agency," in Gary Watson, ed., *Free Will* (Oxford University Press, 1982), pp. 96–110, especially §III.

ours, as Frankfurt has it, but rather are courses of action. Thus, Watson thinks, Frankfurt should say that my wholehearted decision is to endorse my quitting smoking itself rather than my desire to quit, for the question I should ask in deliberation is not "which of [my] desires [I] want to be effective in action" but rather "which course of action is most worth pursuing."[21] This means, Watson thinks, that the whole structure of higher-order desires is irrelevant to understanding what a person identifies with or values; indeed, Watson claims, Frankfurt's solution to the problem of the infinite regress itself "reveals that the notion of a higher-order volition is not the fundamental one."[22] Rather, it is evaluative judgment alone that is relevant for determining a person's values because it is only in judgment that we can articulate our vision of the good.

For both Frankfurt and Watson, then, evaluative judgment is fundamental to an account of import – of caring or valuing – as that to which one's desires ought to conform if those desires are to be a proper part of oneself. Yet their understanding of precisely how judgment is fundamental seems to be incompatible with my account: judgment, they claim, is not simply one element among others in such a pattern (as I have suggested), for it is judgment alone that determines which of our felt evaluations are properly our own as opposed to alien forces that assail us as if from outside. My account of import, therefore, seems to require fundamental revision if not outright rejection.

I agree that evaluative judgment must have a central role in an account of import adequate to persons,[23] and that is why I have been careful to say that the projectible, rational patterns of felt evaluations is only part of what constitutes import. Nonetheless, I do not think that the role of evaluative judgment can be fundamental in quite the way the objection requires. For the objection requires that evaluative judgment be that which determines which of our felt evaluations is truly ours and which are alien forces operating within us, so that felt evaluations that do

---

[21] Ibid., p. 109.

[22] Ibid., p. 108. Part of what is behind Watson's conclusion here is his conception of desires as entirely non-evaluative, as something like inclinations to act that potentially stem from feelings of pleasure or suffering, feelings he in turn understands to be merely phenomenal. Consequently, Watson thinks that desires can provide us with reasons to act only in the sense that the "non-satisfaction of the desire causes suffering and hinders the pursuit of ends of the agent" (p. 101).

[23] Notice the qualification here. I think the account of import I have presented in terms of felt evaluations is adequate for many animals (such as dogs and cats); for arguments to this effect, see my "The Significance of Emotions," *American Philosophical Quarterly*, 31 (1994), pp. 319–31.

133

not accord with these evaluative judgments are consequently irrational; it is therefore fundamentally judgment that is the source of our considered view of the import things have for us. In contrast, I shall argue that, although evaluative judgment does have a kind of priority, that priority is not absolute. To see this, I shall in §5.2 elaborate the case, initially described in §4.1, of Betty, who experiences a kind of conflict that arises between her evaluative judgments and the projectible, rational patterns of felt evaluations she feels. I shall then argue that the conflict involved in Betty's case results in a kind of fragmentation of her identity of a sort that requires understanding felt evaluations and evaluative judgments to be more or less equals in constituting import. Making sense of the example, therefore, requires expanding my account, albeit not in the radical way the objection envisages, so as to incorporate evaluative judgment; I shall do this in §§5.3–5.4.

5.2 INHERENT FRAGMENTATION

Recall that Betty was brought up in the 1950s in a conservative family with what were then traditional values, and naturally came to adopt a subservient role in the family, anticipating and fulfilling the needs, desires, and aspirations of others; after her marriage, she again adopted this role with respect to her husband and children. As the result of her upbringing, Betty takes great pride in fulfilling this role and so in silencing any independent aspirations of her own in order to devote herself completely to those of her family, and she tends to become ashamed of or disappointed in herself for undertaking more selfish pursuits instead of catering to the needs and aspirations of others.

Now assume that Betty eventually comes to be good friends with Linda. Linda is an independent sort of person, with strong interests of her own, though interests that are well integrated with her compassion for others. In coming to respect and admire Linda, Betty comes to see intellectually that there can be more to life than simply subordinating oneself to others, and so comes to have second thoughts – first thoughts, really – about the worthiness of such a subservient role. As their friendship grows, Betty is gradually introduced to some feminist ideas, and she finds that there is some merit in the idea that many women are victimized by a generally chauvinist society. She thus comes to be outraged at how women in general are treated and have been brought up. She eventually comes to see, at least intellectually, that this applies to herself and that she ought to be outraged on her own behalf as well, though she finds herself unable to feel that way. Consequently, as she comes intellectually to appreciate more and more the kind of independence Linda has, she comes to judge that she should not be the kind of person who merely subordinates herself to others. Betty therefore resolves to change herself so as to become more independent, much as Linda is. She struggles to resist the impulse to drop everything, no matter what, to come to the aid of another so as to force herself to develop interests of her own that would otherwise be silenced.

In this example, Betty is faced with a conflict between her evaluative judgments and her felt evaluations. Thus, she wants to subordinate herself to others and she feels reflexive emotions consistent with this desire, but she nonetheless judges that she should not be the kind of person that merely subordinates herself to others. The question is: how should we understand this kind of conflict?

On the account I have provided so far, before Betty meets Linda she values fulfilling a subservient role by virtue of the projectible pattern of reflexive emotions (and, we can assume, second-order desires) she displays. Thus, for Betty, not to be the kind of person who subordinates herself in this way to the needs of others, and so not to be the kind of person who finds things valuable only insofar as they promote the welfare of others, is to be shamefully selfish. After she meets Linda, this projectible pattern of reflexive felt evaluations remains (at least initially) in spite of her judgment that she should not be that kind of person and her subsequent efforts to change herself. Such felt evaluations, I have argued, are a kind of commitment to the import of their common focus, and it is because of this commitment that her emotions and desires both are attuned to that import and are rationally required by it. Because the felt evaluations in this case are reflexive, the import to which she is thereby committed is her being a certain kind of person, and the pattern of felt evaluations therefore constitutes an implicit understanding of herself in these terms. Given the projectibility of the pattern and so the consistency with which she has these felt evaluations, this is a commitment and self-understanding that cannot be ignored.

Nonetheless, it is plausible to suppose that, in making the evaluative judgment and exerting an effort on its behalf, Betty is undertaking a contrary commitment that also constitutes her values and so the kind of person she finds worth being. After all, she comes explicitly to understand herself in terms of her judgment, and this is a self-understanding

135

she endorses: it is her best all-things-considered assessment of what is important and valuable to her.

Of course, merely to undertake in judgment any old commitment to being a certain kind of person is not sufficient to constitute her values. It is not sufficient for Betty simply to say to herself that she values something, for her judgment and explicit self-understanding must make a difference for, and cannot be disconnected from, the rest of her life. Rather, this evaluative judgment must be *sincere* in the sense that it is one she both is willing to make be the grounds for further judgments and is potentially willing to support by further judgments that are themselves sincere. Thus, Betty must, because of her judgment, be willing to evaluate her actions and so her self in terms of the judgment and to say why she finds greater independence so valuable. Insofar as to have import is to be, in part, worthy of attention, such a willingness must involve consistently making these judgments or providing these justifications when the situation warrants it, other things being equal.

Moreover, in order for an evaluative judgment and the self-understanding it makes explicit to constitute her values, undertaking such a commitment to be a certain kind of person must have practical consequences as well, for to have import is also to be, in part, worthy of action. Even if sincere, a judgment that is merely theoretical and idle, having no bearing on what she does or who she becomes through her actions, is an inadequate basis for constituting her identity. Consequently, evaluative judgments that constitute one's values must be practical as well, and so Betty must also consistently motivate herself to act on behalf of her explicit self-understanding. (For the moment I am leaving this requirement of practicality intentionally vague, for understanding it in more detail requires understanding the ways in which one's judgments can both connect with one's desires and emotions and make possible the exercise of one's will. I shall address in more detail the interconnections of judgments and felt evaluations initially in §§5.3–5.4 and again later as these interconnections bear on motivation and the will in chapter 6.)

Assume that all of this is true of Betty: her evaluative judgments and the resulting self-understanding are both sincere and practical in the ways just described. Thus, even as she finds herself subordinating herself to others as the result of her ingrained tendencies, she consistently confronts her subservience, condemning it in judgment and struggling to overcome it in part because of that condemnation. It is for this reason that it makes sense to understand Betty as valuing being a more independent person.

So it seems as though Betty identifies herself with two inherently conflicting things. On the one hand, by virtue of the projectible, rational pattern in her reflexive felt evaluations, she values and implicitly understands herself in terms of being a kind of person who entirely subordinates herself to others. On the other hand, by virtue of her sincere, practical, evaluative judgments, she values and explicitly understands herself in terms of being a more independent person and so as not entirely subordinated to others. The conflict between these two therefore depends not simply on contingent features of the circumstances in which she finds herself, but is rather a part of the content of what she values; it is for this reason that I have described the conflict as "inherent." Consequently, the conflict is such that, no matter what she does, she is divided against herself. When she is successful in restraining her impulse to subordinate herself to others, she judges that she has done what she ought, but, in spite of herself, she is ashamed at her selfishness as unbecoming to a good wife and mother. Although she may tell herself that she is a better person for striving to become more independent, this may only exacerbate her shame. Conversely, when she is unable to overcome these subservient impulses, she finds that she is satisfied with herself no matter how much she may self-consciously condemn that subservience. In this way, her values and, indeed, her identity as a person have become fragmented – indeed, *inherently fragmented* insofar as the conflict between the kinds of person she finds worth being is itself inherent.

Of course, this interpretation of Betty as inherently fragmented is contestable, and I shall now consider and reject three alternative interpretations. First, given the objection concerning the primacy of judgment in §5.1, it might look as though this pattern of reflexive felt evaluations is irrelevant for Betty's identity. Thus, one might think (as Watson and Buss apparently would), what Betty "really" identifies herself with is the content of her judgments, so that what she "really" wants is to change her patterns of felt evaluations to get them to line up with her considered judgments. After all, this is the self-understanding she endorses, and that is what counts for her values and identity. By making such judgments, therefore, Betty rejects this pattern of felt evaluations as alien to her in much the same way the unwilling nicotine addict rejects his desires and emotions focused on smoking: she rejects these felt evaluations as mere impulses that fail to represent the kind of person she thinks it is worth being. Consequently, on this interpretation, we can understand the conflict in Betty's case by appealing to only one source of value and identity: her sincere, practical, evaluative judgments.[24]

This understanding of Betty's case, however, seriously misrepresents the complexity of the conflict she undergoes, for the pattern in her felt evaluations, as a rational pattern, cannot so easily be dismissed as alien to her. As rational, the pattern itself is partly constitutive of the rationality of its elements. Thus, the shame she feels at her failure in a particular circumstance to subordinate herself to others is rational precisely because of the pattern of other felt evaluations focused on such subordination and committing her to its import. The rationality of this pattern is such that not to feel shame in these circumstances is itself a rational failing insofar as it is a failure to be properly responsive to the import to which this pattern commits her. Moreover, insofar as the pattern is a pattern of reflexive felt evaluations, the pattern is both a commitment to, and an understanding of herself in terms of, the value of being the kind of person who subordinates herself to others. Consequently, the emotional pain she feels in the face of her evaluative judgments is far from alien to her; rather, it is a kind of anguish that is, in part, that in terms of which her identity is and has been defined. One cannot simply undo years of identity formation simply by making a judgment, even one that is sincere and practical, for such an identity, ingrained as it is in her rational sensitivity to import, cannot be so easily uprooted. The conflict in

---

[24] This might also be the conclusion Gabriele Taylor would draw from the example. (See her *Pride, Shame, and Guilt*.) According to Taylor, "an agent can be said to value something only if his relevant identifications are reasonably consistent and if he engages in some form of practical reasoning, however rudimentary" (p. 117). Precisely how such identifications are to be understood, however, is a bit unclear. Taylor begins her discussion by understanding such identifications in roughly Frankfurtian terms as having a second-order volition, though she revises and extends this view by an appeal to practical reasoning and the articulation and endorsement of one's desires in judgment so as to make sense of the agent as having control over her evaluations. Does this appeal to judgment supplement or replace the earlier appeal to second-order volition? If the former, then Taylor would claim that Betty has not yet succeeded in identifying herself with anything; such a view would fit the third interpretation of Betty's case, discussed and criticized below. If the latter, then Taylor would agree with Watson and Buss that Betty really identifies herself only with being a more independent person. For Betty fails to endorse and have control over these recalcitrant and alien felt evaluations, and, moreover, she endorses her being such a person both for reasons she can articulate and without the sort of self-deception Taylor thinks undermines her having control over this endorsement.

Betty's case, therefore, must be understood as a kind of fragmentation of her identity.

Of course, this suggests that we ought to look at the case of the unwilling addict more carefully. For, if it is the rationality of the pattern of felt evaluations in Betty's case that makes it be a part of her, rather than an alien force, then it might seem that this ought to be true in the case of the addict as well. Thus, insofar as the addict, as I have described him, feels not only the desire for a cigarette but also frustration, anger, satisfaction, etc., such a desire would seem, therefore, not to be alien, contrary to the conclusion reached in §5.1. Yet we must be careful here. If the pattern of felt evaluations the addict has is focused on smoking as having positive import, then I think it is hard to dismiss the elements of that pattern as alien forces, for such emotions and desires are commitments to smoking being good, are rationally grounded in the coherence of the pattern, and so inherently conflict with the addict's judgment that he ought to quit. However, if the pattern is focused on the addict's ridding himself of the craving for a cigarette, then there is no inherent conflict. The craving is just that: a biologically based urge, with associated bodily pleasures and pains, that does not itself evaluate smoking as good; indeed, the craving is not itself a part of the pattern of felt evaluations.[25] Such a craving is, therefore, an alien force that the addict succeeds in rejecting as a part of himself in making the sincere, practical judgment that he should quit.

A second way of rejecting my interpretation of Betty's case might seem to be suggested by the account I have presented of valuing in terms of reflexive felt evaluations. (I say "might seem to be suggested" by this account because my claim in Part I has been that projectible, rational patterns of felt evaluations are only part of what constitutes import, whereas the current understanding of Betty's case implausibly understands such patterns to be all and only what constitute import.) According to this interpretation, the sincere, practical, evaluative judgments Betty makes are simply irrelevant to constituting her identity. As I indicated a couple of paragraphs back, simply to make an evaluative judgment cannot undo years of identity formation – unless that judgment becomes fully integrated with the patterns of her felt evaluations, which it has not yet done. (Even then, we might think, it is the pattern of felt evaluations that is fundamental, not the evaluative judgment.) So, given

---

[25] Such a craving, therefore, is not a desire in the sense I have articulated, though it is a desire in Watson's sense (cf. note 22 above).

the inherent conflict, Betty "really" identifies herself with the focus of this pattern of felt evaluations and not with the content of her evaluative judgment, and the motivation she has to act in accordance with these judgments must therefore be alien to her.

Yet this interpretation again misrepresents the complexity of the conflict Betty undergoes, for it ignores the fact that, in making such judgments, Betty is committing herself to being a certain kind of person and thereby coming to have a self-conscious understanding of her own worth in its terms. Consequently, to make these judgments is self-consciously to resolve to change who she is by changing the patterns of her felt evaluations. By doing so Betty is putting herself and her worth at stake in exerting herself on behalf of these judgments. Such efforts must therefore be properly a part of her, on pain of ruling out the possibility that one can decide to change who one is, follow through, and do it (as opposed to merely having such change inflicted upon one by alien forces). So the conflict must be within herself, the result of a fragmented identity.

A final way to reject my interpretation of Betty's case is to say that she is simply confused about her identity, that she vacillates between valuing subordinating herself to others and rejecting that subordination as a part of her identity. So it may seem that she really identifies with neither, insofar as identification would seem to rule out such vacillation; the conflict she undergoes is merely a symptom of her confusion. This interpretation might seem to fit Frankfurt's account best, for the whole-heartedness Frankfurt requires involves a kind of harmony among one's judgments and second-order desires, with no higher-order conflicts, a harmony that is missing in Betty's case. Thus, according to this interpretation, Betty's identity is not so much fragmented as unformed.

Again, however, to adopt this interpretation is to refuse to acknowledge the special character of the conflict at issue in Betty's case. For far from vacillating between valuing subordinating herself to others and rejecting such subordination as a part of herself, Betty simultaneously both embraces and rejects it. To see this, consider what happens in particular circumstances. As the result of her judgment that she should be more independent, Betty actively and consistently tries to make room for that independence by rejecting the impulse simply to subordinate herself to others. If on a particular occasion she fails, she will castigate herself for that failure while simultaneously taking pride or self-satisfaction in the very subordination of herself that is that failure; or, if she succeeds, she will praise herself for that success while simultaneously feeling shame or regret at that very success. This castigation or praise is the result of her self-consciously understanding herself in terms of the rejection of such subordination and the conviction that a life can be a good one only if it makes room for oneself. Nonetheless, the simultaneous pride, self-satisfaction, shame, or regret she feels is the result of a stable, projectible, rational pattern of felt evaluations that is partly constitutive of her finding her own worth in her subservient role. Consequently, far from vacillating between valuing this subordination of herself to others and rejecting it, Betty simultaneously values both, and it is the inherent conflict between these values that makes intelligible the depth and complexity of her predicament: an inherently fragmented identity.

What underlies Frankfurt's, Watson's, Buss', and G. Taylor's accounts of valuing is the idea that emotions and desires are best understood as alien forces when they are disconnected from the subject's own evaluations simply because they are contrary to her evaluative judgments. Although this may be true in cases in which a single emotion or desire, even if habitual (as in the case of Frankfurt's unwilling addict), conflicts with one's evaluative judgments, it is at least highly questionable that this idea can be sustained when it is such projectible patterns of reflexive felt evaluations that conflict with evaluative judgment, as Betty's case shows. In combination with the initial (though still partial) account of import, in particular of value, given in chapters 3–4, this forms the beginnings of a powerful argument against simply subordinating emotions and desires to evaluative judgment. To fill in the argument, the precise relationship between these felt evaluations and evaluative judgment must be clarified; this will be my aim in §§5.3–5.4.

Nonetheless, there is something right about Frankfurt's appeal to wholeheartedness, for too much conflict can indeed undermine the idea that something has import to an agent. Thus, although the projectible, rational patterns of felt evaluations partly constitutive of import can tolerate some isolated gaps or anomalies, too much ambivalence concerning a single focus leaves no coherent pattern and so no import that is constituted by this pattern and to which its elements are properly responsive. Thus, consistently to feel both pride and regret in a situation, where these emotions have the same focus, is to fail to have a single commitment to the import of that focus. Insofar as such conflicts are widespread, the rationality and projectibility of the pattern, as instituted

141

by such commitments, are unintelligible, and so no pattern has been defined. (Of course, it is entirely possible – and may even be rationally required – to feel both pride and regret in the same situation when these emotions have different foci, for given their different foci these emotions belong to different patterns of felt evaluations. Ambivalence of this kind poses no threat to the coherence of either pattern.) Inherent fragmentation, therefore, is not possible solely within the patterns of one's felt evaluations, for the very conflict such fragmentation requires destroys the rationality and projectibility of the pattern necessary for import. Likewise, inherent fragmentation is not possible solely within one's sincere, practical, evaluative judgments, for roughly the same reason: the very conflict such fragmentation requires destroys the sincerity necessary for such judgments to constitute one's identity.

The possibility of inherent fragmentation therefore requires that one be in a sense divided against oneself, but not too divided lest it become unintelligible that the two sides of the division are both parts of oneself. As the example of Betty shows, inherent fragmentation is possible when we understand the two fragmented identities to have their sources largely in the projectible, rational patterns of felt evaluations and in the rational patterns of sincere, practical judgments respectively: each pattern can remain largely intact in the face of the other, and so these sources of one's identity are potentially separable. For this reason, inherent fragmentation is not a psychosis or a neurosis, nor does it require that we postulate the existence of two or more persons within a single body.

Nonetheless, it should be clear that such a separation of felt evaluation and evaluative judgment is not the normal state: we should not understand one's felt evaluations and one's evaluative judgments each to operate within its own distinctive sphere, conforming to each other if at all only by coincidence. Inherent fragmentation, it must be remembered, essentially involves a kind of rational conflict, and it is a conflict at the limits of intelligibility. What is needed at this point is a clearer understanding of the kind of rational conflict involved between evaluative judgments and felt evaluations and so, ultimately, of the kind of rational coherence between them that is the norm.

5.3 SINGLE PERSPECTIVE ON IMPORT

In the account of felt evaluations presented in chapter 3, I argued that felt evaluations involve a kind of assent or commitment to the import of their targets and foci: to be angry at the neighbor kid for smashing your vase is to assent not only to the kid's having offended or wronged you but also to the import of the vase. In §3.1, I distinguished this kind of assent from that involved in ordinary judgment or belief in two ways.

First, the kind of assent involved in our felt evaluations is passive not just with respect to its initial acquisition, but also with respect to the kind of control we are able to exercise over it: it is a commitment to how things are that gets thrust upon us and which we cannot change by simply withdrawing that assent. By contrast, the kind of assent involved in judgment and belief is active at least in the sense that we can have such direct, unmediated control over whether to continue to assent, if not also over whether to assent in the first place, and in this way we have a kind of freedom with respect to our active assents that we do not have with respect to our passive assents. (I do not intend to imply that we have complete control over our active assents. After all, it is a condition of the intelligibility of having the capacity for judgment that one's judgments be responsive to the evidence, so that one cannot normally make a judgment contrary to the evidence one has. My claim here is only that the control we do have over our judgment, especially in those cases in which a judgment call is required, is, in an intuitive sense, direct and unmediated by other capacities. Nonetheless, it should be clear that this understanding of the kind of active assent characteristic of judgment is still only intuitive; I shall offer an explicit account of the kind of active assent characteristic of evaluative judgment in chapter 6 in articulating the ways in which such judgments enable us to take control over both what we do and what we feel, and in chapter 7 in my account of self-interpretation and the elucidation of concepts.) In virtue of this distinction between active and passive assents, I claimed, judgment normally has a kind of priority over our felt evaluations both as an articulation of our understanding of how things are and as rational, insofar as in cases of conflict between emotion and judgment it is emotion as passive that usually seems to thrust a vision of the world upon us contrary to what we in some sense really think.

Second, the kind of assent implicit in felt evaluations is disclosive as opposed to cognitive assent. Cognitive assent, with its mind-to-world direction of fit, is assent to an object whose existence is independent of the subject's pattern of assents: whether the cat is on the mat does not depend in any way on my assenting to it or not. Such cognitive assent is characteristic of ordinary judgment and belief. By contrast, disclosive assent is not independent of the existence of its object, even though that object serves as a standard of correctness for one's assent. Thus, as I have argued, whether or not something has import to a subject is not intelligible apart from that subject's pattern of assents to import, even while that import is itself a standard of warrant for these assents. Consequently, import and our felt evaluations come together as a conceptual package, and it is in this sense that the kind of assent to import implicit in felt evaluations is disclosive assent.

The distinction between active, cognitive assent and passive, disclosive assent now needs to be clarified as a part of a careful discussion of the connections between judgment and felt evaluations. In particular, two features of the distinction just sketched need to be articulated more fully and defended. First, in the distinction between active and passive assents I claimed that active assents "normally" have a kind of priority over passive assents. That this is merely normally so implies that this priority is not absolute, and part of my aim in this section is to argue that our felt evaluations can in some cases correct our judgments and so in these cases have a kind of priority over judgment. Second, in the distinction between cognitive and disclosive assent, I claimed that "ordinary" judgment and belief are cognitive assents. My intent in qualifying the claim in this way is to leave open the possibility that evaluative judgment is a kind of disclosive, albeit active, assent. Indeed, another part of my aim in this section is to argue for precisely this conception of evaluative judgment by revealing it to have a place in the same projectible, rational pattern of felt evaluations constitutive of import. I shall argue this first in §5.3.1 by concentrating on cases of conflicts between particular emotions and evaluative judgments over the target of the evaluation, and then, what will turn out to be much more important, by examining in §5.3.2 cases of conflicts between patterns of felt evaluations and patterns of evaluative judgments over the focus of their respective evaluations, before summing up the implications this has for our understanding of the rational interconnections between them in §5.3.3.

5.3.1 *Conflicts of target*

Ordinarily, when things go right, a subject will have a single, unified perspective on the world, a perspective that is partly emotional and partly judgmental. This is because the objects one apprehends in one's emotions and in one's judgments are the same, so that conflicts between

144

emotions and judgments are conflicts about how things are. Thus, at dusk you may see a large brown dog charging through the trees directly at you and respond simultaneously with the thought that it is a vicious Rottweiler and with fear of it. The coherence of judgment and emotion in this case is no coincidence, for it is rationally required by virtue of their responsiveness to a common object. Indeed, it is this joint emotional and judgmental response that constitutes your overall perspective on your circumstances.

Of course, this perspective might be mistaken, and we can rationally assess both the judgment (as right or wrong) and the emotion (as warranted or not) in terms of whether the perspective they afford reveals the world, their common object, as it is. Thus, assume that, as the dog rushes at you, you hear the owner, whom you had met earlier, of the friendly, toothless Bernese mountain dog yelling, "Stay!" In hearing this sound, you make the inference that the dog rushing at you is not a Rottweiler bent on injuring you but instead poses no threat to you at all. The resulting judgment, by enabling you to perceive the brown blur more accurately and thereby to achieve a measure of confirmation, provides you with a clearer perspective on the world that supersedes and corrects your previous perspective. Insofar as to make this judgment is to commit yourself to the world's being a certain way, it is a commitment that affects not only your other judgments but your entire perspective on the world. Given that emotions and judgments share a common object, the perspective achieved as a result of this inference ought to affect your emotion accordingly: your fear rationally ought to disappear.

One's emotions and judgments can, of course, come apart and so present one with inconsistent perspectives on the world. In such cases, we ordinarily think of the emotion as being at fault. Thus, if upon realizing that the dog must be the friendly Bernese your emotion does not change, then it would seem the emotion is unwarranted because it conflicts with your considered judgment. As I indicated above, your judgment normally has a kind of rational priority insofar as it, as an active assent potentially resulting from deliberation, represents your considered view on how things are. Moreover, in this case that rational priority is supported, in part, by the stability and coherence of that judgment with other things you believe, a coherence that enables you to perceive the situation differently and in a way that achieves a measure of confirmation in a more careful scrutiny of the animal rushing at you. For these reasons, the judgment in this case corrects the emotion.

In virtue of this correction, the judgment imposes *rational pressure* on the felt evaluation to conform. By this I mean not merely that the failure to conform is irrational, but also that you come to have at least an increased propensity to feel felt evaluations in conformity with the judgment precisely because of that irrationality. After all, insofar as rationality is the constitutive ideal of the mental, to be intelligible as having the capacity for felt evaluations, one's felt evaluations must generally be rationally responsive to the evidence. This means that, although cases of irrationality are clearly possible, any manifest irrationality must involve pressure to change one's mental states so as to resolve that irrationality, for a failure to do so in general, by substantially increasing one's irrationality, thereby undermines the idea that one has the capacity for such mental states at all. Thus it is a condition of the possibility of having the capacities both for judgment and felt evaluation that one's judgments be able to impose rational pressure on one's felt evaluations. Indeed, this idea is implicit in the notion of commitment: to be *genuinely committed* to the world's being this way, a commitment with this sort of rational priority over other commitments, is to have a perspective on the world that normally rules out alternative, inconsistent perspectives. Consequently, other things being equal (for example, in the absence of new and substantial evidence to the contrary), this perspective will project into the future, and shape one's subsequent awareness of the world, including not only one's judgments but also one's felt evaluations.

Not all cases of rational conflict between emotions and judgments need to be like this, however. When an inexperienced camper camps alone for the first time, the rustling noises coming from the nearby undergrowth may cause him to be afraid. In the face of this fear, he may try to calm himself by telling himself that it is probably just a harmless rabbit bedding down for the night and so is not dangerous. Nonetheless, his fear may persist: the noises continue, and he continues to feel them to be vaguely threatening. Because of this rational conflict with a persistent emotion, it may well look like this judgment, isolated as it is from other judgments, is much more akin to wishful thinking than a considered judgment. It seems plausible, therefore, that the best way to resolve this conflict is to give up (at least by withholding) on the judgment. In such a case, the emotion may well turn out to be more rationally appropriate and so to correct the judgment in the minimal sense that it provides a reason to reconsider that judgment in order to achieve clarity of perspective. Consequently, we might say, the commitment implicit in fear is a commitment not only to have subsequent felt evaluations with the same focus in the appropriate circumstances, but also to make the relevant judgments concerning how things are. Given this correction by the emotion, the commitment explicit in the judgment is not genuine because it fails to provide the camper with a perspective on the world that rules out alternative, inconsistent perspectives.

One might object that the wishful thinking in this example is not a genuine belief insofar as it can be quickly doubted and shown up as irrational by the emotion; thus, one might think, the case is not one of the emotion correcting a belief. Yet, just because the camper's assent is wishful thinking does not mean that it does not function as a belief in the relevant ways: as a cause of behavior, as a premise in inferences, etc. Moreover, its content is something to which the camper explicitly assents. What is doubtful, therefore, is not so much whether he believes it, but rather whether this belief represents his point of view on the world, whether it involves a genuine commitment. Doubt on this point must be based on his having the emotion, a doubt that is well grounded only in light of the rationality of the emotion. Consequently, the passive assent implicit in one's emotions can impose rational constraint on one's active, judgmental assent by virtue of the commitment it involves to the world's being a certain way.

Notice the asymmetry in the way I have described how judgments and emotions can correct each other. When judgments correct emotions it is by repudiating the view of the world they provide because it conflicts with that to which one has actively committed oneself in judgment; judgments consequently exert rational pressure on emotions to conform. In contrast, when emotions correct judgments it is by providing reason to reconsider the commitments explicit in judgment, and thereby undermining their genuineness in virtue of the contrary passive commitments implicit in the emotions. In terms of this asymmetry, we can understand more clearly the sense in which judgments normally have a kind of priority over felt evaluation, both as articulations of one's considered view and as rational. Such priority should not be understood in terms of emotions being always less rational and always repudiated by judgment, for emotion can correct judgment as well. Rather the priority of judgment results only in this asymmetry in the ways in which judgments and emotions can correct each other.

5.3.2 Conflicts of focus

In the examples just provided, the conflicts between emotions and judgments concern the target of the emotion and whether it is appropriately related to the focus so as to have the evaluative property defined by the formal object. As I shall now argue, a similar moral applies when we turn to conflicts over the import of the focus: felt evaluation and judgment are each rationally responsive to the same thing, and each can correct the other in cases of rational conflict. This understanding of the rational interconnections among felt evaluations and judgments is possible only because import itself is a kind of object about which we can be right or wrong. Of course, the objectivity of import is limited and should not be thought to have the same status of the objectivity of ordinary physical objects, as I argued in §2.4. All that is claimed here is that import is objective in the sense that it can serve as a standard of warrant for our assents to it, even if it is not a standard that is independent of those assents themselves. This is clear in the case of felt evaluations, as I have already argued in chapter 3: particular emotions or desires might be unwarranted insofar as they respond to things which, by failing to be the focus of a broader pattern of felt evaluations, do not really have import to us. The same is true of evaluative judgments: to judge that something is important to one does not by itself mean that it really is so; rather, one's judgment can be mistaken, as may be the case when one is self-deceived or merely makes an evaluative judgment that is not sincere in my technical sense. In such cases, one's evaluative judgments misrepresent the import things have for one. In this way, import is a common object of the assents implicit in our felt evaluations and explicit in our evaluative judgments: a common object of our evaluative perspective.

Nonetheless, the moral in the case of conflicts over the import of the focus is not exactly the same as that for conflicts over that of the target. This is because import is perspectivally subjective: its existence is intelligible only as the proper object of a certain perspective, which I argued in Part I is afforded in part by one's felt evaluations. By arguing that evaluative judgment is a part of this perspective, and so by articulating the rational connections among felt evaluations and evaluative judgments, I shall thereby articulate more fully the kind of rational pattern constitutive of the import things have for one. Consequently, the interesting cases for making sense of these connections will be cases of conflicts not merely between particular judgments and felt evaluations, but rather between patterns of judgments and inferences and patterns of felt evaluations.

Consider the following example: Cassie pays much attention to her personal appearance by, for example, keeping up with the latest trends, eagerly buying current fashions and scorning those who are out of style; she is fastidious about the condition of her clothes and often gets upset when the dry-cleaner fails to clean or press them just so; etc. In short, she invests considerable time and emotional energy (not to mention money) in her appearance, resulting in a pattern of felt evaluations that constitute the import it has for her. Eventually, however, Cassie begins to think and read systematically about ethics, becomes a confirmed utilitarian, and is articulate about the reasons why. As a result, she judges that the time, energy, and money she has been spending on fashion is excessive, and that the excess should be used instead to promote worthy causes, such as helping the needy. She therefore resolves to eliminate or at least to reduce these excesses by, for example, buying new clothes only when the old ones are truly worn out, and then buying only practical, durable clothes: fashion and appearance, she judges, are not very important in the larger scheme of things. In spite of this resolve, however, Cassie continues to feel emotions and desires consistent with her earlier pattern of concern, and becomes increasingly dissatisfied with her appearance and annoyed at her newfound principles, even as she intellectually rejects these emotions and desires as groundless. Here Cassie faces a conflict between her felt evaluations (and the coherent, projectible pattern they form) and her judgments (and the pattern of inferences she has come to endorse as well as efforts on their behalf).

In the face of this conflict, what can we say about the import her appearance has for her now? If we focus narrowly on this pattern of felt evaluations, it seems clear that she still does care about her appearance, yet if we focus narrowly on the pattern of judgments, inferences, and efforts on their behalf, it seems clear that she does not (at least to the same extent). Nonetheless, in this case it might seem that her judgments ought to have priority: her considered view is that fashion should not matter so much to her, that it does not have this much import to her, and so this might seem to be where her genuine commitments lie. Insofar as we can say that her judgments constitute a genuine commitment, they have corrected her emotions and so impose rational pressure on them to fall in line, for genuine commitments afford an evaluative perspective that ought to rule out inconsistent evaluative perspectives. The failure of her felt evaluations to conform to her considered view, therefore, would merely exhibit the irrationality of these felt evaluations. If this is right, judgment, at least in this case of evaluative conflict, would have a kind of rational priority over her felt evaluations: by virtue of the genuineness of its commitment, it corrects them by repudiating them and exerting rational pressure on them to conform.

Why should we say that these evaluative judgments involve a genuine commitment to import and so correct her conflicting felt evaluations? In the case of the friendly Bernese discussed above, the answer was that the judgment presented me with a clearer perspective on the world: a perspective that enabled me to perceive things differently in a way that received a measure of confirmation. It was for this reason that the perspective afforded by my judgment could be said to correct that afforded by my emotion. This tack, however, will not succeed in Cassie's case, for there is no fact about what import fashion has for her independent of her evaluative perspective: import, as perspectivally subjective, depends for its existence on that perspective. Consequently, to be able to say that the evaluative perspective provided by Cassie's judgments is confirmed by import and therefore corrects that provided by her felt evaluations, we must already be able to say that former perspective represents her considered view. This is, apparently, too tight a circle to be helpful, and something more needs to be said about how to adjudicate such conflicts so as to determine the conditions under which one takes precedence over the other.

Part of what makes these judgments intelligible as articulating her considered view is their sincerity: her ability to justify them in light of a broader evaluative framework and her willingness to use them to justify further evaluative judgments. For to make an evaluative judgment is to undertake a commitment to the import things have that is genuine only if it is both a commitment to draw the relevant evaluative inferences when appropriate and a commitment that is bolstered by being in turn justified by other evaluative commitments. Consequently, a failure of sincerity reveals one's judgment to be defective as a commitment to import. Given the way in which her evaluative judgments are grounded in a broader ethical commitment, we can assume that Cassie meets this standard of sincerity.

Equally important, however, is the way in which this evaluative framework of judgments generally resonates with her felt evaluations insofar as it provides her with an evaluative perspective on the world that in general both is consistent with, and is that in terms of which she can make sense of, those felt evaluations. For to commit oneself to import is not only to commit oneself to making subsequent evaluative judgments, but, more generally, to responding as that import demands, since to have import is to be worthy of both attention and action. This means, in particular, that making the evaluative judgment commits her to having the relevant felt evaluations; isolated failures of her felt evaluations to conform to her sincere evaluative judgments are rational failures – typically failures of these felt evaluations to respond to the imports things have. It is because Cassie's evaluative judgments concerning utilitarianism generally resonate with her felt evaluations, that the failure of her felt evaluations focused on fashion to conform to the inferences she draws from utilitarianism is intelligible as an isolated failure, in spite of the fact that these felt evaluations themselves form a projectible, rational pattern: although she does in a sense care about fashion, her overall evaluative perspective is one that rejects its import. In this way, the evaluative perspective on fashion offered by her judgments takes precedence over the conflicting perspective on fashion offered by her felt evaluations and so can be said to correct it.

Why bother with this appeal to a general resonance of her evaluative judgments with her felt evaluations? Why not instead assert, as Sarah Buss does (cf. chapter 4, p. 116 above), that the priority of judgment as an articulation of one's considered view always takes precedence in cases of conflict with felt evaluations and end the discussion there? The answer is that, in the absence of such resonance, the idea that her pattern of felt evaluations focused on fashion is an isolated part of her cannot be sustained.

To see this, assume the opposite: that Cassie's intellectual assent to utilitarianism does not generally resonate with her felt evaluations. She finds more and more cases where the dictates of utilitarianism clash with her felt evaluations, as when she is forced to make choices between loyalty and devotion to her loved ones and helping others selflessly, and finds herself consistently drawn in her emotions and desires to the former in a way that suppresses those focused on the latter. In this context, Cassie's commitment to utilitarianism is at best fragmented in much the same way Betty's commitment to independence was fragmented (cf. §5.2), for, by virtue of these felt evaluations, she is committed to the import of particular individuals in a way that is inconsistent with her

151

judgmental commitment to utilitarianism. Such a widespread failure of her felt evaluations to conform to her sincere evaluative judgments is, once again, a rational failure, but here, because the failure is widespread, it is not so easy to pin that failure on her felt evaluations rather than her judgments. For, if the commitment to import she undertakes in judgment is to be genuine and so to represent her considered view, it ought to rule out inconsistent evaluative perspectives, and yet it fails to do so not merely in isolated cases but across a broad range of cases.

Consequently, without this general resonance of evaluative judgment with felt evaluation, it seems that there is no clear fact of the matter about what her considered view really is: the commitments to import she undertakes both in judgment and in felt evaluation are both defective. In such a case, therefore, judgment is not rationally prior to her felt evaluations and, we might say, her felt evaluations have corrected her judgment at least in the minimal sense that, so long as the alternative evaluative perspective provided by these felt evaluations persists, she has reason to reconsider. In effect, this is to say that the commitments she has by virtue of her felt evaluations are not only to have other felt evaluations with the same focus, but also to make the relevant judgments, in each case as appropriate to the circumstances.

5.3.3 Rational interconnections

The upshot of this discussion of conflicts between judgments and felt evaluations concerning both the targets and the focus of evaluation is that judgments, whether evaluative or not, and felt evaluations are tightly rationally interconnected in several ways. First, they each involve assent to the same object, namely how things are, and so are each rationally assessable in terms of whether things really are that way. Second, the kind of assent in each case is a commitment to things being that way, where this is a commitment to make the relevant other judgments and having the relevant other felt evaluations. Conflicts among judgments and felt evaluations are irrational precisely because they involve inconsistent commitments to how things are. Third, judgments and felt evaluations can correct each other by virtue of these commitments to how things are: each can rationally constrain the other, although there is an asymmetry in these constraints that makes intelligible the normal priority of judgment over felt evaluations. This means that when things go right, it is not that two separate faculties of judgment and felt evaluation merely happen to converge on a single object; rather, our judgments and felt evaluations normally provide us with a single, unified perspective on the world. Of course, things can go wrong, but the normal unity of perspective is generally preserved by the way in which judgments and felt evaluations correct each other.

That felt evaluations and judgments are rationally interconnected in this way is fundamental to understanding (1) import, that which constitutes import, and how we can control what has import to us, (2) the nature of judgment as active assent and in particular evaluative judgment as disclosive assent, and (3) the nature of felt evaluation and the way in which felt evaluations are informed by the conceptual resources of judgment. Consider these in turn.

(1) The way in which felt evaluations and evaluative judgments can correct each other by virtue of their commitments to import reveals them each to be a part of the same projectible, rational pattern with a common focus. Consequently, import is constituted by this whole projectible, rational pattern of felt evaluations and sincere judgments. Of course, isolated gaps or inconsistencies in this pattern are tolerable without destroying the pattern or the import it constitutes, so long as they remain isolated. Thus, felt evaluations and evaluative judgments need not always be in harmony with each other or even with themselves. Moreover, we should not forget that the very import constituted by such a pattern is the standard of warrant for the elements of that pattern: felt evaluations and evaluative judgments can each go wrong by failing to be properly responsive to the import things have for one. (This means in particular that the sort of assent involved in evaluative judgment is disclosive, as opposed to cognitive, assent; I shall return to this point in (2), below.)

Evaluative judgment, however, is also a matter of active, as opposed to passive, assent, and this gives it a prominent place in the pattern constitutive of import by virtue of its normal priority over felt evaluation. In particular, deliberation resulting in sincere evaluative judgments is a means of having control over, and taking responsibility for, what has import to one. For such deliberation can issue in a genuine commitment that, by achieving a new clarity of evaluative perspective, exerts rational pressure on one's felt evaluations to conform. Nonetheless, as I have just argued, deliberation on its own does not guarantee the genuineness of commitment required here, for one's felt evaluations may be resistant to the evaluative perspective one tries to achieve through deliberation, and

153

such resistance, so long as it is systematic and so provides one with an inconsistent evaluative perspective, provides one with reason to reconsider. (I shall discuss the possibility of such control and the nature of such deliberation in chapters 6 and 7, respectively.)

(2) These rational interconnections among felt evaluations and judgments are important for understanding the nature of judgment. Given their connections to felt evaluations, we cannot understand judgment to be purely intellectual, the point of which is simply to get one's thoughts to correspond to how things are. This is most obviously true in the case of evaluative judgments, which I have argued involve disclosive assent rather than simply cognitive assent. My first point here, however, is about not disclosive as opposed to cognitive assent, but rather active as opposed to passive assent. For actively to assent to the world's being a certain way is self-consciously to adopt what purports to be a univocal stance on how things are; indeed, this is the point of my claim that judgment, as active assent, has a kind of priority as an articulation of one's view of things. Consequently, a failure of such assent to bring one's felt evaluations along with it can, at least in some cases, be a defect not so much in those felt evaluations as in one's active assent itself.

To see this, consider the following example.[26] Upon learning from a trustworthy source that my father has died, I may intellectually assent to it and so begin making the necessary travel arrangements to attend his funeral, notifying other relatives, etc. Nonetheless, it may take a while for this knowledge to "sink in": I may be left unaffected emotionally by this news – not because I find it necessary to suppress these emotions as a temporary means of continuing to function, but because I fail to have any such emotions to be suppressed – and the process of grieving may not begin until I actually see my father's lifeless body. Yet, beforehand, the complete failure of emotional response in this context cannot be written off as an isolated gap in the pattern of my caring about my father; nor can it be indicative of my ceasing to care about my father, especially in light of my subsequent grieving. Rather, such a failure of response can only mean that I do not in a sense "really" believe that my father has died: the view of the world expressed in my judgment is not fully my

---

[26] This example is derived from Robin Dillon's "Self-Respect: Moral, Emotional, Political" (*Ethics*, 107 (1997), pp. 226–49), in which she distinguishes intellectual from experiential understanding. See also Alison Jaggar's "Love and Knowledge: Emotion in Feminist Epistemology," *Inquiry*, 32 (1989), pp. 151–76, and Michael Stocker's "How Emotions Reveal Value and Help Cure the Schizophrenia of Modern Ethical Theories," in Roger Crisp, ed., *How Should One Live?* (Oxford: Clarendon, 1996), pp. 171–90.

view. My judgment in this case has not succeeded in defining a univocal perspective on the world, not merely because, as in the case of Cassie, I have a conflicting perspective implicit in my emotions, but rather because, lacking an emotional perspective where one is manifestly required, the perspective defined by my judgment is not fully mine.

In short, the point of judgment, even those judgments involving cognitive assent, is not merely truth or correspondence to how things are; rather, its point is to define one's perspective on the world by virtue of a responsiveness to how things are, a perspective that necessarily involves one's passive assents as well.

A second point about judgment concerns evaluative judgment in particular. Evaluative judgment, I have argued, involves not cognitive but disclosive assent insofar as it is simultaneously both constitutive of and rationally responsive to import. This means, in part, that having the capacity for evaluative judgment presupposes that one is already a subject of import. (It does not also mean that being a subject of import presupposes that one have the capacity for evaluative judgment. As I indicated above [note 23], many animals such as dogs and cats can be subjects of import without having such a distinctively human capacity for evaluative judgment.) Yet, as I argued in chapter 3, being a subject of import and having the capacity for felt evaluations must come as a conceptual package, neither part of which is prior to the other. This means that having the capacity for evaluative judgment presupposes that one also has the capacity for felt evaluations.

(3) Finally, these rational interconnections between judgments and felt evaluations are important for understanding the nature of felt evaluation. As I have argued, by making judgments we commit ourselves in part to having certain felt evaluations in the relevant kinds of situations. Yet these kinds of situations are defined by the concepts we deploy in deliberation and judgment. Consequently, in order for felt evaluations to be properly responsive to the perspective on the world made explicit in judgment, they must be conceptually informed. Our emotions and desires, but not those of non-linguistic animals, are therefore rich and complex states that are shaped by the conceptual and inferential skills our capacity for judgment brings with it. This means that our capacity for discrimination need be no less refined in our felt evaluations than it is in our judgments. Indeed, as I shall argue in chapters 6–7, because felt evaluations are conceptually informed and can exhibit, in some cases, a capacity for discrimination that is more refined than that explicit in

evaluative judgment, they can correct not only particular evaluative judgments but also our understanding of the relevant evaluative concepts, thereby shaping our understanding of these evaluative concepts and so the reasons we come to have for having certain values. Consequently, that felt evaluations are conceptually informed will play a central role in my solution to the deliberative problem as well as, I shall argue, to the motivational problem.

5.4 FELT EVALUATIONS AND JUDGMENTS OF PREFERENCES

In the kinds of examples I have been discussing so far in this chapter, I have tried to avoid cases that can properly be described as conflicts among the various things that have import to one. Thus, for both Betty and Cassie the question was not about how to reconcile two things they care about but rather, given the incompatibility of the choices, about which to care about at all. In many cases, however, we find our conflicting cares and values to be not inconsistent in that we cannot coherently continue to care about or value both, but rather in competition given our current situations. In these cases, the question is about how to balance our cares or values against each other: how, at least in given circumstances, should we adjudicate these conflicts? My aim in this section is to lay the groundwork for answering this question, which will be addressed explicitly in §7.4.2, by discussing the connections between our judgments of priorities and the sense of relative import implicit in our felt evaluations.

Consider the following example.[27] Tom is a high-school student who has his heart set on getting into Harvard – it has a very high degree of import to him; indeed, we can imagine that he decides, as a matter of evaluative judgment, that getting into Harvard is more important at this point in his life than maintaining his active social life. Although he has considerable academic ability, in order to be a serious candidate for Harvard, Tom must continue to work hard on his studies. When faced with the prospect of working on his science project or writing his application essay, however, Tom often finds himself in the mood instead to engage in various social activities with his friends. It is not that Tom lacks the motivation to apply himself, for he does care about getting into Harvard, worries about his prospects for getting in, and occasionally does

[27] Thanks to Yaroslava Babych and Aleksandra Markovic for proposing this example and discussing it with me.

find time to study his vocabulary or practice solving math problems. Yet, when faced with the choice of studying or spending time with his friends, he consistently is inclined to the latter. As a result, Tom fails to live up to his potential, ultimately resulting in his rejection from Harvard.

What is going on here? The evaluative judgment Tom makes fails to motivate him because he consistently finds himself in the mood to do other things. To say that he is *in the mood* to do something on a particular occasion is to say that the import of that activity or its end impresses itself on him more strongly than, and so dampens, the import of other things. Thus, on a particular occasion, Tom may find that his desire to play video games with his friends fails to be dampened by a reminder that the SATS are coming up, even though he recognizes that running through some practice tests would help him do better (in a way that is instrumental to getting into Harvard) and judges that now is the appropriate time to do so. Yet his being in such a mood is not merely a passing fancy or a momentary bout of laziness, for Tom consistently feels doing things instrumental to getting into Harvard to be of lesser importance than his social life. That is, although in situations in which he otherwise would feel the import of Harvard impressing itself on him and motivating him to study, given the prospect of doing something with friends the import of the latter impresses itself on him more strongly, dampening the import of Harvard, and so motivating him to act accordingly. In this way he commits himself by virtue of this pattern of dampening relations in his felt evaluations to the preference for engaging in his social life over academic work. So, in spite of his commitment in judgment to apply himself academically, the consistency of this pattern within his felt evaluations both constitutes and reveals the place Harvard really has among his preferences, and his pursuit of social activities is therefore to some extent rationally defensible in light of the evaluative orientation implicit in these felt evaluations.

One might object that this is merely a case of weakness of will, insofar as Tom's judgment about what he should do here and now fails to motivate him in a way that overcomes contrary motivations, and so does not show that these contrary motivations are in any way rationally defensible. Yet this case differs in an important way from standard cases of weakness in which either the contrary motivation is in a clear sense an alien force, as in the case of the unwilling addict, or the strength of the contrary motivation is clearly out of proportion with the subject's preferences, as when we succumb to temptation. Although Tom judges that getting into Harvard is more important, such a judgment is defective precisely because of the pattern of felt evaluations he has. For such a consistent pattern of dampening relations within his felt evaluations defines a perspective on relative import that has at least some claim to being his perspective; thus, we might say, "actions speak louder than words." Nonetheless, just as with conflicts between evaluative judgments and felt evaluations, judgment – especially sincere judgment – normally has some priority as an articulation of one's perspective on things, given its status as active assent. So my claim is only that the sense of relative import implicit in his felt evaluations has some claim, though perhaps not equal claim, to being his own view.

In light of this pattern of commitments in felt evaluation, we can criticize Tom's judgment as not representing an evaluative perspective that is fully his. The genuineness of his commitment to the content of his judgment is thereby brought into question, and he therefore has reason to reconsider that judgment. Nonetheless, similar things might be said about his preferences as constituted by these patterns of felt evaluations: these commitments are defective insofar as they conflict with his evaluative judgment and can be criticized in light of the reasons justifying that judgment. Consequently, both his judgments of preferences and these patterns of felt evaluations in effect commit him to have a certain perspective on relative import that, in part, involves the other. The conflict arises, therefore, out of the incompatibility of these commitments with each other, and, because of the conflict, Tom is not of a single mind about where his preferences lie: they have become fragmented.

This means that judgments of relative import and felt evaluations together define what is normally a single rational pattern with a common object, relative degree of import, which both is constituted by this pattern and serves as a standard to which each element of the pattern must be properly responsive. Isolated gaps or inconsistencies within this pattern can be written off as noise, with clearly identifiable sources of irrationality. Yet, when these gaps or inconsistencies become wide-spread, they can undermine the coherence of the overall pattern and so the relative degree of import that pattern constitutes, or even divide that pattern in two, fragmenting one's preferences. Moreover, just as the rational interconnections among evaluative judgments and felt evalua-tions enable us to understand how felt evaluations generally are concep-tually informed, so, too, the rational interconnections among judgments of relative import and the pattern of dampening relations among felt evaluations enable us to understand our implicit sense of relative import as conceptually informed. For our sense of relative import must normally be sensitive to rational pressure from our judgments and so must be shaped by the conceptual and inferential skills judgment makes possible.

In light of this account of the rational interconnections among evaluative judgments and felt evaluations, we can now see what it is to have an *integrated* evaluative perspective, one that involves an appropriate and reasoned balance among the various cares and values a person has. Such integration requires not only that what she cares about or values by virtue of her felt evaluations are just what she cares about or values by virtue of her evaluative judgments. Rather, as I argued in §5.3, these felt evaluations and evaluative judgments must coincide non-accidentally, with each being properly responsive to rational constraint from the other. Moreover, being integrated requires that, for any normal situation in which a conflict might arise among the various things she cares about or values, she is able for the most part, both explicitly in judgment and implicitly in the dampening relations among her felt evaluations, to recognize without ambivalence where in this situation her commitments lie and so what she should do. A person who is completely integrated, then, has a clear understanding of import, an understanding that is truly wholehearted not in Frankfurt's weak sense of having no contrary second-order desires (cf. §5.1) but in the more robust sense of having the sort of overall pattern just described in her evaluative judgments and felt evaluations.

Of course, this notion of an integrated evaluative perspective is an ideal that is not something we can entirely attain in practice. Nonetheless, as an ideal it represents the standard against which defects, in this case rational defects, are to be measured. However, it should be clear how limited this idea is so far, for it defines only standards of consistency and so provides no guidance at all for the content of one's cares or values. I shall return in chapter 7 to expand this account so as to provide a solution to the deliberative problem.

5.5 CONCLUSION

My claim in this chapter has been that a person normally has a single evaluative perspective instituted by the commitments he makes to import, both explicitly in evaluative judgment and implicitly in his felt evaluations. In virtue of these commitments, outliers to the overall pattern are thereby revealed to be irrational, not properly responsive to the imports things have, and so potentially corrected by other states that are elements of this pattern. Judgment, as a matter of active assent, has a special place in this pattern as normally prior to felt evaluation both as an articulation of the perspective that is genuinely one's own and, therefore, as rational. Nonetheless, I have argued, this priority can be overturned in particular cases.

Because judgment has a place in this pattern of evaluations, the resulting perspective is informed by the concepts we can bring to bear in judgment. As I shall argue in chapter 6, it is because the conceptual resources made available by judgment can be actively brought to bear on our perspective on a situation that we can exercise control over what we are motivated to do. This will provide me with an account of two distinct kinds of freedom, freedom of the will and freedom of the heart, in terms of which I shall solve the motivational problem. Finally, as I shall argue in chapter 7, it is once again the way in which these conceptual resources enter into our overall evaluative perspective that enables us to solve the deliberative problem. Just as felt evaluations can correct our evaluative judgments, they can also correct the concepts we apply in making those judgments, thereby making intelligible the kind of discovery relevant to deliberation about value. Nonetheless, by exercising our freedom of the heart, we can exert some control over our felt evaluations and so over our cares and values, thereby making intelligible the kind of autonomous invention relevant to deliberation about value. Such discovery and autonomous invention, I shall argue, are essentially interconnected in a way that provides a solution to the deliberative problem.

Finally, two further ways in which I reject the cognitive–conative divide are implicit in this account of the rational interconnections among evaluative judgments and felt evaluations. For, first, in addition to my arguments in Part I concerning why emotions and desires as disclosive assents cannot properly be understood in terms of that divide, we can now see that evaluative judgment, as itself a disclosive assent, cannot be understood in terms of that divide either. Second, although I allow that judgment in general, as a kind of active assent, normally has a kind of priority over our emotions and desires, my conception of this priority is not one that proponents of the divide would be happy to accept. For on my account, emotion and desire can correct judgment both by under-mining its status as representing our view on things and by undermining its status as rational.

6

Rational control: freedom of the will and the heart

In chapters 2–5, I developed a detailed account of emotions and desires as felt evaluations and of their rational and conceptual interconnections with judgment, especially evaluative judgment. It is now time to return to the two problems of practical reason raised in chapter 1, namely the motivational problem and the deliberative problem, and exploit this account in solving them. My concern in this chapter will be the motivational problem; I shall address the deliberative problem in chapter 7.

6.1 THE MOTIVATIONAL PROBLEM REVISITED

The motivational problem, recall, is the problem of how we can have control over what we are motivated to do by exercising our judgment. As I argued in chapter 1, the kind of control at issue in the motivational problem is very different from that which we exercise over ordinary objects in our environment. For the latter kind of control we exercise simply by exploiting causal connections, as when I control the computer I am typing this on by pressing keys or moving the mouse. Although I need not know the precise nature of the causal relationship between my pressing these keys and, ultimately, words being printed on paper, I do know enough to use them to get the computer to do what I want, even in some cases overcoming a degree of recalcitrance when the computer "acts up" – in short, enough to control it. Control over our motivations, by contrast, involves an exploitation not merely of causal connections but of rational connections: it is my appreciation of the reasons for pursuing a course of action that can and should motivate me to act accordingly. When things go wrong and I find myself motivated contrary to the reasons I articulate in practical judgment, I am motivated

161

irrationally, and it is precisely in such cases that I need to exercise control in order to overcome my irrationality: I must exploit my capacity for reason itself. Control over our motivations, therefore, is a matter of having our motivations be susceptible to our appreciation of our reasons: it is a matter of rational control.

Our capacity for rational control may initially seem straightforward, something we might try to capture intuitively in terms of the following two attractive principles:

(1) When we deliberate and arrive at a practical judgment, that judgment is properly and fully ours by virtue of our committing ourselves to its contents self-consciously and actively.

(2) A practical judgment that is properly and fully ours is a judgment that motivates us to act accordingly, for anything less would be a hollow commitment, one not fully made.

The motivational problem arises, however, when we notice that practical judgment is not always motivationally effective. Thus, we can be motivated contrary to our practical judgments (weakness of will) and we can fail to be motivated at all by those judgments (listlessness). In such cases, our motivations have somehow become disconnected from our reasons for acting in a way that seems to undermine our joint acceptance of these two principles. The motivational problem, therefore, is the problem of how to understand, in the face of the persistent possibilities of weakness and listlessness, the connection between our practical judgments and our motivations in virtue of which rational control is possible.

In my discussion in §1.3, I tentatively argued that a solution to the motivational problem is impossible if we make the assumption of the cognitive–conative divide. For to make this assumption is to understand cognition and conation to have opposite directions of fit and therefore to be mutually exclusive: the same mental state cannot both be a cognition and a conation. Moreover, to be committed to some content having one direction of fit in no way requires or presupposes that one is committed to a similar content with the opposite direction of fit. Consequently, cognition and conation must be distinct existences: one can always have a cognition, with its mind-to-world direction of fit, without having any relevant conation, with its world-to-mind direction of fit, and vice versa. Practical judgments, it seems, cannot be conations for then it would be unintelligible that we could make such a judgment and be wholly unmoved by it. Yet if our practical judgments are cognitions, then, given the cognitive–conative divide, there must an inevitable gap between these judgments and our motivations, and the motivational problem therefore gets reconceived in light of that gap: how can such a gap be bridged? Insofar as it is rational control at issue, what bridges the gap must be intentional and so, given the cognitive–conative divide, either a cognition or a conation. It cannot be a cognition, for cognition on its own can have no direct effect on conation: they are distinct existences. Yet it cannot be a conation, for this would merely push the problem back one step without helping: how could rational control over this conation be any easier than rational control over any other conation? Thus it seems that the motivational problem cannot be solved if we assume the cognitive–conative divide.

At this point the general outlines of my solution should be apparent. Having rejected the cognitive–conative divide, I understand felt evaluations to be motivating precisely because they are responsive to the import things have for us and so the reasons that import provides for action. The motivational problem, therefore, should not be understood as the problem of how to bridge an inevitable motivational gap, as it gets understood in light of the assumption of the cognitive–conative divide. Rather, in the normal case where everything goes right, there is no gap between evaluation and motivation to be bridged, for evaluation (and responsiveness to reasons) and motivation are ineliminable parts of the same mental states. What makes this kind of account possible is my understanding of felt evaluations as involving disclosive assent: assent that is both rationally responsive to import (and so, in a sense, having mind-to-world direction of fit) and constitutive of that import (and so, in another sense, having world-to-mind direction of fit). For, to simplify a bit, felt evaluations motivate because of the kind of responsiveness to import they are, and they constitute that import in part because of the way in which they motivate. Hence, rational control is no problem: insofar as our evaluative judgments disclose the import things have for us, our desires will normally be responsive to them, and so we can exercise rational control by bringing these judgments to bear on particular situations. (I shall return in §§6.3–6.4 to fill in the details of this account.)

6.2 MOTIVATIONAL INTERNALISM AND EXTERNALISM

The argument two paragraphs back that, given the assumption of the cognitive–conative divide, we cannot solve the motivational problem is, as I said, so far only tentative. For it ignores a crucial distinction between two fundamentally different kinds of accounts of the connection between practical judgment and motivation, namely motivational internalism and motivational externalism; these two kinds of accounts would object to this tentative argument at different stages, and these objections need to be addressed.[1] The differences between motivational internalism and motivational externalism and how they each respond to the motivational problem can perhaps best be described in light of the two "attractive principles" concerning rational control articulated in §6.1:

(1) When we deliberate and arrive at a practical judgment, that judgment is properly and fully ours by virtue of our committing ourselves to its contents self-consciously and actively.

(2) A practical judgment that is properly and fully ours is a judgment that motivates us to act accordingly, for anything less would be a hollow commitment, one not fully made.

According to *motivational internalism* there is a conceptual connection between practical judgment and motivation. Thus, motivational internalists accept principle (2) as true of properly practical judgments. Of course, in order to make sense of the possibilities of weakness of will and listlessness, motivational internalists cannot simply accept principle (1) as it stands and so attempt to offer more sophisticated versions of it. Consequently, motivational internalists, even those who accept the cognitive–conative divide, might resist the claim in my tentative argument that a gap between practical judgment and motivation is inevitable, for all the argument shows, they might say, is that a gap between cognition and conation is inevitable. It remains to be seen whether we can make sense of how practical judgment, while still being a cognition, can be properly and fully ours in a way that might motivate us directly (and not by means of an intermediary conation) and still allow for the possibility of weakness of will and listlessness.

By contrast, *motivational externalism* rejects this idea that there is a conceptual connection between practical judgment and motivation: when it is in place, externalists claim, the connection is always contingent, the result of our psychological make-up, which might have been

---

[1] I call these views "motivational" internalism and externalism so as to distinguish them from other accounts, also labeled "internalism" and "externalism," of the nature of our reasons; cf. Bernard Williams' "Internal and External Reasons," in *Moral Luck: Philosophical Papers 1973–1980* (Cambridge University Press, 1981), pp. 101–13.

different. Thus, motivational externalists reject principle (2) but accept principle (1). Of course, in order to make sense of the possibility of our having rational control over our motivations, externalists must propose some way to bridge the motivational gap, and at this point they might resist my claim that what bridges the motivational gap cannot be susceptible to rational control. My aim in the remainder of this section is to strengthen my tentative argument in the face of these challenges, discussing motivational externalism and internalism in §6.2.1 and §6.2.2 respectively before filling in my positive account in §§6.3–6.4.

6.2.1 Motivational externalism

Michael Smith has forcefully made the case for motivational externalism.[2] According to Smith, part of the mistake motivational internalists make is to fail carefully to distinguish between normative and justifying reasons. In arriving at an evaluative judgment, Smith claims, we consider *normative reasons* – i.e., reasons that rationally justify a particular course of action and so show why we ought to act in this way. Normative reasons thus underwrite our judgments about what we should do, and they are what we consider in deliberation (prototypically before we act) from what Smith calls the "*deliberative perspective.*" Consequently, our practical judgments, resulting from such deliberation, are rationally grounded in the normative reasons we advance in the course of that deliberation. On the other hand, Smith claims, from the *intentional perspective*, from which we explain our actions (prototypically after we act), what are in view are the causes of our actions. Such causes are psychological states that serve as our *motivating reasons*, explaining in such causal terms why we actually engage in some activity. Typically, our motivating reasons will be a desire–belief pair; indeed, Smith thinks motivating reasons must always involve some cognition and conation. For he accepts the idea, fundamental to the cognitive–conative divide, that cognition and conation have opposite directions of fit, such that our being motivated requires some conation specifying the end we are disposed to achieve and a cognition specifying the means we think will produce that end.

Normative reasons are reasons we can discover in deliberation, and so are something about which we can be right or wrong; they are,

---

2 *The Moral Problem*, especially chapters 4–5. (All page citations to Smith in the text are to this book.)

therefore, objects of cognition.[3] Consequently, Smith claims, they must be fundamentally different from motivating reasons. For, although conation is the source of a creature's being motivated (and thus serves this distinctive role in the creature's motivating reasons), conation is not in any way entailed by our normative reasons precisely because they involve opposite directions of fit: "It is a commonplace, a fact of ordinary moral experience, that practical irrationalities of various kinds . . . can leave someone's evaluative outlook intact while removing their motivations altogether" (pp. 120–21); Smith cites listlessness as one such practical irrationality. The acceptance of a normative reason in judgment, because that judgment has mind-to-world direction of fit, can leave entirely untouched our conations, with their world-to-mind direction of fit. Consequently, Smith accepts that there is an inevitable motivational gap between our practical judgments and our desires, and he understands the motivational problem as the problem of understanding how this gap can be bridged.

Smith's solution to the motivational problem is to postulate a causal disposition to have desires with motivational strength equal to the deliberative weight we give the corresponding normative reasons.[4] This means that, when we reach a practical judgment as the result of deliberation, this disposition is engaged and so we are caused to have the relevant motivations. Such a disposition, Smith claims, can afford properly rational control, for it is nothing other than "*pure practical reason*":[5] that capacity of ours in virtue of which our motivating reasons non-accidentally coincide with our normative reasons just is our capacity for practical reason. To exercise rational control over our motivations, therefore, is simply a matter of engaging this capacity by making practical

---

[3] This is, of course, contestable, even among those who accept the cognitive–conative divide. As I briefly indicated in §1.4, non-cognitivists claim that our values, and so our normative reasons, are fundamentally conative, and they would reject this assumption. If practical judgment has a substantive role in instituting what normative reasons we have, however, then such judgment must be conative rather than cognitive, and the resulting account of motivation would therefore be internalist. Again, I shall address motivational internalism in §6.2.2.

[4] See, e.g., Philip Pettit and Michael Smith, "Practical Unreason," *Mind*, 102 (1993), pp. 53–79; Jeanette Kennett and Michael Smith, "Philosophy and Commonsense: The Case of Weakness of Will," in Michaelis Michael and John O'Leary-Hawthorne, eds., *Philosophy of Mind: The Place of Philosophy in the Study of Mind* (Boston: Klewer, 1994), pp. 141–57; and Smith's *The Moral Problem*, pp. 177–80.

[5] For this language, see Pettit and Smith's "Practical Unreason."

judgments or focusing our attention on those features of our situation relevant to our normative reasons.[6]

This solution, however, is untenable, for Smith's claim that "pure practical reason" is a kind of responsiveness to reasons cannot be sustained, whether we construe the relevant disposition to have desires in accordance with our practical judgments as itself a desire or not. To see this, compare the case of ordinary desire. I want to do something, but am unsure about what means to take to accomplish it; consequently, my desire fails to motivate me to do anything. I then come to see that a means is available, and this engages my desire, motivating me to perform a particular action. In a sense, this is a case in which my motivation to act this way is responsive to the reason I come to have in recognizing the means, and so, in a sense, the desire is responsive to reasons. Yet the case of "pure practical reason" is different. For, in the case of ordinary desire, my having the desire is itself part of the reason for my being motivated in this way: the reason is a motivating reason that explains my action, not a normative reason justifying my having the desire in the first place. After all, desires, as they are understood in terms of the cognitive–conative divide, must in general be responsive to our beliefs as the other half of our motivating reasons in order for them to be a source of motivation at all. Yet, in the case of "pure practical reason," it is rather our normative reasons that are at issue, and the question is: how can "pure practical reason" be responsive not merely to motivating reasons but to normative reasons as well?

In exercising rational control, according to Smith, we focus our attention on those features of the situation relevant to our normative reasons: for example, on the fact that cigarettes contain carcinogens or that eating more cake now is to ingest too many empty calories and too much cholesterol (and, in each case, that health is more important than momentary pleasure). Yet, for these reasons to engage my disposition of "pure practical reason," that disposition must be responsive to these reasons *as reasons*. It is not enough that I merely have a disposition to

[6] Like Smith, Alfred Mele accepts the cognitive–conative divide and insists that phenomena like listlessness and weakness show there to be an inevitable motivational gap. Mele likewise appeals to something outside cognition to bridge that gap: in Mele's case, a desire to act as one judges best. (See, e.g., Mele's *Autonomous Agents: From Self-Control to Autonomy* [Oxford University Press, 1995], especially §2.5, and his "Internalist Moral Cognitivism and Listlessness," *Ethics*, 106 [1996], pp. 727–53.) Indeed, Smith would agree with Mele that what bridges the gap is a desire, for Smith understands desire simply to be a disposition to attain some end.

have motivational strength equal to deliberative weight, for, in order for me to exercise rational control, this disposition, when it has initially failed to produce its usual effect (as in cases of weakness of will or listlessness), must be responsive not merely to the features of the situation to which I call my attention but to these features as the relevant features – as, that is, providing normative reasons. Otherwise, merely calling my attention to the facts of the situation that happen to constitute these reasons would have no more effect on my "pure practical reason" than my calling my attention to extraneous, irrelevant facts.

At this point, however, it becomes clear that Smith's appeal to such a disposition fails. For, if the disposition is to be responsive to features of our situation as normative reasons, it must be an intentional disposition and so, according to the assumption of the cognitive–conative divide, be either a cognition, having mind-to-world direction of fit, or a conation, having world-to-mind direction of fit. Yet it cannot be a conation, for then we could not make sense of it as being responsive to features of the situation as normative reasons: given the cognitivism about normative reasons that underwrites externalism (cf. note 3), such responsiveness can only be a matter of mind-to-world direction of fit, which conations cannot have. Nor can it be a cognition, for then, assuming externalism, it could have no direct connection to motivation. Consequently, the appeal to such a disposition cannot, in the context of the cognitive–conative divide, provide us with an account of rational control nor, therefore, with a solution to the motivational problem.

It should be clear that my objection here is not merely to Smith in particular, but to any externalist who accepts the cognitive–conative divide. Something must bridge the inevitable motivational gap between cognition and conation, and, if this something is to provide the basis for rational control, it must be responsive to normative reasons as such and so be intentional; yet, given the divide, it can be neither a cognition nor a conation, and so cannot be intentional. Consequently, rational control over our motivations is impossible given these assumptions. Moreover, it should be clear that my objections are not to the idea that in each particular case there is a contingent connection between practical judgment and motivation, such that the connection might not obtain in any given case. That has to be true if we are to make sense of weakness of will and listlessness as persistent possibilities. Rather, as will become clear in §6.3, my objection stems from the possibility that we succeed in having normative reasons supporting a particular practical judgment and yet in no case are motivated to act by those normative reasons: that, as Smith puts it, it is possible to remove motivation entirely and leave the evaluation intact.[7] Indeed, given the assumption of the cognitive–conative divide, this has to be a plank in any motivationally externalist platform, for, given that divide, practical judgment and desire are distinct existences, and, given the externalism, there is no sort of conceptual connection between any particular practical judgment and our being motivated.

6.2.2 Motivational internalism

My diagnosis for what has gone wrong in the case of motivational externalism, as I have said, lies with the implicit assumption of the cognitive–conative divide. Yet it is possible to keep that assumption and offer an alternative diagnosis for the failure of externalism.

Recall that motivational externalists try to make sense of our having rational control in the face of the persistent possibility of weakness and listlessness by accepting principle (1), that we have direct control over our practical judgments, but rejecting principle (2), that there is a conceptual connection between making a properly practical judgment and being motivated to act. For, given the manifest phenomena of weakness and listlessness, they claim, (2) must embody a misguided understanding of the connection between practical judgment and motivation as conceptual. At this point, one might think, it is precisely externalists' acceptance of (1) rather than (2) that is the mistake, for anything short of the sort of conceptual connection between practical judgment and motivation articulated in (2) must fail to account for our motivational responsiveness to normative reasons, and therefore for our having rational control. We are not merely intellectual beings, as externalism's emphasis on (1) seems to suggest, but are also and essentially practical beings. We must therefore insist on (2) and reject (1). Such a position, accepting (2) and so understanding there to be a conceptual connection between practical judgment and motivation, is motivational internalism.

On the face of it, motivational internalism seems to be inconsistent

---

[7] *The Moral Problem*, pp. 120–21. See also Smith's claim at p. 178: "the mere fact that we actually desire not to φ gives us no reason to change this belief [that we have a normative reason to φ]."

with the assumption of the cognitive–conative divide, for if, according to the cognitive–conative divide, belief or judgment and desire are distinct existences, it seems as though there can be no conceptual connection between them. Yet internalists can try to make a distinction between judgments that are practical in their content and judgments that are practical in their issue.[8] The former are cognitions having no essential connection to motivation; indeed, internalists can even accept that (1) is true of them. Yet the latter might be understood to be a special kind of cognition, having mind-to-world direction of fit, that nonetheless is conceptually connected to motivation insofar as such a connection is a condition of the possibility of our being full-blooded agents, in line with the intuition expressed by (2). Consequently, motivational internalists, even those accepting the cognitive–conative divide, would reject my contention in the tentative argument of §6.1 that there is an inevitable gap between practical judgment and motivation, for, in the case of judgment that is practical in its issue, there is a conceptual connection to motivation and so no gap at all. This needs to be spelled out more clearly – and in a way that makes sense of the possibilities of weakness and listlessness.

Consider David Velleman's account of rational control.[9] According to Velleman, standard conceptions of the notion of direction of fit conflate two distinctions that need to be kept separate. On the one hand is the distinction between *accepting* (i.e., regarding something as true) and *approving* (i.e., regarding it as to be made true); this distinction is what accounts for the distinction between cognitions and conations. On the other hand is the distinction between receptive acceptances and directive acceptances – a distinction of kinds of cognitions. A *receptive belief* is the kind of acceptance we ordinarily understand cognitions to involve: accepting something as true by way of trying to reflect its truth. (Of course, as Velleman correctly notes, there are other kinds of receptive cognitions that do not involve receptivity to the truth, such as hypothesizing.) A *directive belief*, however, is the kind of acceptance involved in properly practical cognitions: accepting something as true so as to make it true. As Velleman says:

---

[8] Cf. Donald Davidson, "How is Weakness of the Will Possible?" in *Essays on Actions and Events* (Oxford: Clarendon, 1980), pp. 21–42, at p. 39.

[9] See his *Practical Reflection*; "The Guise of the Good," and especially "The Possibility of Practical Reason." (All page references for Velleman in the text will be to this latter article.)

Note that the latter method [i.e., directive believing] does not entail regarding the proposition as *to be made* true. It entails attempting to make the proposition true by regarding it as such, but attempting to make a proposition true by regarding it as true is quite different from regarding it as to be made true [i.e., from approving it]. The proposition is regarded as fact, not *faciendum*, and so it is accepted, in a cognitive rather than a conative attitude. What's more, the proposition is accepted seriously, not hypothetically or frivolously. For in attempting to accept something so as to make it true, one attempts to reach the position of accepting a genuine truth, no less than when one attempts to accept something in response to its being true. In either case, one's acceptance aims at a correspondence between what's regarded as true and what is true, and so it is a serious cognitive attitude, whose success deserves to be called knowledge. (p. 721)

This distinction between receptive and directive believing is important for understanding how directive belief, a cognition, can play a role in defining the ends by which we are motivated, rather than merely in defining the means to ends already defined by conation. To understand this more fully, consider first receptive believing. Receptive believing differs from hypothesizing in its *constitutive aim* (roughly what I have called the "formal object" in the case of emotions). Whereas the constitutive aim of hypothesizing is more "polemical or heuristic,"[10] the constitutive aim of receptive belief is truth in the sense that a condition of the possibility of having receptive beliefs is that we have an inclination to sustain or modify our receptive beliefs in the face of evidence of their truth or falsity. Hence, it is a condition of the possibility of one's having a receptive belief that this belief be responsive to truth. This means that to continue to accept a proposition that presents itself as false is not receptively to believe that proposition: "a proposition that presents itself as false cannot be the object of an attitude that aims at getting the truth right."[11]

In the account of a receptive belief as accepting something as true so as to reflect its truth, this "so as to reflect its truth" specifies its constitutive aim. The same, *mutatis mutandis*, is true of directive belief: if a directive belief is the accepting of something as true so as to make it true, this "so as to make it true" specifies its constitutive aim. As Velleman puts it thus:

When one accepts a proposition in response to its truth [i.e., has a receptive belief], one registers the influence of evidence and other reasons for belief, thereby manifesting an inclination to conform one's acceptance to the facts.

---

[10] "The Guise of the Good," p. 14.
[11] Ibid., p. 18; cf. "The Possibility of Practical Reason," p. 711.

Accepting a proposition in such a way as to make it true [i.e., having a directive belief] would simply require a converse inclination, to conform the facts to one's acceptance. (pp. 721–22)

Hence, it is a condition of the possibility of having directive beliefs that we have an inclination to be motivated in accordance with what we directively believe.

Velleman's understanding of this inclination to make true what one directively believes, it will be observed, is similar to Smith's understanding of "pure practical reason" as a disposition to be motivated in accordance with one's practical judgments. The difference is that Velleman understands our having this inclination to be not merely an empirical fact about us that might come and go without affecting our status as agents (as Smith does), but rather to be a condition of the possibility of our having directive beliefs and so being full-blooded agents at all. In this way, Velleman's directive beliefs have a conceptual connection to motivation, and his account is therefore a form of motivational internalism.

It should be clear, therefore, how Velleman understands the nature of rational control and so would claim to solve the motivational problem: by forming directive beliefs we can directly shape the course of our motivations. Moreover, such shaping counts as rational control insofar as our directive beliefs, as cognitions, are formed on the basis of, and with a responsiveness to, normative reasons: it is, as Velleman says, an account of "rational guidance."[12] Consequently, Velleman would object to my earlier tentative argument against an account of rational control that accepts the cognitive–conative divide by arguing that an acceptance of the divide, and so of there being an inevitable gap between cognition and conation, does not require accepting that there is an inevitable motivational gap – between cognition and motivation. For directive cognition has a conceptual connection to motivation directly, and not indirectly via conation.

Nonetheless, Velleman's account of rational control fails because, in the context of the cognitive–conative divide, the three-way distinction between receptive beliefs that are practical in their content, directive beliefs that are practical also in their issue, and desire cannot be sustained in a way that allows for rational control.

To see this, consider first directive beliefs and desires (or conations more generally). Both involve an inclination to change the world to

12 Ibid., p. 4.

172

conform to some proposition; how then are they to be distinguished from each other? The central difference, Velleman would say, is that desire, as a conation, involves approval (i.e., regarding the proposition as to be made true and so as a pattern for the world to follow), whereas directive belief, as a cognition, involves acceptance (i.e., regarding the proposition as true and so as "patterned after the world").[13] It is not, of course, the mere fact that one regards a proposition as true (even if that acceptance is directive) that makes it true; one must thereby be motivated to act accordingly, and it is one's actions that make it true. Yet, insofar as directive belief essentially involves an inclination to change the world to conform to the proposition, it seems also essentially to involve regarding the proposition as a pattern for the world to follow, and this seems to break down the distinction between directive belief, as a cognition, and conations: Velleman's talk of directive belief as a belief, as involving an acceptance of the proposition, seems to amount to nothing more than mere confidence in one's ability to conform the world to one's thoughts – a confidence that seems to have no essential connection to the motivation. The distinction between directive belief and desire, therefore, seems merely to be that directive belief involves such confidence. This is hardly a sound basis for an account of rational control.

Velleman would surely regard this interpretation as a distortion of his view. After all, directive beliefs are not compound states of cognition and conation; rather, they are entirely cognitive, entirely a matter of accepting a proposition as true. Part of what is behind this insistence on directive belief as an acceptance is that this is something we do; indeed, Velleman thinks, it is only for this reason that we can get the agent into the picture as in control of her actions rather than as merely a passive observer of the desires that move her. Moreover, it is only in this way that normative reasons can get into the picture: a directive belief "presents the behavior, if you will, as fit for (en)action, given the constitutive aim of action, just as theoretical reasons present a proposition as fit for [receptive] belief, given the constitutive aim of belief" (p. 725). So the account of properly rational control comes through the way such an acceptance, as involving normative reasons, is tied to motivation via the constitutive aim of directive belief.

The trouble now is to distinguish directive belief from receptive

---

[13] Ibid., p. 8. As I discussed in §3.5, Velleman argues that we should not understand desire as itself being evaluative, a matter of regarding its object as a good to be pursued. So he explicitly rejects understanding the relevant notion of approval in these terms.

belief, at least in a way that helps solve the motivational problem. The distinction between them concerns not the proposition we accept, but rather the way in which we accept that proposition: whether we accept it as true so as to reflect the truth, or whether we accept it as true so as to make it true. As such, they both "aim at correspondence between what's regarded as true and what is true" (p. 721); the difference is that receptive belief aims at achieving that correspondence by changing the belief, whereas directive belief aims at achieving it by changing the world. In other words, the difference is that receptive beliefs motivate changes of belief, whereas directive beliefs motivate intentional action. Now, however, it becomes puzzling how that distinction can help make sense of rational control.

Assume, for example, that I believe it is good for me to eat broccoli and so try to motivate myself to eat some. If I am faced with a bout of listlessness, however, then this belief cannot be a directive belief, for it is a condition of the possibility of its being a directive belief that I am thereby inclined to act accordingly, an inclination that is absent given my listlessness. This means that my belief is merely a receptive belief, albeit one that is practical in its content.[14] In order to exercise rational control over my motivation, however, I must somehow turn my receptive belief into a directive belief. But how is this possible? – How can I exercise control over whether my acceptance of a proposition is a receptive or a directive belief? At this point no answer is forthcoming, and so the distinction looks merely stipulative and *ad hoc* as the basis for a solution to the motivational problem.

Donald Davidson's earlier account of rational control in terms of a kind of motivational internalism faces a similar problem. According to Davidson, weakness of will, or incontinence, poses a philosophical problem insofar as the following three principles seem to form an inconsistent set:

[14] Perhaps we could relax this requirement somewhat: it is a condition of the possibility not, as Velleman says, of one's having a particular directive belief that one thereby be inclined to act accordingly, but rather of one's having the capacity for directive believing that one in general be so inclined. This would allow us to say that in cases of listlessness one still has a directive belief, albeit one that is defective. Nonetheless, this would not help matters any. For a solution to the motivational problem must explain how it is possible to exercise rational control over what we do especially in cases of weakness or listlessness. On the current suggestion, this means explaining how, by the exercise of cognitive abilities, we can come to acquire the missing inclination to act so as to make our directive belief no longer be defective. In effect, this just is a restatement of the motivational problem, and on this matter Velleman is silent.

P1   If an agent wants to do *x* more than he wants to do *y* and he believes himself free to do either *x* or *y*, then he will intentionally do *x* if he does either *x* or *y* intentionally.

P2   If an agent judges that it would be better to do *x* than to do *y*, then he wants to do *x* more than he wants to do *y*.

P3   There are incontinent actions.[15]

This problem is in essence the motivational problem, for *P2*, in conjunction with *P1*, provides an account of rational control that seems to be thwarted by the possibility of weakness (*P3*).

Davidson's solution to the problem is to distinguish prima facie judgments from unconditional judgments. A *prima facie judgment*, Davidson says, is a judgment made in light of particular evidence or considerations – in the case of practical judgments, that there is something to be said in favor of a course of action. Thus, I might judge that the fact that the cake tastes good prima facie makes it worth pursuing; or I might judge that the fact that the cake is fattening prima facie makes it worth avoiding. Even the judgment that all relevant things considered the cake is worth avoiding, Davidson claims, is a prima facie judgment insofar as those considerations are an intrinsic part of the judgment. By contrast, an *unconditional judgment* is a judgment that has been detached from these considerations, such as the judgment that, in effect, the cake is worth avoiding, full stop. In light of this distinction, Davidson claims that the account of rational control in *P2* should be understood in terms of unconditional judgments, for to make such a judgment is a sufficient condition of having the relevant desire, a desire which, by *P1*, can motivate us to act. Weakness of will, on the other hand, should be understood in terms of a conflict between an all-things-considered prima facie judgment and the desire that moves one to act; such conflict is clearly possible insofar as "reasoning that stops at conditional [i.e., prima facie] judgments . . . is practical only in its subject, not in its issue."[16]

This distinction between prima facie judgments and unconditional judgments is, on the face of it, similar to Velleman's distinction between reflective and directive judgments, and it suffers similar problems. After all, unconditional judgments are not "detached" from considerations in the sense that one makes them without any reasons. As Davidson says

---

[15] "How is Weakness of the Will Possible?" in *Essays on Actions and Events*, pp. 21–42, at p. 23.

[16] Ibid., p. 39.

elsewhere, an unconditional judgment is "a further judgment that the desirable characteristic was enough to act on – that other considerations did not outweigh it."[17] But what is this if not an all-things-considered prima facie judgment?[18] At this point it seems as though the only distinction between the two is that unconditional judgments motivate action, but prima facie judgments, even all-things-considered, do not. If that is the way the distinction gets made, then it seems the best we can do as an exercise of our capacity for practical reason is to make an all-things-considered prima facie judgment and hope that this judgment achieves the status of an unconditional judgment by engaging our desires: unconditional judgments are not themselves under our rational control. In the context of the motivational problem, therefore, such a distinction simply begs the question.

These difficulties are not peculiar to Velleman's or Davidson's accounts; they are rather endemic to any motivational internalist account that takes the cognitive–conative divide seriously. For, given that divide, it seems that the only way to establish the sort of conceptual connection between judgment and motivation the internalist is after is to define a distinctive kind of cognition. The problem, therefore, will be to distinguish this kind of cognition that is practical in its issue from ordinary cognitions that are practical only in their content. Such a distinction can be in terms of either the content of the proposition or the attitude one takes towards it. If the former, the account implausibly rules out either the possibility of one's having ordinary cognitions with the same content or the possibility of listlessness. If the latter, the account must find a path between turning the distinctively practical cognition into a conation (and thereby raising again the question of how we can have rational control over it) and making a merely stipulative distinction that begs the question of rational control; yet, given the cognitive–conative divide, there is no room for such a middle path.

Motivational internalism and motivational externalism are mutually

---

[17] "Intending," in *Essays on Actions and Events*, pp. 83–102, at p. 98.

[18] One might think that an unconditional judgment just is a conation, albeit one that, as a judgment, we have direct control over. (Indeed, this might be a part of a non-cognitivist account of import and normative reasons.) Yet such an account would seem to rule out the possibility of listlessness: to make such a conative judgment just is to be motivated. (Of course, one might try to understand such conative judgments as not always under one's control, but then one needs a principled way of distinguishing those judgments that succeed in being conations and so in motivating us from those judgments that fail in this regard. This just returns us to the motivational problem without seeming to have advanced the issue at all.)

exclusive and exhaustive as accounts of rational control, since externalism is defined as the denial of internalism. I have argued that, if we grant the assumption of the cognitive–conative divide, both internalism and externalism fail to provide an adequate account of rational control and so to provide an adequate solution to the motivational problem. The answer, therefore, is to reject the cognitive–conative divide, thus confirming the conclusion I already reached in chapters 2–3 in my discussion of the problem of import.

6.3 RATIONAL CONTROL

I have argued that the proper solution to the motivational problem requires giving up the assumption of the cognitive–conative divide, for then we can understand desires themselves as responsive to normative reasons. This may make it seem as if there is no motivational problem at all, but that would be a mistake. As I initially described it (before the redescription I gave in light of the assumption of the cognitive–conative divide), the motivational problem is the problem of how we can have and exercise rational control over our motivations. However, felt evaluations cannot be that by virtue of which we exercise control over our motivations, for exercising control is something we do actively, whereas our felt evaluations are passive assents, a matter of import impressing itself on us as the result of our general attunement to it. Rather, the exercise of control over motivation must be understood in terms of practical judgments, which are active assents. Consequently, the motivational problem is, broadly speaking, a problem of how to understand the connections between practical judgment and motivation such that by means of the former we can exercise control over the latter.

The solution to the motivational problem, therefore, can be given in terms of the account of the interconnections between practical judgments and felt evaluations provided in chapter 5. As I argued in §5.3, evaluative judgments and felt evaluations are rationally interconnected insofar as (a) they each involve assent to the same object, namely the import things have for us, and so are each rationally assessable in terms of whether things really have that import; (b) the kind of assent is in each case a commitment to import and as such involves a commitment to making the relevant other evaluative judgments and having the relevant other felt evaluations; and (c) in cases of rational conflict between them, each can in a sense correct the other in light of the rational constraints these mutual commitments impose on each other, although there is an asymmetry in these constraints that makes intelligible the normal priority of judgment over felt evaluations. Consequently, evaluative judgments and felt evaluations provide us with and commit us to what is normally a single evaluative perspective that constitutes the imports things have for us. Of course, our perspective on import is, in part, a perspective on relative import, on what takes priority over what in particular situations in which the various imports things have impose competing demands on our attention and activity. As I argued in §5.4, there are similar rational interconnections among judgments of relative import and felt evaluations by virtue of which they each impose rational constraints on the other, thereby making intelligible the possibility of each correcting the other. Consequently, judgments of relative import and felt evaluations together commit us to what is normally a single evaluative perspective that constitutes the relative degree of import things have for us.

I indicated that our judgments have a kind of rational priority over our felt evaluations insofar as the evaluations explicit in our judgments are active, whereas those implicit in our felt evaluations are passive. For actively to make an evaluative judgment is explicitly to commit oneself to a perspective on import that is also an emotional and desiderative perspective, and the evaluative judgment thereby imposes rational pressure on these felt evaluations to conform. Other things being equal, therefore, one will normally come to have the relevant felt evaluations as a rational response to this perspective. Such an imposition of rational pressure is itself the exercise of rational control over our felt evaluations and consequently over our motivations, for in this way our motivations are susceptible to our reasons in precisely the way required by the notion of rational control. Hence, the solution to the motivational problem lies in my understanding of evaluative judgments as active rather than passive assents, and in my understanding of both evaluative judgments and felt evaluations as disclosive assents, simultaneously responsive to and constitutive of import by virtue of the projectible, rational patterns they form.

Nonetheless, this quick sketch of an account needs further explication in several respects. First, the notion of active assent that I have claimed is characteristic of judgment and that is supposed to explain the kind of control we can have over our motivation stands in need of clarification. Without such clarification, it can look like this solution to the motivational problem merely begs the question in just the way Davidson's appeal to the notion of an unconditional judgment does. Second, it is not yet clear how my account is able to explain cases of weakness of will or listlessness. Indeed, the need for control over our motivation arises precisely in such cases, cases in which we fail to be motivated as we judge we ought to be. My strategy in the remainder of this section and in §6.4 will be to tackle cases of weakness and listlessness head-on, allowing the account of active assent to emerge in the process.

Assume that on some occasion I am faced with the prospect of having a second piece of chocolate cake. I judge that I ought to refrain from eating it, and yet I find myself wanting it and drawn to it. How, on my account, can I control this akratic desire and so motivate myself to act in accordance with my judgment? The answer lies in my understanding of the nature of that akratic desire. As a felt evaluation, it involves passive assent to the chocolate cake as worth pursuing, whereby that import impresses itself on me and enthralls me, and I am thereby drawn to eat the cake. Controlling how I am motivated, therefore, requires controlling the way import impresses itself on me – that is, the evaluative perspective I have on the current situation. To this end, I can remind myself of my practical judgment and the reasons supporting that judgment, and thereby try to reconceptualize the cake accordingly. Thus, I generally care about my health and, in particular, my weight and cholesterol levels and, although I think it is well and good on special occasions such as this to have one piece of cake even after having eaten a rather heavy meal, I judge that my concern for my health is more important than the pleasure to be derived from having a second piece of cake. So I come to understand the cake in these terms: not as delicious (though it is that) and not merely as empty calories but, more fundamentally, as excess, as the undoing of my more important aim of restoring and maintaining good health, and therefore as here and now an improper object of desire. By actively reconceptualizing the cake in these ways in light of my normative reasons, I am altering my perspective on the current situation, thereby imposing rational pressure on my felt evaluations to conform by virtue of their responsiveness to these reasons.

Whether this rational pressure is successful or not depends in large part on one's appreciation of the reasons supporting the practical judgment. Thus, the mere existence of such a reason (such as a moral reason), if one were unaware of it, would be insufficient to make sense of the judgment's exerting such rational pressure. Moreover, one cannot merely think that there is such a reason, but it must actually be a reason for one: in effect, the object of the practical judgment must truly have both the import and relative import the judgment commits one to. In short, the evaluation one makes in judgment must be *complete* in the sense that the commitments one thereby undertakes to import or relative import fit into the relevant broad, projectible, rational pattern of similar commitments implicit in one's felt evaluations and other evaluative judgments. Complete evaluations are expressive of the normative reasons one has for action. Consequently, one will normally come to have occurrent desires in accordance with the evaluative perspective undertaken in complete evaluation because such desires, as elements in this broader projectible, rational pattern, are themselves responsive to the normative reasons for action that evaluation expresses. In the case of complete evaluation, therefore, the rational pressure practical judgment exerts on one's desires will normally be sufficient to alter one's motivation, and in this way we can exercise rational control. (Of course, evaluation need not always be complete; I shall return in §6.4 to discuss how we can exercise rational control over our felt evaluations in such cases.)

My appeal to this notion of a complete evaluation in providing an account of rational control may seem objectionable. After all, one may think, a complete evaluation is one that, by definition, involves having the relevant desires so that of course, defined this way, there will be no gap between our practical judgments and motivation. Simply to stipulate a definition of a particular kind of judgment where there is no gap, however, cannot solve the motivational problem, which concerns in particular how we can make sense of our maintaining rational control over our motivation even in cases in which there is such a gap, at least initially. Indeed, this is in essence the same criticism I offered in §6.2.2 of other internalist accounts of motivation.

In reply, this objection misses my point in using the notion of a complete evaluation to articulate a conceptual connection between practical judgment and motivation. This connection is not merely stipulated in a definition, but earned by philosophical analyses (a) of the rational interconnections among felt evaluations and evaluative judgments constitutive of import and our normative reasons, and (b) of the way in which these felt evaluations motivate (as itself a part of what constitutes import and normative reasons). Hence, once we understand complete evaluation in terms of these analyses, we can see that this connection to motivation is a substantive claim about what it is to have reasons. The view is, therefore, a kind of motivational internalism, but it differs from Velleman's version of internalism insofar as, by rejecting the cognitive–conative divide more fully than he, I am able to account for the rational interconnections between practical judgments and desires while sustaining the distinction between them as, respectively, active and passive assents to import. (It remains to be seen, however, how I can distinguish between judgments that are practical in their issue and judgments that are practical merely in their content. I shall return to this point below in my reply to a second objection.)

The account so far makes room for the possibility of weakness of the will and listlessness, for I have claimed that the rational pressure one's (complete) practical judgments exert on one's desires is normally sufficient to bring one's desires in line, yet this leaves room for abnormal cases in which one's desires irrationally fail to conform. Such cases are possible even in the context of complete evaluation because the requisite projectible, rational patterns of judgments and felt evaluations constituting one's normative reasons can tolerate some (but not too much) "*noise*": isolated failures to respond in judgment, emotion, or desire as one ought. Consequently, it can be contingent in each situation in which action is called for that a gap does or does not arise between practical judgment and motivation; yet, because these patterns are rational, it is necessary that in general this gap does not arise in order for the requisite pattern of felt evaluations and evaluative judgments to constitute import and so for us to have normative reasons at all. This means in part that, contrary to Smith's claim, it is unintelligible that we could remove the motivation entirely and leave the evaluation intact. For, given the rational connections among felt evaluations and judgments, this would be to undermine not only the rationality of the pattern constitutive of import but also therefore import itself (and the normative reasons it provides).

Nonetheless, one might at this point raise a second objection: although my account may make sense of our rational control in the normal cases, it does not make sense of it in the abnormal cases – in the very cases in which we need most to exercise such control. For, if all I can do actively is to make the judgment, then it would seem as if it is not up to me, not under my control, whether I have the relevant desire or not. So, as was the case for motivational externalism, it seems that on my account all we can do, at least in these abnormal cases, is to make the judgment and hope that the gap to motivation will be bridged for us, and that is insufficient as an answer to the motivational problem.

In reply, this objection overstates our helplessness in the abnormal cases in two respects. First, there is something more we can do in the face of weakness of will or listlessness than simply to make the judgment and hope. Indeed, Smith's description of what we can do to exercise rational control in such cases is essentially correct (though his account of why that should amount to rational control was not): we can bring to mind the reasons supporting our judgment and call our attention to the relevant features of the situation as relevant. According to Smith, doing such things will naturally engage "pure practical reason," the causal disposition to have one's desires match one's practical judgments, but (as I argued in §6.2.1), given his acceptance of the cognitive–conative divide, Smith can have no account of how or why that disposition will be engaged in these ways. By contrast, on my account doing these things is a matter of self-consciously adopting an evaluative perspective on the current situation defined by the reasons justifying my evaluative judgment. It is, therefore, this active reconceptualization of the situation in light of my reasons that imposes rational pressure on my desires to conform precisely because these desires are themselves responsive to normative reasons. So, even though my initial attempts at such reconceptualization fail and my akratic desires continue to present an alternative, irrational perspective on the situation, continued efforts at rejecting this alternative perspective and adopting the rationally justified one will amount to continued rational pressure and so to continued attempts to exercise rational control. Consequently, in contrast to Smith's account of merely causal connections between practical judgment and desire, on my account the connection is conceptual and fundamentally normative, an essential part of the rationality of evaluation itself.

This first reply, however, may seem to miss part of the point of the objection. For what is behind the objection is, in part, the idea that, on my account so far, when we are motivated it is only as the result of a passive occurrence within us, namely our felt evaluations. The objection therefore stems from the sense that we should make room for the possibility that we can actively and directly control our motivations rather than waiting and hoping for a passion to mediate our activity and our motivation. This leads to the second way in which the objection overstates our helplessness in the abnormal cases: on my account such a notion of active motivation is implicit in the idea that evaluative judgment is a commitment to import. This needs further discussion.

To have import, as I argued in chapter 3, is to be worthy of attention and action. Consequently, to be committed to something's having import is to commit oneself to attend to it and act on its behalf when such attention and action are called for. In the case of felt evaluations, I cashed out these commitments in terms of an attunement to import and a preparedness to act on its behalf. Insofar as felt evaluations are passive, we can make sense of both their attunement and preparedness as a kind of rational responsiveness to import: import impresses itself on us and enthralls us by engaging both our attention and our motivation. By contrast, evaluative judgments are active commitments to something's having import and so also to attend to it and act on its behalf. Thus, I argued, to make an evaluative judgment is to commit oneself to certain inferences and demands for justification, and therefore to making the relevant other evaluative judgments; the sincerity of a judgment is, therefore, a measure of this attentive aspect of one's active commitment to import, such that a failure of sincerity is a failure genuinely to be committed to that import (cf. §5.2). Consequently, we can now see that to undertake this kind of commitment to make further evaluative judgments that actively focus one's attention on the import of something just is a part of what it is actively to assent to its having that import.

Yet there is also what I there labeled a "practicality" requirement on evaluative judgment: such judgments must not be merely theoretical and practically idle, but must have a bearing on what one does, such that a failure of such practicality is once again a failure genuinely to be committed to import. One way to spell out the practicality requirement on evaluative judgments is in terms of their rational connections to our felt evaluations, connections I articulated in chapter 5. As the objection rightly points out, this seems inadequate – both as the basis for an account of rational control and, we might now add, as the basis for understanding judgmental commitment to import. What more is needed to fill out the account of active assent and so of rational control?

The answer is to understand evaluative judgments themselves as directly motivating action. If in felt evaluation our passive recognition of and commitment to the reason import provides for action can directly motivate us to act, why not think that our active recognition of and commitment to that very same reason in judgment also directly motivate us?

What apparently rules out this possibility is the ordinary understanding of the cognitive–conative divide: on the one hand, cognition, with its mind-to-world direction of fit, is active and fully rational, and in the case of a perceived lack of fit it can motivate merely a change of mind; on the other hand, conation, with its world-to-mind direction of fit, is passive and less rational, though in the case of a perceived lack of fit it can motivate action so as to change the world. If we accept this divide, we cannot make sense of an active judgment being simultaneously both responsive (with mind-to-world direction of fit) to normative reasons and itself motivating action in the world (and so having world-to-mind direction of fit).

However, I have rejected this divide as it applies to our felt evaluations and evaluative judgments. Although we can distinguish between evaluative judgments and felt evaluations in terms of whether they are active or passive assents to import and the reasons it provides for action, this distinction is irrelevant for understanding motivation. For it is a condition of the possibility of our being committed to import that, other things being equal, we be motivated to act in particular situations in which we recognize that this import provides us with a reason for so acting, and this is true whether that commitment and recognition are active or passive. To have the capacity for evaluative judgment just is to have the capacity in general to motivate oneself in light of that evaluation; the exercise of anything less than this capacity would fail to be the exercise of properly evaluative judgment. Consequently, by actively committing oneself to import and recognizing the reasons it provides for action, judgment can and normally does have a direct connection to motivation, one not mediated by our passive felt evaluations.

This understanding of evaluative judgment as actively motivating should not be taken to imply that we have complete control over our actions, for our active motivations may have to compete with other sources of motivation, which we may be unable to overcome, as in cases of weakness of will. Nonetheless, we can exert effort to act on behalf of our judgment by renewing our commitment to the import it involves in the ways already described: other things being equal, actively to commit oneself to import by reconceptualizing one's circumstances in light of the reasons supporting one's judgment is not only to attend to those features of these circumstances relevant to action, but also to motivate oneself directly to act accordingly. Moreover, this understanding of evaluative judgment as actively motivating should not be taken to imply that simply to make a practical judgment is to be motivated to act accordingly. Just as practical judgments can be defective by virtue of a failure of sincerity, so, too, they can be defective by virtue of a failure of practicality, thereby leading to listlessness; in each case, the failure lies with the commitment one undertakes in so judging. Nonetheless, that we are generally able actively to motivate ourselves by undertaking such commitments in judgment is a condition of the possibility of our having the capacity both for such commitments, and so for genuinely evaluative judgments, at all. Consequently, these defective cases are intelligible only as parasitic on the normal case, lest it become unintelligible that the subject has the capacity for evaluative judgment at all.

The *will*, therefore, can be understood as our ability to motivate ourselves directly by virtue of an active, judgmental recognition of and commitment to import and the reasons it provides for action. We have *freedom of the will* to the extent to which we are successful in exercising this ability; freedom of the will, therefore, is not equivalent to freedom of action: physical restraints that prevent my acting, for example, need not thereby prevent my being motivated all the way to action.

Smith, following J. E. J. Altham,[19] labels such practical judgments, that simultaneously are commitments to things being a certain way and are directly motivating, *"besires"* insofar as they share features of beliefs and desires. He claims that such a view requires "that it is *impossible* for agents who are in a belief-like state to the effect that their φ-ing is right not to be in a desire-like state to the effect that they φ; that the two cannot be pulled apart, not even modally," and he goes on to argue that this is manifestly false (pp. 119–20, Smith's emphasis). It should be clear that such an impossibility is not something I am committed to. For on my view the practical commitments we undertake in judgment can in some, abnormal cases be defective precisely because they fail to motivate us, either directly or by means of a desire or other felt evaluation. There can be, therefore, a degree of helplessness in the face of recalcitrant akratic desires; our rational control over our motivations is not complete, and our wills need not be free. Nonetheless, that we normally have such control is, as I have said, a condition of the possibility of our having the capacity for evaluative judgment at all.

It might be thought that this account of rational control in terms of evaluative judgments is independent of felt evaluations, contrary to my claim at the beginning of this section (p. 177), for it may seem that I

---

[19] "The Legacy of Emotivism," in Graham Macdonald and Crispin Wright, eds., *Fact, Science, and Morality: Essays on A. J. Ayer's Language, Truth and Logic* (Oxford: Blackwell, 1986), pp. 275–88.

have just given an account of a *"pure will,"* an ability directly to motivate ourselves that is wholly independent of our emotional and desiderative lives. This would be a mistake. Evaluative judgment, as I argued in §5.3, must be understood as simultaneously rationally responsive to import and partially constitutive of that import. This means that the kind of active commitment to import evaluative judgment essentially involves, as that which makes intelligible our ability to exercise our wills, is disclosive rather than cognitive assent, and as such presupposes the more general account of disclosive assent given in terms of rational patterns of evaluative judgments and felt evaluations. Hence, the capacity for evaluative judgment (and so for the will) presupposes the capacity for felt evaluations and is unintelligible otherwise. Consequently, our capacity to exercise our wills presupposes these rational interconnections among evaluative judgment and felt evaluations; although I do think we can make sense of particular cases in which we can exercise our wills in the absence of such rational interconnections to felt evaluations, such cases are intelligible only as parasitic on the normal case in which actively to commit oneself to import by virtue of making an evaluative judgment is also to exert rational pressure on one's felt evaluations to fall in line by virtue of one's coming to adopt a particular evaluative perspective that is essentially an emotional and desiderative perspective as well.

6.4 FREEDOM OF THE HEART

In §6.3, I presented an account of how we can exercise rational control over our motivation in two ways: one indirectly by exerting rational pressure on our felt evaluations so as to feel motivated to act appropriately, and the other directly by exercising our wills. Recall, however, that the first of these means of rational control was restricted to cases of complete evaluation, in which one's evaluative judgments and felt evaluations together form a single projectible, rational pattern constitutive of import and degree of import; in such cases, akratic desires must be exceptions: mere noise in the pattern that does not undermine the rational coherence of that pattern. (Notice that the second means of rational control was not subject to this restriction: an exercise of will depends not on the completeness of the evaluation expressed in judgment, but rather on the character of the commitment undertaken in so judging. This will prove important later on.) Yet, in a wide variety of cases calling for rational control, it will not be true that evaluative judgment is complete. An extreme example is that of Betty, described in §5.2, whose felt evaluations and evaluative judgments pull her in opposing directions, thereby fragmenting her evaluative perspective and her identity; somewhat less extreme is the case of Cassie from §5.3. A more natural example is the following.

Martin is a corporate executive for whom work and career are very important. He puts in long hours attending important meetings and finishing reports, and he often has to travel away from his family for days at a time. When he does get home, he finds himself unable to muster the physical and emotional energy required to interact meaningfully with his wife and two kids. It is so difficult to make the transition between being a good executive and a good father that making that transition just feels like an unwelcome chore. He is, after all, providing for them as well as he can, and he is proud of how well he has done in his career. Nonetheless, he appreciates that this single-minded devotion to his career is having deleterious effects on his family. His wife tells him how disappointed and hurt their children are when he misses, for example, his son's school play or his daughter's soccer games. Though he does think he is setting a good example for his children, he remembers how his own father was such an important part of his life, and he comes to see that in focusing so much on his career both he and his children are missing something: their lives are slipping away without him, and, what is worse, he finds that he *feels* no great loss. He resolves, therefore, not just to take a more active part in their lives and to spend more time at home – he has tried doing that and not yet succeeded because he finds it such a chore; in addition, he resolves to come to care about and take an interest in his family's interests as a part of his caring about them, thereby achieving a new balance in what is important to him.

As in the case of Betty, Martin's evaluative judgments are not complete, though unlike Betty this is not because Martin has felt evaluations directly opposed to these evaluative judgments but rather because he fails to have felt evaluations in accordance with them. How, given the failure of completeness, can Betty, Cassie, and Martin exercise rational control over their felt evaluations so as to achieve completeness? If such control were never possible, then my reply to the first objection of §6.3 would be incomplete: I would not have presented an account of rational control except by defining a special kind of judgment (i.e., complete judgment) the making of which is not itself under my rational control.

To make an evaluative judgment and then exercise rational control so as to make that evaluation be complete is to achieve a projectible, rational pattern in one's evaluative judgments and felt evaluations that constitutes the import of the focus of that pattern. Consequently, what is needed is an account of how we can exercise rational control over what we care about or value – over our *hearts*; being able successfully to exercise such control is to have *freedom of the heart*. The question, therefore, is: how is freedom of the heart possible?

As I argued in §3.3, felt evaluations form projectible, rational patterns that are, in effect, attunements of one's sensibilities to the foci of those patterns as having import. Indeed, it is in part for this reason that felt evaluations play a central role in constituting import, for such an attunement is the sort of passive vigilance necessary for the focus of that pattern being worthy of attention and so having import. This attunement therefore consists of habits of emotional and desiderative response to import, including the habits of attention to and of preparedness to act on behalf of that focus, that provide one with an evaluative perspective that is partially constitutive of its import. If freedom of the heart is to be possible, therefore, we must be able to exercise control over not merely particular felt evaluations, but also over these habits of emotional and desiderative attention and response.

So far, this is merely a redescription of the problem, but it does aid in formulating a solution. For in general we can change our habits or acquire new habits by successfully and consistently, over a period of time, controlling our behavior by exercising our will. This suggests that the same might be true of our habits of emotional and desiderative response to import: to control such habits we need to control our attention and behavior so as to respond actively as if we had the relevant felt evaluations when warranted, and, if we simulate these felt evaluations long enough, eventually such attention and behavior may well become habitual and so genuine.[20] Indeed, something similar was recommended by Pascal to get ourselves to believe in God: if belief is something like a habit of responding in certain rationally appropriate ways to circumstances, both by behaving in accordance with that belief and by making

---

[20] In effect, this is a point Aristotle insists upon in the *Nicomachean Ethics*: the moral excellences (i.e., those states of character by virtue of which we feel the right emotions and desires at the right times), and consequently the emotions and desires themselves, "come about as the result of habit" (1103a16) and so are things that we can acquire only "by first exercising them" (1103a30).

the relevant inferences, we can get ourselves to believe in God by consistently behaving and inferring in these ways, and eventually the habits – and genuine belief – might well follow.

Along these lines, Justin Oakley provides some details for how we are to proceed in the case of emotions.[21] According to Oakley, we must first develop the conceptual and discriminative capacities to identify both which emotions we approve or disapprove of and the kinds of situations in which these emotions are appropriate (p. 138); part of this task, he suggests, may require engaging ourselves in great works of literature and film (p. 137). In this way we can come to "understand why we feel" these emotions and so how we can "modify our emotions by changing ourselves" (p. 136). We can do this, he suggests,

> by engaging in actions which are characteristically associated with particular emotions, and by doing so in such a way that is deliberately aimed at the inculcation of the capacities for having those particular emotions, and, after some time and effort, the emotions themselves may come more naturally. (p. 137)

Clearly, there is some sleight of hand here. For even granting that consistently behaving this way will produce the habit of doing so, all one can get, it seems, is the habit of behaving as if one has the relevant felt evaluations when they are warranted. Simulated felt evaluations, however, are no less simulated when the simulation is habitual, so the proposed solution does not seem to address the problem. Indeed, deliberately to aim at inculcating certain emotions by engaging in the simulation, as Oakley suggests, is part of the problem here.[22] This is no less a problem for Pascal's account of how to acquire the belief in God: simply behaving as if one has a certain belief, even if that behavior becomes habitual, is still only a simulation. Pascal recognizes this difficulty in claiming that genuine belief will come only after divine

---

21 *Morality and the Emotions* (New York: Routledge, 1992), especially chapter 4. Actually, Oakley's discussion consists of roughly five separate methods to control one's emotions, with little attempt to articulate connections between them. I have tried to work these methods into a single account.

22 Oakley understands the problem to be the idea that in deliberately acquiring an emotion in this way one is learning to respond spontaneously with the emotion, where such "learned spontaneity" is apparently self-contradictory. Oakley argues that such an appearance is mistaken: we can learn to be spontaneous in playing jazz saxophone by "deliberately practising various scales, phrases, and progressions" so that eventually we can improvise "*without* having to deliberate" – spontaneously (p. 139). As I shall argue in the text below, this merely masks the underlying problem, which concerns the nature of the reasons one has for responding as if one has the relevant emotions, even if that response is spontaneous or habitual.

grace, to which one becomes more open by behaving as if one believes. The question, then, is: what is the emotional equivalent of divine grace?

The answer depends on what habit one acquires by behaving as if one has the relevant pattern of felt evaluations. If, as the above objection rightly points out, one acquires the habit of simulating these felt evaluations whenever they are warranted, then such simulation cannot be genuine no matter how habitual. This is because a felt evaluation is a response of a certain sort to import impressing itself upon one, so that to have a felt evaluation is to respond passively and in the right way when such a response is warranted because it is warranted. In simulating felt evaluations, however, one is responding in the characteristic ways when appropriate but for the wrong reason: because one judges one ought to have the felt evaluation. To simulate a felt evaluation, therefore, is not genuinely to have it because the motivation for responding in this way is mediated by one's judgment that one should behave in this way here and now, even though that judgment is itself a response to the (judged) warrant of the felt evaluation in the situation. What is needed, therefore, is for this mediating judgment to drop out, so that one is habitually moved in the right ways directly by those features of the situation that warrant the felt evaluation – by import itself. What does it take for this mediating judgment to drop out?

The answer lies in the interconnection between two habits that must, in the course of one's exercising rational control over one's heart, be developed separately but must ultimately come together as a single habit of response. The first is a habit of perception and attention to those situations in which, as one judges, emotional or desiderative response is warranted; the second is a habit of acting on behalf of the focus of one's attention as if one had the relevant felt evaluations deemed to be warranted as a result of an application of the first habit. In inculcating these habits, it is evaluative judgment that mediates in each case between one's active commitment to import and the application of the habit, resulting in merely simulated felt evaluations. Yet, as I shall now argue, given the kind of habits these are and their interconnections, once they are both acquired the responsiveness of the second habit will follow immediately on the recognition resulting from the first habit in a way that just is to have the relevant felt evaluation. I shall first consider how we can acquire these two habits and then how, once they are acquired, they can become interconnected.

First is the habit of attending to the way in which one's evaluative judgment bears on particular situations and so coming to conceive these situations accordingly. Acquiring such a habit requires first that one consistently undertake such attention and perception actively and self-consciously in judgment. In doing so, one is bringing to bear on these situations certain concepts relevant to both one's evaluative judgment and the reasons supporting that judgment. In somewhat dramatic cases, such as Cassie's adoption of utilitarianism, these concepts may be newly acquired and so may have the potential to change her understanding of these situations fairly radically; somewhat less dramatically, these concepts may receive expanded application, as when Martin understands caring about his children's interests to be a part of being a good father and so of the kind of person it is worth his being. Nonetheless, the acquisition of such a habit comes about largely through the exercise of one's will.

It should be clear that what is at stake in the acquisition of such a habit of attention and conception is not only one's coming to have the relevant felt evaluations in accordance with the evaluative perspective it provides, but also the dampening or silencing of alternative, inconsistent perspectives on the relevant situations implicit in one's existing patterns of felt evaluations, in each case by means of the rational pressure one's judgments bring to bear on these conflicting felt evaluations. For any change in what one cares about or values must include a revision of one's preferences so as to fit these changes into one's overall evaluative framework. Consequently, implicit in my discussion of these habits of attention and conception in accordance with one's evaluative judgments are habits of attention to and perception of relative degree of import. This means that at stake in acquiring such habits are not only the patterns of commitments in felt evaluation to the import of a common focus, but also patterns of commitments to relative degrees of import and so to the relevant dampening effects.

Second is the habit of getting oneself to respond as if one has the relevant felt evaluations, acting on behalf of its focus, when, according to one's conception of the situation in light of one's evaluative judgment, these felt evaluations are warranted. Once again, this is a task one can undertake by exercising one's will: one must consistently go through the motions of having the relevant felt evaluations, in particular those motions rationally expressive of these felt evaluations (cf. §3.4), for it is such expressions that make intelligible that behavior as a responsiveness to import and so that are relevant for simulating the emotion. This

191

means, in part, that one must by force of will both resist acting on felt evaluations that conflict with one's evaluative judgment and subsequently get oneself to respond emotionally according to whether these attempts are successful or not.

It would be a mistake to understand these two habits as simple stimulus-response dependencies, for in each case the habit is a habit of rational response. Thus, in acquiring the habit of attending to and conceiving of situations in accordance with one's evaluative judgment, the relevant stimulus will be a situation of a certain kind, namely the kind specified in the resulting conception of that situation that is the response. Consequently, the connection between the stimulus and the response is mediated by the rationality of the correct application of these concepts. Likewise, in acquiring the habit of responding as though expressing the relevant felt evaluations when one recognizes that they are warranted in the situation, not just any response will do. As I argued in §3.4, the stereotyped conception of fear as causing us to run away from danger is oversimplified precisely because it ignores the rational connection between the situation as warranting avoidance of danger, the opportunities the situation presents for doing so, and the resulting expression of one's fear. Thus, the response must in general be intelligible as worthwhile in light of the way in which one conceives the situation in line with the felt evaluation. Once again, the connection between the stimulus and the response is mediated by rationality.

Moreover, these habits are expressive of commitments, in each case to the import that justifies the response. In the case of the first habit of attention and perception, the relevant response is not merely the appearance that a situation is a certain way, but rather a commitment or assent to its being so. This is because, in inculcating this habit, one starts out with an active commitment in judgment to that import, and one tries self-consciously to identify when and how particular situations bear on that import; such an identification is itself a continued commitment to that import because its rationality presupposes that commitment. By doing this consistently, the habit one seeks to inculcate is precisely the habit of attending to and recognizing how situations bear on the import to which one is committed when such recognition is called for by that commitment. The same goes for the second habit of acting as though expressing certain felt evaluations, given a certain conception of the situation as warranting those felt evaluations. In inculcating this habit, one starts out by self-consciously identifying what behavior the felt evaluation would warrant in the situation given one's commitment (initially in judgment) to the import of its focus, and so exercising one's will so as to behave in those ways precisely because it is warranted. Thus, as in the case of the first habit, here, too, the rationality of the action as a response to this stimulus is intelligible only in terms of a commitment to import. In this sense, these habits are expressive of such a commitment.

We can now begin to see how the acquisition of these two habits can result not merely in the habit of simulating felt evaluations when warranted, but rather in the habit of genuinely having these felt evaluations. Assume that Martin has acquired the relevant habit of attention to and recognition of situations in accordance with his judgmental commitment to the import his children's interests have to him, a habit that succeeds in reshaping other existing habits of attention and recognition of import that bear on this one. For example, he no longer conceives his attendance at his daughter's soccer games as an unwelcome chore interfering with his work (in line with his previous habit of attending more exclusively to the import of his career); rather, he has acquired the habit of conceiving this attendance as an expression of his love for her and so as an opportunity for action worthwhile in its own right (in line with his newly acquired habit of attention and recognition). Assume also that Martin has acquired the habit of acting as though expressing the relevant felt evaluations when he recognizes, in accordance with his judgmental commitment to import, that the situation warrants them. In each case, these are habits of response: no self-conscious effort is required (as was the case in inculcating the habits) to make judgments or exercise his will in order to engage them. Moreover, the responsiveness of the second habit follows immediately on that of the first: having responded passively to his circumstances with a recognition that these circumstances warrant a particular felt evaluation, as the result of the first habit, there is nothing Martin needs to do self-consciously to engage the second habit, which itself is a passive response to such a recognition: in effect, the habits have merged to become a single habit.

The upshot is that Martin has acquired the sort of passive vigilance and preparedness to act resulting from a commitment to import that, especially in conjunction with his sincere evaluative judgments and active efforts on their behalf, is constitutive of that import – import that had not yet clearly been constituted prior to his acquisition of these habits. This means that the first habit can now be redescribed not merely as the habit of attending to situations in accordance with his evaluative judgments and their commitment to import (though, of course, it remains that) but, what is more important, as the habit of attending to import itself. The same goes for the second habit: it is not merely the habit of acting as though expressing the relevant felt evaluations in response to his recognition, in accordance with his judgmental commitment to import, that the situation warrants them; rather, this habit can be redescribed as that of acting as called for by these emotions when he recognizes that the situation does warrant them. Consequently, having acquired these habits of response, Martin is motivated to respond passively in the right ways because of, and out of a commitment to, the import of his situation. This just is to have genuine felt evaluations: the mediating judgment has dropped out.

In providing this account of how we can acquire new patterns of felt evaluation, I have assumed not merely that Martin's exercise of will and self-conscious attention has succeeded in instituting the relevant habits of attention and response, but also that old, potentially conflicting habits of both the attunement of his felt evaluations to the import of their common focus and his preparedness to act accordingly have been replaced or modified. It should be clear that this latter assumption is non-trivial, for the conflict between the relevant habits is a conflict of commitment to import and relative degree of import. Thus, previously Martin was committed to the import of his career as overriding that of his participation in his children's lives, whereas in acquiring the new habit he would be committing himself to a new balance here. Consequently, the assumption is, in effect, that Martin has succeeded in substituting one habitual set of commitments for another. That success depends, therefore, not merely on the strength of his will in consistently focusing his attention and acting as he judges he ought, for that the conflicting commitment is already habitual will interfere with the new judgmental commitment itself becoming habitual. In addition, success depends on the quality of the reasons supporting that judgment, for the conflicting felt evaluations are, of course, themselves responsive to such reasons. Consequently, the reasons supporting this judgment and the import to which he thereby commits himself are fundamental to understanding how, through an exercise of will, he can have rational control over his felt evaluations. (Of course, it need not be impossible to get oneself to care about or value something for no reason. It may be possible to institute the relevant habits simply by strength of will. My claim, though, is that it would be mysterious why in such a case this would happen, and it is not clear, therefore, in what sense this would be properly rational control.)

Because these conflicting felt evaluations are responsive to reasons, they may simply fall in line with Martin's evaluative judgments relatively easily, as the result of the sort of rational pressure already discussed. The theoretically interesting cases, however, are cases in which they prove resistant to persistent attempts to control them. In such cases, it is important to notice that when, as in Martin's case, the conflict between these evaluations is not inherent, the range of situations in which the conflict arises will be only a (possibly small) subset of those situations in which, as he judges, application of the new habit of evaluation is warranted. It may therefore be possible to institute this habit robustly in the remaining situations, thereby acquiring the relevant pattern of attention and response that, even though the pattern has gaps resulting from the interfering evaluation, is constitutive of import because these gaps are isolated. Moreover, he may be able to get this import to fit into the rest of his preferences in such a way as to institute further rational pressure on his conflicting felt evaluations to conform. Thus, Martin may be an extremely serious amateur golfer, having once considered turning professional, and find his devotion to golfing to rival his devotion to his career. Martin may find it easier, at least in many cases in which his commitment to golfing conflicts with his commitment to his children, to come to feel, by virtue of the relevant pattern of dampening relations, that his children come first. Nonetheless, the relative balance between his commitments to golfing and to his career may remain the same. In such a case, he has an apparent inconsistency in his preferences, and Martin can exert rational pressure, by means of articulating in judgment normative reasons for how to resolve the inconsistency, on his felt evaluations, as essentially rationally responsive to such reasons.

Even so, his conflicting felt evaluations may prove resistant to these attempts at rational control. Such resistance should not be understood in every case to be irrational stubbornness; indeed, given that the conflict is within his commitments to import, it may become clear that Martin is not of a single mind about what has import to him. In some such cases, it may be that there is no clear fact of the matter about what imports things really have for him in particular situations and so no clear fact of the matter about what felt evaluations and motives for action he ought to have. Consequently, questions of whether he has or fails to have rational control over his felt evaluations are premature because of this indeterminacy in what his reasons really are. Further deliberation is called for, and, as I argued in chapter 5, it is precisely in this sense that his felt evaluations can correct his evaluative judgments.[23]

In other cases, however, the resistance provided by these felt evaluations may be irrational stubbornness which we may find ourselves unable to overcome. There are limits on our freedom of the heart, just as there are limits on our freedom of the will: we cannot come to care about or value just anything, nor can we motivate ourselves to do just anything. Nonetheless, such limits are possible only against the background of our generally having freedom of the heart and so being able to exercise rational control over our felt evaluations. For, as I argued in §6.3, it is a condition of the possibility of our being able to make evaluative judgments that we generally be able successfully to exercise our wills on their behalf, and it is therefore only against this background of success that limitations on our freedom of will are intelligible. Likewise, given that we have the capacity for evaluative judgment, it is a condition of the possibility of our having both that capacity and the capacity for felt evaluations that we generally be able successfully rationally to control our felt evaluations and thereby our hearts.[24] For such control, as I have argued, is in part a matter of our being able to exercise our wills, and in part a matter of having our evaluative judgments and felt evaluations each being in general rationally responsive to the other; the former is already required by our having the capacity for evaluative judgment, and the latter is required as a part of the kind of rationality that is the constitutive ideal of distinctively human commitment to import. Failures to exercise control over our hearts, therefore, are intelligible only against the background of such cases of success, and they do not threaten but rather presuppose the idea that when we succeed it is by virtue of an exercise of rational control.

6.5 CONCLUSION

The motivational problem is therefore solved – almost. I have argued that, in order to solve this problem, we must reject the assumption of the

[23] I shall discuss the nature of such deliberation in chapter 7.

[24] Notice that this way of putting the point makes room for animals lacking the capacity for evaluative judgment nonetheless to have the capacity for felt evaluations; such animals will not, of course, have even the possibility of exercising rational control over their hearts

cognitive–conative divide and thereby come to see our motivations themselves as rationally responsive to the normative reasons we acknowledge in judgment. By exploiting the account, developed in chapter 5, of the rational interconnections between evaluative judgments and felt evaluations, I argued that we can exercise rational control over our motivations in three interconnected ways. First, we can exercise our wills, here understood to be the ability to motivate ourselves by virtue of an active commitment in judgment to import and the normative reasons it provides for action. Second, we can exercise control over our motivations in a way that is mediated by our desires. By self-consciously adopting an evaluative perspective on our current situation in accordance with the normative reasons we acknowledge in judgment, we can exert rational pressure on our desires to conform precisely because those desires, as felt evaluations, are themselves responsive to import. Such an exercise of control, however, is normally successful only in the case of complete evaluations – evaluations reflecting a commitment to import that arises out of a projectible, rational pattern of both evaluative judgments and felt evaluations, presenting us with what is largely a single evaluative perspective. Achieving such a complete evaluation, however, may require that we exercise control in a third way: over our hearts. This requires, through an exercise of the first two means of control, acquiring rational habits of response to situations that reflect one's judgmental commitment to import, habits which, once acquired, can become genuine felt evaluations. In shaping our felt evaluations in this way, we can acquire the sort of single evaluative perspective that is constitutive of complete evaluations.

Each of these kinds of control is intelligible as a condition of the possibility of the capacity to commit ourselves to import, both actively through evaluative judgment and passively through felt evaluation. Failures of control, as in cases of weakness of will and listlessness, do not, therefore, threaten to undermine our having such control in cases in which things go right because their intelligibility as failures instead presupposes the background of normal cases in which we clearly have such control.

In every case, the kind of control we exercise over ourselves is rational control. As such, it depends on the quality of the reasons that support our evaluative judgments. As I indicated in §6.4, when our felt evaluations prove resistant to our attempts to control them, it may be that this resistance amounts to a kind of correction of our evaluative judgments, calling for a re-examination of just what our reasons are. In order to provide a complete solution to the motivational problem, we must therefore understand how deliberation about both import and priorities is possible. This is the task for chapter 7. Indeed, as I shall argue in §§7.3–7.4, the possibility of deliberating about value presupposes the possibility of freedom of the will and the heart as well. Consequently, the motivational and deliberative problems are essentially interconnected and cannot be answered in isolation from each other; this is why I have claimed that the motivational problem is "almost" solved.

7

Deliberation about value

My aim has been to understand the kind of practical rationality distinctive of persons so as to be able to solve certain problems of human practical reason. To this end, first, I have given an account of a distinctive kind of rationality governing the interconnections among our felt evaluations and evaluative judgments: a *rationality of import*, as we might call it. Why is such a rationality of import distinctive? These felt evaluations and evaluative judgments, I have argued, are disclosive commitments to import. By this I mean that they are neither cognitive commitments having mind-to-world direction of fit to an antecedent fact, nor conative commitments that project that import by virtue of their world-to-mind direction of fit. Rather, our commitments to import are simultaneously both responsive to that import and constitutive of it by virtue of their complex rational interconnections. This rationality of import, therefore, is distinctive insofar as it is neither instrumental nor epistemic and so is intelligible neither in terms of specifying how to get the world to fit our conations nor in terms of specifying how to get our cognitions to fit the world.

Second, in articulating an account of human practical reason, I have provided an account of how we can exploit this rationality of import in controlling both our motivations and our felt evaluations, potentially coming to have both freedom of the will and freedom of the heart. For, by identifying in judgment reasons for acting, we thereby exert rational pressure on our felt evaluations and motivations to conform. Again, this rational pressure stems from the rationality of import: insofar as a creature's overall conformity to the rationality of import as well as both epistemic and instrumental rationality is a condition of the possibility of being a human agent at all, our having the capacity to control (and our generally succeeding in controlling) ourselves in these ways is conceptually necessary, even if it is a contingent fact in each case whether or not our attempts at control are successful.

199

Nonetheless, as I noted in §6.5, the account of freedom of the heart presented so far is incomplete. For the rational pressure our evaluative judgments can apply to our felt evaluations depends on the quality of the reasons supporting those judgments. When our felt evaluations resist our attempts to control them by means of evaluative judgment, they can thereby correct our evaluative judgments and so call for further deliberation. Understanding how freedom of the heart is possible, therefore, requires understanding how deliberation about value is possible. Achieving this latter understanding is my task for this chapter. It should be clear, however, that my aim here is not to provide a recipe for deliberation about import: there is no such thing. It is, rather, to understand the source of the norms governing our choice of import – as both genuinely normative and partially internal to our evaluative sensibilities.

7.1 THE DELIBERATIVE PROBLEM REVISITED

The deliberative problem arises from the question of how deliberation about value – and import quite generally – is possible. As I indicated in §1.4, what makes an answer to this question so difficult is the way in which our concept of value is pulled in seemingly opposed directions of objectivity and subjectivity. On the one hand, to value something is to find it to be a part of one's identity, of the kind of person one finds worth being (cf. §4.1). Part of what distinguishes us as persons from mere animals is the possibility that we can have a say in the kind of creature it is worth our being. This "having a say" is our *autonomy:* our freedom to govern not merely our actions but, more fundamentally, our selves. Consequently, we can in a sense *invent* which values we ought to have, and these values are in this sense subjective. On the other hand, the choice of values as the result of deliberation is not arbitrary, for the point of deliberation is to justify these choices by an appeal to reasons. Justification, as I intend it here, is a success notion: the claim is not merely that certain reasons can seem to justify our values, but that these reasons can truly justify them. Consequently, which values we ought to hold is something we can *discover* through a consideration of reasons, and such discovery is what makes possible a kind of depth of meaning in our lives that would otherwise be missing.

Both these ideas of invention and discovery of value seem central to our understanding of persons, and yet they are seemingly in conflict. For if by virtue of our autonomy we are the ones that determine what kind of person it is worth our being and so what values we ought to hold, what room is left for this being something we also discover? The notion of discovery seems to imply that there are independent standards for correctness, and so seems to rule out precisely the kind of self-determination involved in autonomy. This is what I called the *apparent paradox of simultaneous autonomous invention and rational discovery*, and it is this apparent paradox that causes difficulties for understanding how deliberation about value is possible: both invention and discovery seem to be required by our understanding of persons, and yet both, it seems, cannot simultaneously be true. The deliberative problem, therefore, is the problem of finding a satisfactory way of understanding deliberation about value that enables us to resolve (or dissolve) this paradox.

As I suggested in §1.4, the deliberative problem cannot be solved if we assume the cognitive–conative divide. For, according to that divide, our reasons for choosing certain values are either prior to our thoughts, and so are fit objects of cognition and discovery, resulting in a cognitivist account of values; or our reasons are posterior to our thoughts and so are fit objects of conation and invention, resulting in a non-cognitivist account of values. Both cannot be true simultaneously on pain of violating that divide, and (according to the divide) there is no third option. Consequently, the deliberative problem gets conceived in terms of a genuine paradox of simultaneous invention and discovery. As I claimed in §1.4, this forces us, unsatisfactorily, to give up one or the other of these dimensions of ourselves as persons. Nonetheless, this argument was too quick, and my task in §§7.1.1–7.1.2 is to discuss particular cognitivist and non-cognitivist views more carefully, arguing that a proper understanding of the notion of rational discovery presupposes the notion of autonomous invention, and vice versa. I shall then turn in §7.2 to examine and criticize as inadequate several attempts to dissolve the paradox by rejecting the cognitive–conative divide and so finding a middle path between cognitivism and non-cognitivism, before turning in §§7.3–7.4 to present my own account so as to resolve these inadequacies.

7.1.1 *Cognitivism*

According to cognitivist theories of value, there are facts about what values things have for me that are independent of the evaluative perspective I adopt, and so are independent of the evaluative concepts I bring to bear on the world in adopting that perspective.[1] In this way, the cognitivist construes the notion of discovery relevant to deliberation about value in terms of a recognition of such a mind-independent fact, analogous to our recognition of non-evaluative facts. The relevant rational standards we bring to bear in deliberation, therefore, are primarily standards of epistemic rationality. (Of course, a cognitivist need not rule out a role for instrumental rationality. After all, we might think, part of what must go into the determination of whether the pursuit of an end is worthy of the kind of person we should be is an assessment of the necessary means to that end and whether such means undermine or support other values. Nonetheless, such a role for instrumental rationality is only secondary.) Consequently, it seems as though cognitivism can provide a straightforward account of the element of discovery and that problems for this view must arise only on the side of autonomy. As I argued in §1.4, the difficulties in reconciling this cognitivist account of discovery with an adequate notion of autonomy are insurmountable: given the cognitivist conception of the values things really have as wholly independent of my evaluative perspective, there is no room for my having a say in what these values shall be. Nonetheless, what I shall now argue is that cognitivism must fail even on its apparent strengths, for the way in which it conceives of discovery makes a proper account of the objectivity of value impossible.

To see this, consider first Peter Railton's account of personal value. According to Railton, to understand what values one should adopt we need to appeal to the notion of an *ideal advisor*. Thus, imagine that I am perfectly epistemically and instrumentally rational and am fully cognitively informed about the world, including my current psychological states, dispositions, aptitudes, etc. What I should value, Railton claims, is what this idealized version of myself would want his values to be were he in my position. In this way, Railton hopes, the standards of correctness of value can be located in the world (which includes facts about my psychology, etc.).

On the face of it, this account might seem to violate the cognitivist requirement that facts about values be independent of the subject's evaluative perspective. After all, when the ideal advisor takes into account my psychological states in rendering his verdict, that may seem just to be a matter of taking my evaluative perspective into account.

---

[1] For an explicit account of such independence, see Peter Railton's "Moral Realism," p. 172.

Nonetheless, Railton tries to preserve independence by his understanding of the relevant kind of psychological facts the ideal advisor is apprised of and takes into consideration (cf. p. 173). Thus, the sense in which the ideal advisor knows about my "subjective interests" – my desires – is as a responsiveness of "positive valence" to situations of certain kinds, where these kinds of situations can be specified as a "complex set of relational, dispositional, primary qualities" wholly independent of my perspective on them. Railton claims that we should understand such a set to be the "reduction basis" of my subjective interests: "an objective notion that corresponds to, and helps explain, subjective interests." In this way, we can see that the task of the ideal observer is to determine in light of his perfect information about the world and, in particular, of the reduction bases of my subjective interests, what interests I should have in order to maximize the positive valence I experience in the long run. It is precisely because the relevant worldly properties are independent of my evaluative perspective that the task of deliberation about value is intelligible as a cognitive task.

A central difficulty with Railton's account, however, is why deliberation about such reduction bases should be of any use in determining the reasons we have for valuing something: what in this account is the source of that value? It might seem that the answer is to be found in his characterization of the notion of an interest as a response of "positive valence," for this description suggests that our interests are such a source. Yet we must be careful in how this gets understood. As a first pass, we might construe Railton's talk of "positive valence" as something like an inclination towards something, so that to have an interest is to be disposed to pursue it. This construal is consistent with his account of the task of the ideal advisor as concerned with the reduction bases of one's subjective interests, but it requires that we give up on it as the source of value. For, as I argued in chapter 2, such goal-directedness must be carefully distinguished from genuine desires precisely in that the latter but not the former involves import. Consequently, if goal-directedness is all Railton means by "interest," the resulting deliberation about reduction bases is inadequate to an account of what values we should adopt.

This suggests that what Railton has in mind is not mere goal-directedness, but genuine desire, so that his talk of positive valence can be construed as a properly evaluative response. This would at least begin to make sense of the task of the ideal advisor as one of coming up with reasons for valuing, but it prevents us from understanding the relevant properties the ideal advisor appeals to as independent of my evaluative perspective. For genuine desire, as I have argued in chapter 3, is a felt evaluation and so is responsive to import only insofar as it is also simultaneously constitutive of import by being a part of a broader evaluative perspective. This means that when the ideal advisor considers my current desires and attempts to extrapolate from them, given his perfect knowledge about the world, to the desires I should have, he must do so only in light of the point of view those desires partly constitute. For otherwise no such extrapolation is possible: to ignore that point of view is to ignore precisely that feature of desire that makes it intelligible as constituting import and so as relevant to my reasons for valuing. Consequently, the independence of my point of view cognitivism requires cannot be sustained if the account is to be intelligible as an account of the objectivity of value.

This same basic criticism also applies to Richard Boyd's account of moral values.[2] According to Boyd, we can discover what is morally good by coming to see what promotes "important human goods, things which satisfy important human needs," where it is "a potentially difficult and complex empirical question" what these goods and needs are – a matter for biology, psychology, and perhaps sociology (p. 122). As for Railton, the problem for Boyd is to give an account of these "goods" and "needs" as a source of value, for it is not clear how anything discoverable solely within empirical science, independent of any evaluative point of view we take, could be such a source. After all, an appeal to merely biological facts cannot be the answer without presupposing that such things as health or life itself (the continuation of the species or of an individual) have import, but that is a normative presupposition that is not a part of biology. Moreover, an appeal to psychological facts can support the normative notion of import, but only through an appeal to a robust notion of desire. (Again, mere goal-directedness will not suffice.) As I have argued, this requires accepting a conception of import as perspectivally subjective and so rejecting the kind of independence cognitivists are after.[3]

[2] "How to Be a Moral Realist," in Stephen Darwall, Allan Gibbard, and Peter Railton, eds., *Moral Discourse and Practice*, pp. 105–35. Although Boyd offers this as an account of moral value, specifying values we all ought to hold, we might imagine its extension to personal values as well, insofar as my goods and needs might be different from yours; I shall assume that this extension is unproblematic.

[3] This same criticism applies as well to Elijah Millgram's account of practical induction as a method for arriving at reasons for valuing. (See his "Pleasure in Practical Reasoning,"

Ironically, therefore, cognitivists fail to provide an adequate account of the discovery of value precisely because, in their quest for objectivity, they omit the point of view from which alone value is intelligible. Indeed, as we shall see, part of the point of the demand for autonomy is that the personal point of view not be missing in order to make sense of value as potentially an object of discovery. We must therefore reject the idea that the values things have are ontologically and rationally prior to our evaluative point of view. This seems to push us to non-cognitivism; indeed, if we accept the cognitive–conative divide, it forces us to non-cognitivism as the only alternative.

7.1.2 *Non-cognitivism*

In rejecting the idea that values are ontologically and rationally prior to our evaluations, non-cognitivists assert that our evaluations are ontologically and rationally prior to the values things have. Such a reversal of priority is demanded by the assumption of the cognitive–conative divide, for if our evaluations are not cognitions, responsive to how things antecedently are, they can only be conations, at least purporting to establish a standard the world ought to fit. Values therefore exist in the world only as ontologically posterior to, and so as a projection of, our conations and the evaluative perspective they provide. In this way, non-cognitivism seems to make good sense of our autonomy, that we can have a say in what values to have, for, if the values themselves exist only as internal to our evaluative perspective, then the standards for what we ought to value – standards that themselves must be intelligible as values – are also internal to that perspective. Consequently, non-cognitivists can seem to make sense of our being actively responsible for our values by holding out for an account of how we can control our conations.

As I argued in §1.4, however, non-cognitivism cannot make good sense of the notion of discovery. For the notion of discovery requires that there be non-arbitrary reasons for valuing something, such that the mere appeal to the internal coherence of one's evaluations is insufficient

Monist, 76 [1993], pp. 394–415; and his *Practical Induction*.) According to Millgram, practical induction starts from feelings of pleasure and displeasure, which he understands to be "signs or symptoms, evidence as to how well things are going" ("Pleasure in Practical Reasoning," p. 397; cf. p. 401). Yet, as I argued in chapter 3, an adequate account of pleasure and displeasure as properly evaluative must understand them to be simultaneously not only responsive to import (as Millgram has it) but also constitutive of that import, and cannot, therefore, be the basis of a cognitivist account of import.

to explain why one has these values rather than others. Yet, given the non-cognitivist's commitment to the ontological and rational priority of our evaluative perspective over the values things have, they can appeal to nothing other than such internal coherence. (Simon Blackburn explicitly rejects the idea that internal coherence is all that a non-cognitivist can appeal to. For, he claims, we can appeal as well to other virtues of thought, such as "maturity, imagination, sympathy, culture. An imma-ture, unimaginative, unsympathetic and uncultivated ethic might be quite coherent, in the way that the decalogue is quite coherent. But that does not make it the last word."[4] However, for these further virtues of thought to do some work beyond that specified by mere coherence, they must be values that have precisely the sort of independence of our evaluative perspective that non-cognitivists deny. The best non-cogniti-vists can do is to conceive of such virtues as emerging from within our evaluative attitudes, and once again internal coherence seems to be the only standard to which they can appeal.) Consequently, non-cognitivism forces us to give up on this dimension of our conception of ourselves as persons.

Nonetheless, what I shall now argue is that non-cognitivism fails even on its apparent strengths because, given its conception of values as projected, it cannot sustain a conception of conation that makes intelli-gible the idea that value is what it projects. To see this, consider the accounts of Allan Gibbard and Simon Blackburn.[5] As Gibbard and Blackburn note, not just any conation succeeds in projecting values onto the world, for we may repudiate some emotions or desires, or find them to be otherwise inappropriate in a way that undermines any value they may purport to project. How, then, is this distinction between appro-priate and inappropriate conations to be understood? Although a cogni-tivist about value can understand this distinction in terms of whether or not these conations reflect independently existing values, such a route is not open to a non-cognitivist given their understanding of values as projected by our conations and so as not independently existing. Rather, the basic answer Gibbard and Blackburn provide involves an appeal to norms of response that emerge within a process of conversing with others.

According to Gibbard, a *norm* is a rule or prescription permitting or

---

[4] *Ruling Passions*, p. 310.
[5] Gibbard, *Wise Choices, Apt Feelings*; Blackburn, *Ruling Passions* and *Spreading the Word: Groundings in the Philosophy of Language* (Oxford University Press, 1984).

requiring some action or response; as such norms are what underlie our values. To *accept a norm* (and the underlying value) is to be disposed not only to feel emotions and desires (and so be motivated) in accordance with it, but also to express that norm in conversation and so be prepared to stand up for it in the face of conversational pressures to change. The claim is not, Gibbard would insist, that we should stubbornly hold onto the norms we accept, simply refusing to change in the face of others' objections. Rather, what others say can have a strong influence on what we think and feel: in part by articulating demands of consistency and in part, perhaps through an appeal to our sympathies, by getting us to see things differently. As a result, Gibbard claims, the norms it is *rational* for us to accept are those that survive this sort of confrontation with others' attempts to influence us through the expression of the norms they accept. Consequently, such rationality is a standard of correctness for norm acceptance, and it therefore underwrites the idea that values are projected by the resulting complex of dispositions to feel emotions and desires and to respond in conversation to others in this way. As Blackburn puts essentially the same point, to value something and so successfully to project that value is to have:

a relatively stable disposition to conduct practical life and practical discussion in a particular way: it is to be disposed to be *set* in that way, and to be set against change in this respect.[6]

In this way, value is understood as emerging wholly from within one's evaluative perspective, and, insofar as this is an evaluative perspective we can control, the account seems to make sense of our autonomy.

This account of the "rationality" of norm acceptance, however, fails as an account of the relevant sort of appropriateness of conations that enables those conations to project value. For, if my continuing to accept certain norms in the face of conversational pressure from others is to be anything other than a stubborn and arbitrary refusal to change, that refusal must be intelligible as responsive to reasons. Thus, I ought to take into consideration what you say only insofar as you give me reasons for valuing something, and my taking what you say into consideration means my giving those reasons some weight in an attempt to justify my valuing. Gibbard and Blackburn, however, substitute stubborn refusal as a thin surrogate for reason: according to them, from my point of view reasons just are those conversational moves that in fact strengthen or

---

6 *Ruling Passions*, p. 67.

weaken my acceptance of norms. However, these are not reasons at all. We cannot, as the non-cognitivist does, understand the relevant standards of rationality or appropriateness to emerge simply because my acceptance of these norms actually survives such conversational pressure; rather, the relevant standards of appropriateness themselves define which acceptances of norms ought to survive that pressure, whether or not they in fact do. Actual survival of norm acceptance might be a reliable indicator of what the standards of appropriateness are, but we cannot understand these standards simply in terms of that actual acceptance. Insofar as the standards of appropriateness of conations are meant to distinguish those conations that succeed in projecting value from those that do not, a failure to articulate such standards is a failure to make sense of value as that which is projected by these conations.

This difficulty is not merely characteristic of Gibbard's and Blackburn's accounts; it must plague any non-cognitivist account of value. For non-cognitivists, by insisting on the ontological and rational priority of our conations over the values things have, thereby rule out the possibility of appealing to those values as themselves the source of the relevant standards of appropriateness. Consequently, whatever standards a non-cognitivist can appeal to in distinguishing appropriate from inappropriate conations, the question will arise as to whether the conations thus identified as appropriate actually project value or not. Of course, a non-cognitivist will insist that what enables the question to be answered is precisely that we are dealing here with emotions and desires – states that are essentially evaluative, so that internal constraints of appropriateness will suffice to make intelligible which of these states succeed in projecting value. Nonetheless, this insistence merely begs the prior question of the conditions of the intelligibility of a response as emotional or desiderative, a question that is implicit in the problem of import and that, as I argued in chapters 2–3 (most explicitly in §2.4), can only be answered by giving up the non-cognitivist assumption of the ontological and rational priority of our conations over the values they serve to constitute: mere internal standards of coherence are an inadequate basis for distinguishing those evaluative states that are appropriate because they project value from those that are not.[7]

Ironically, therefore, non-cognitivists fail to provide an adequate

---

[7] For an alternative way of making essentially this same argument, albeit one framed within an explicitly ethical debate, see Justin D'Arms and Daniel Jacobson's "Sentiment and Value," *Ethics*, 110 (2000), pp. 722–48.

account of the invention of value precisely because, in their quest for subjectivity, they omit the non-arbitrariness of the standards that alone can make intelligible the idea that conation can project value. As we have seen, part of the point of the demand of discovery is precisely that such standards make ineliminable appeal to the values things have. We must therefore reject the non-cognitivist insistence that our evaluative point of view be ontologically and rationally prior to such values.

7.2 DISSOLVING THE PARADOX

Cognitivism and non-cognitivism seem to be the only options for making sense of value precisely because of the implicit assumption of the cognitive–conative divide: the values things have must be either objects of cognition, and so be independent objects of discovery, or objects of conation, and so be in effect the inventions of our evaluative perspectives. As a result, the deliberative problem gets conceived in terms of a genuine paradox of invention and discovery. On the surface, this understanding of the deliberative problem forces us to choose unsatisfactorily either invention or discovery at the expense of the other. More deeply, as I have just argued in §7.1, this understanding of the ideas of invention and discovery in the end prevents an adequate conception of value as the object of either invention or discovery. For, to insist on value as a mind-independent object of discovery is to omit the point of view essential to making sense of value as what is discovered, and to insist on value as merely the product of our conations is to make unintelligible the kind of rational standards that enable our conations to project value. Consequently, in order to solve the deliberative problem we must reject both the idea that the values things have are ontologically and rationally prior to our evaluative point of view and the idea that our evaluative point of view is similarly prior to the values things have. In short, we must reject the assumptions of priority that form the core of the cognitive–conative divide.

The solution to the deliberative problem, therefore, must involve not so much resolving the paradox of invention and discovery as dissolving it as merely apparent, thereby treading a middle path between cognitivism and non-cognitivism. Such a position has been advocated by David Wiggins and John McDowell.[8] The basic idea, in line with my rejection

---

[8] See, for example, David Wiggins' *Needs, Values and Truth: Essays in the Philosophy of*

of the cognitive–conative divide, is to reject any claim of ontological or rational priority among the values things have and our evaluative sensibilities. As McDowell puts it, values should be understood as *subjective* in the sense that they are properties "not adequately conceivable except in terms of certain subjective states," namely our evaluative sensibilities; in this way, he rejects cognitivism (p. 113). Nonetheless, he claims, value is also *objective* in the sense that it is "there to be experienced, as opposed to being a mere figment of the subjective state that purports to be an experience of it" (p. 114); such objectivity, he thinks, can be explained largely in terms of the possibility of criticizing our experiences as of objects that do not merit these responses. Thus, McDowell claims:

> we make sense of fear by seeing it as a response to objects that *merit* such a response, or as the intelligibly defective product of a propensity towards responses that would be intelligible in that way. For an object to merit fear just is for it to be fearful. So explanations of fear that manifest our capacity to understand ourselves in this region of our lives will simply not cohere with the claim that reality contains nothing in the way of fearfulness. (p. 119)

In this way, he rejects non-cognitivism as well.

In forging a middle path between cognitivism and non-cognitivism, therefore, Wiggins and McDowell try to conceive of the standards of criticism which underwrite objectivity as simultaneously subjective insofar as they are "at least partially internal to [our] perceptions" – i.e., our evaluative sensibilities.[9] However, this raises a fundamental difficulty: the risk of vicious circularity. This risk is in essence a manifestation of the apparent paradox of simultaneous invention and discovery in a new guise. For these standards of criticism must, in order to underwrite objectivity, be independent of our evaluative sensibilities insofar as we assess these sensibilities for warrant in terms of these standards. Simultaneously, however, these standards are said to be dependent on our sensibilities as "partially internal" to them – as somehow emerging out of patterns of warranted response. If the warrant of our sensibilities depends on there being standards, but these very same standards depend on what sensibilities it is warranted to have, we have a circle that seems too tight to be informative.

Value, 2nd edition (Oxford: Blackwell, 1991), and John McDowell's "Values and Secondary Qualities," in Ted Honderich, ed., *Morality and Objectivity*, pp. 110–29.

[9] Wiggins, "A Sensible Subjectivism?," in *Needs, Values, and Truth*, pp. 185–214, at p. 196.

Wiggins and McDowell intend their rejection of any ontological or rational priority between the values things have and our evaluative sensibilities to rebut any such charge of vicious circularity. After all, they would claim, the circle is vicious only if we assume a priority in one direction or the other: so long as the values things have are not prior to our sensibilities, there can be no problem in understanding those values to depend on our sensibilities; moreover, so long as our sensibilities are not prior to the values things have, there can be no problem in understanding our sensibilities as depending for their warrant on those values. However, the trouble is that the relevant notion(s) of dependence must remain vague and elusive until we have a clear understanding of the precise nature of our evaluative sensibilities and their relation to value that can support such a rejection of priority; yet this is an understanding neither Wiggins nor McDowell has provided. As they stand, therefore, these accounts are inadequate as solutions to the deliberative problem. (My account of felt evaluations and their connection to import also involves the rejection of priority between them and is, therefore, a step in the right direction, but this account must be extended in order to make intelligible the kind of reasons it is possible to have for valuing and, consequently, the possibility of exercising freedom over our hearts; that will be my aim in §§7.3–7.4.)

A closely related attempt to solve the deliberative problem, a solution that both rejects any claims of priority and attempts to specify more clearly how deliberation about value is possible, is offered by Charles Taylor.[10] Taylor claims that the task of deliberation about value, in particular what he calls *radical reevaluation*, in which "by definition the most basic terms, those in which other evaluations are carried on, are precisely what is in question" (p. 40), is largely a task of self-interpretation. For, he claims, what has import to us has its source in our "deepest unstructured [or 'largely inarticulate' – cf. p. 38] sense of what is important, which is as yet inchoate and which I am trying to bring to definition" (p. 41). Such a sense is initially more or less inarticulate in that one has not yet spelled it out in judgment; as a result, it is somehow implicit in the kind of experiences and reactions one has, in particular one's emotional experiences. Deliberation, therefore, is largely a matter of articulating this sense more clearly, and that is a task for self-interpretation. Given this central role for self-interpretation, Taylor claims, we can understand how elements of both invention and discovery

---

[10] See his *Human Agency and Language*, and *Sources of the Self*, especially Part I. (Page references to Taylor in the text will be to *Human Agency and Language*.)

are simultaneously at issue, for, in articulating our experiences more clearly, we must strive to be faithful to those experiences (hence the element of discovery), and yet the very act of self-interpretation can change those very experiences (hence the element of invention).

To see this, consider the following familiar phenomenon. When you feel vaguely hungry but do not really know what you want, you may have to run through several options (perhaps staring into the refrigerator in the process) until something strikes you as being what you wanted all along; or when you try to figure out where to go for a vacation, you must articulate what kind of trip you want more fully, perhaps rejecting several possibilities before settling on one that ultimately strikes you as right. In each case, the articulation of what you want changes your desire by making it more determinate. Here we can shape and invent these desires, possibly in light of deliberation; thus, you might reason that, since you have just a couple of hours ago stuffed yourself with a large meal, eating something light is now appropriate, and so start looking for fruit that will satisfy your craving. Of course, you cannot just shape your desire any old way you want: eating a lemon probably will not satisfy it (a fact you can test by eating it and seeing if the craving remains unfulfilled). In this way, your vague hunger imposes a constraint on how you interpret and so articulate it. Consequently, in the process of settling on an apple as what you wanted all along, there are elements both of discovery (insofar as you are constrained) and invention (insofar as you nonetheless shape the desire).

Likewise, Taylor claims, by using self-interpretation to articulate our sense of import, we thereby change that sense in a way that involves both invention and discovery. In deciding whether to make a career change, for example, it is common to lay out the pros and cons on each side and then to use one's sense of what is more important to guide one's choice. Insofar as this is deliberation and not guesswork, however, it must involve having something to say about why one made the choice this way: why, to oversimplify, a profession that involves helping the underprivileged has more going for it than one that merely pays a lot of money. One can articulate this by saying that it is a nobler life, and in this way, Taylor thinks, one is articulating more fully one's deepest sense of what is important. To do this is to provide some shape to one's understanding of value and so is in part a matter of free choice: invention. Nonetheless, not just any choice is possible here, and mistaken choices may leave one with a sense of being unfulfilled: maybe that to which one aspires is not nobility but a kind of high culture only the high-paying job will enable one to afford. Consequently, one's unstructured sense of import can impose constraints on choice in a way that enables one to discover what one really values: it is that to which our judgments must "strive to be faithful" (p. 38). Invention and discovery are simultaneously possible because of the role self-interpretation plays in this special kind of deliberation. As Taylor puts it:

> That description and experience are bound together in this constitutive relation admits of causal influences in both directions: it can sometimes allow us to alter experience by coming to fresh insight; but more fundamentally it circumscribes insight through the deeply embedded shape of experience for us. (p. 37)

There is much that is right about this outline of how deliberation about value is possible, and I shall in §§7.3–7.4 exploit this notion of self-interpretation as a way of making sense of simultaneous invention and discovery. Nonetheless, there are problems with Taylor's account as it stands.

Taylor is vague about the precise connection between our experiences, in particular our emotions, and the values they somehow constitute, and this hurts his account in two ways. First, he conceives of the sense of import implicit in these experiences to be unstructured, at least initially. Yet if that sense is unstructured, what purchase does it provide for interpretation? Indeed, this idea that our sense of import is unstructured makes appropriate the analogy to the vague hunger presented above, but it is surely a strain to talk of "interpreting" one's hunger and so coming to a better understanding of it. Rather, interpretation must be a matter of identifying the structure that is in some sense already there in what is interpreted, and this is fundamental to the possibility of getting the interpretation right in a way that underwrites the notion of discovery. This leads to a second difficulty. Even if we grant that there is enough structure in our experiences to make sense of self-interpretation, it is not clear how the resulting notion of discovery is sufficient for solving the deliberative problem. For, in order for a choice of values to be non-arbitrary, there must be reasons supporting that choice, reasons it is the point of deliberation to uncover. Yet, no matter how well grounded it is in the structure of our current experiences, self-interpretation seems inadequate on its own as an account of how to uncover such reasons and so the experiences we ought to have, as opposed to those we in fact have. Consequently, it is not clear how such self-interpretation can amount to deliberation.

Elizabeth Anderson proposes a model of deliberation about value that is in many ways similar to Taylor's.[11] According to Anderson, deliberation about values is a matter of interpreting one's circumstances in such a way as to make sense not only of these circumstances, but also of our evaluative attitudes in response to them. Anderson differs from Taylor, therefore, by appealing to social standards: it is *our* attitudes that in part determine the appropriateness of a given interpretation, attitudes that are sustained from within social practices of criticism within which each member "acknowledge[s] the equal authority of others to offer criticisms and proposals, giving them weight in discussion" (p. 93). However, this appeal to social standards does not seem to enable Anderson to provide a proper account of the subjectivity of personal values and so of the role of individual autonomy. Moreover, insofar as Anderson systematically ignores questions concerning the ontological status of values (cf., e.g., p. 99), she fails as well to provide a satisfactory account of the objectivity of values. For without such an account it seems the best she can do to show that an interpretation of our circumstances is the right one is to say that it makes sense of our current evaluative attitudes (perhaps as shaped by that interpretation), and not that it makes sense of the evaluative attitudes we ought to adopt. Of course, Anderson might claim that the evaluative attitudes we ought to adopt just are those made intelligible by such interpretation, but now we have a circle that is too tight to be informative.

At this point we can see how my account of felt evaluations and their connections to evaluative judgment can help. For felt evaluations are defined by their place within a certain kind of rational structure, and it is this structure that provides purchase for self-interpretation. Moreover, insofar as the connections between felt evaluations and evaluative judgment are rational (and bi-directional), there may be room to see how the way in which the structure of our felt evaluations rationally constrains our interpretation can support the discovery of reasons to value. It is to this task that I now turn, arguing first in §7.3 for a precise account of how through self-interpretation we can shape the rational patterns of our felt evaluations in a way that is distinct from those already discussed in §§6.3–6.4, and then in §7.4 for an account of how the elucidation of concepts (an element McDowell and Wiggins insist on) can be a part of self-interpretation in a way that makes intelligible the discovery of

---

[11] *Value in Ethics and Economics* (Cambridge, MA: Harvard University Press, 1993).

reasons for valuing and so of rational improvement in our values. My aim, therefore, is to show that, on a proper understanding of the relevant notions of autonomous invention and rational discovery, no paradox arises in the first place.

7.3 SELF-INTERPRETATION AND CHANGE OF IMPORT

The appeal to self-interpretation can help make sense of the possibility of simultaneous invention and discovery when there is some lack of clarity, some indeterminacy, in what felt evaluations one has. For it is in such cases that the articulation of feeling through self-interpretation can enable one to achieve a new clarity in what was felt all along (thereby making sense of discovery) by shaping the patterns of felt evaluation through the concepts one thereby brings to bear on them (thereby making sense of invention). The relevant unclarity might be located either in the precise target or focus of one's felt evaluations or in their depth as reflexive or non-reflexive.[12] Moreover, insofar as such patterns of felt evaluations partly constitute import itself, indeterminacy in what those felt evaluations are is, in part, indeterminacy in that import. Consequently, processes of self-interpretation can help determine both which object has import to one and the kind of import at issue – whether one cares about or values it.

This needs to be spelled out in more detail. In doing so I shall consider two examples, one (in §7.3.1) concerning indeterminacy in the focus of the relevant felt evaluations, and the other (in §7.3.2) concerning indeterminacy in their depth. Nonetheless, it should be clear in advance that, although I shall discuss elements of both invention and discovery, the notion of discovery (of what we were feeling all along) at issue here falls short of the kind of discovery necessary for an account of deliberation about value, for the latter requires discovering not merely what I now value but what I should value. I shall return to this richer, more interesting notion of discovery in §7.4.

7.3.1 Indeterminacy in focus

Consider first an example of indeterminacy in the focus of one's felt evaluations. Ed finds himself increasingly interested in and excited about

---

[12] As I shall argue in §7.4, this unclarity in one's feelings need not be there in advance but can emerge out of self-interpretation in the process of elucidating the relevant concepts.

going to volunteer every weekend at a local homeless shelter but is puzzled as to the source of his excitement for this: is it a newfound concern for helping others, or is it a growing love for Lisa, one of the other volunteers? The question here is not about the target of his excitement; I have already specified that in saying that he is excited about going to volunteer. Rather, the question is about the focus of his emotion: he is wondering about the background object the import of which makes this intelligible as something to get excited about. Insofar as rationality is a canon of interpretation for the mental, answering this question requires identifying the projectible, rational pattern of other felt evaluations with the same focus, a pattern to which his present excitement is beholden as a necessary condition of its warrant.

Determining the focus of his excitement, then, depends in part on what felt evaluations Ed has had in the past. On the one hand, has his past excitement been a kind of hopefulness that has become disappointment when Lisa has not shown up? If he did feel bad in these circumstances, that would suggest that the focus is Lisa. (It might be, however, that he felt bad in these cases for other reasons, and it was just coincidence that those were the times she did not show up; that would undermine this suggestion.) On the other hand, has he felt excited about similar opportunities to help others in contexts in which Lisa is not present? This would suggest that the focus of his excitement is helping others. (Again, however, we can ask about whether the presence or absence of excitement in these other cases can be explained away by other factors; again, that would undermine this suggestion.) These are further questions for interpretation, and in each case they are questions of exactly what the relevant patterns in his past felt evaluations are and how these patterns are connected to his present excitement.

What is interesting about this case is that Ed's interest, whether it is in Lisa or in volunteering, is only recently beginning to grow, and there may be indeterminacy in how to understand the relevant patterns of rationally connected felt evaluations. Consequently, in trying to answer these questions, Ed himself is in the special position of being able, to a certain extent, to invent himself through self-interpretation. To arrive at a single understanding of himself and what has import for him requires making interpretive decisions whose effect is to delineate patterns of felt evaluations where antecedently there were no clear lines to be drawn. Such decisions will therefore change his understanding not only of his current excitement but also of his past felt evaluations. What is important here is that these patterns commit him to feeling subsequent felt evaluations with the same focus, thereby imposing rational pressure in order to sustain the projectibility of the patterns. By making these interpretive decisions and delineating these patterns more precisely, Ed is not only making the pattern in his past felt evaluations more determinate; he is also instituting rational commitments that shape the future course of his felt evaluations, thus providing a new direction to his sensitivity to import as a whole.

Of course, Ed cannot just make any old interpretive decision about what his felt evaluations are, have been, and so should be, and have that be the last word. Self-interpretation like any interpretation must be constrained by its object; as Taylor says, the articulation of import must "be faithful" to something, and we can now understand this "something" to be in part the projectible, rational patterns in one's felt evaluations generally. By being held accountable to these patterns, such articulation of import runs the risk of getting it wrong. It may be that the subsequent felt evaluations one feels are not consistent with the patterns of felt evaluations one has delineated in self-interpretation, and this failure of the pattern to project into the future indicates that one's interpretation is inadequate.[13] In this way, successful interpretation is intelligible as a kind of *discovery* of what has import to one.[14]

---

[13] One way, but not the only way, one might have gone wrong here is through self-deception. Consider, for example, Dickens' *A Christmas Carol*, when Scrooge first meets the ghost of Marley:

> "You don't believe in me," observed the Ghost.
> "I don't," said Scrooge.
> "What evidence would you have of my reality beyond that of your senses?"
> "I don't know," said Scrooge.
> "Why do you doubt your senses?"
> "Because," said Scrooge, "a little thing affects them. A slight disorder of the stomach makes them cheats. You may be an undigested bit of beef, a blot of mustard, a crumb of cheese, a fragment of an underdone potato. There's more of gravy than of grave about you, whatever you are!"
>
> Scrooge was not much in the habit of cracking jokes, nor did he feel, in his heart, by any means waggish then. The truth is, that he tried to be smart, as a means of distracting his own attention, and keeping down his terror; for the spectre's voice disturbed the very marrow in his bones.

Here, in an attempt to reinterpret the terror he feels, Scrooge tries to reinterpret his experience as the effect of "an undigested bit of beef" – as an upset stomach – rather than as terror in the face of what his life has become. This attempt at reinterpretation, however, fails in the light of the shape his subsequent experiences take, revealing it as a bit of self-deception.

[14] One might object that because such "discovery" is merely a matter of coherence, it is

Nonetheless, it is not true, in cases in which one's subsequent felt evaluations are consistent with the pattern as one interprets it to be, that one has merely discovered the pattern that was there all along, for that would be to ignore the rational interconnections among felt evaluations and evaluative judgments and so the ways in which making self-interpretative judgments can shape one's subsequent felt evaluations. We should not conceive of the role of judgment as one of offering up an interpretation, as something like a prediction that can be shown to be right or wrong as one's subsequent felt evaluations take their course. For, first, having made the decision to interpret oneself one way, one has thereby undertaken a commitment to import, and there may be considerable work both in casting about to reinterpret apparently anomalous felt evaluations one comes to have in a way that is consistent with the interpretation, and in exerting effort on behalf of one's judgment so as to get one's felt evaluations to conform. Second, and more important, self-interpretation aims at understanding not merely the past pattern of one's felt evaluations, but also, through them, the imports things have for one. To make good sense through self-interpretation of the past pattern of one's felt evaluations, thereby making them intelligible as rational in a way that, given the initial indeterminacy, was not available antecedently, is to have evidence for both the truth of that interpretation and so of the attendant understanding of import.

This means that self-interpretation can impose rational pressure on one's subsequent felt evaluations to conform, and this rational pressure is, so to speak, internal to one's felt evaluations as a continuation of the patterns one has felt all along. In this way, the rational pressure applied on subsequent felt evaluations through self-interpretation differs from that discussed in §§6.3–6.4, for there the rational pressure was applied from outside one's felt evaluations, the result of evaluative judgments one arrives at through deliberation and inference. Indeed, this notion of the role of self-interpretation in controlling our felt evaluations helps fill out the sense in which evaluative judgments are active assents to import.

not a very interesting notion of discovery and therefore cannot be that which underlies our deliberation about import. This is right, as I already acknowledged (p. 215): we need to be able to articulate a conception of how a change in import can be an improvement even when it results in no net increase (or even a net decrease) in coherence. I shall address this issue in §7.4 by arguing that the articulation of import must be accountable not only to the rational patterns in one's emotions but also to a correct elucidation of the relevant evaluative concepts in terms of which such improvement is intelligible.

Of course, in practice there will be no sharp boundary between these two kinds of rational pressure. Nonetheless, when this pressure is successful, it institutes a new evaluative perspective that can properly be understood as a kind of *invention*, for, antecedent to the interpretive judgment, there was no clear fact of the matter about what the focus of one's felt evaluations was.

It should be clear that the rational pressure one applies on one's subsequent felt evaluations as the result of self-interpretation is defeasible. One's subsequent felt evaluations may be stubbornly recalcitrant and, precisely because of this recalcitrance, reveal the self-interpretation to be inadequate; indeed, it is precisely this fact that makes intelligible the element of discovery. Nonetheless, given the antecedent indeterminacy in the patterns of one's felt evaluations, such discovery is not possible apart from the element of invention that resolves that indeterminacy by delineating these patterns more precisely. Consequently, invention and discovery are both possible here because of the mutual readjustments felt evaluation and interpretive judgment must make by way of each being responsive to rational pressure from the other.

7.3.2 Indeterminacy in depth

Consider now another example, one in which the indeterminacy involved lies with whether one's felt evaluations are non-reflexive or reflexive. Thus, imagine Fran, a mother who, having decided that she wants to resume her career now that her children are in secondary school, has recently gone back to work full time and is consequently faced with a readjustment of her relationships with her husband and children. As her commitments at work begin to encroach on her previous commitments to her family, she begins to feel bad about missing important events in their lives. In part, the questions she faces in feeling this way concern whether the relevant felt evaluations are non-reflexive like frustration or disappointment, or reflexive like shame or guilt: is her absence at these family events merely an unfortunate consequence of conflicting cares and concerns, or is it, more deeply, a failure to be the kind of person to which she aspires? In this case neither the target of her felt evaluations (her missing important events in the lives of her family) nor their foci (her family and her work) are in question; rather it is the depth of the felt evaluations themselves and so whether the relevant import is that of caring or valuing.

As before, this question must be answered in large part in terms of the broader, rational pattern of other felt evaluations into which this negative emotion fits. Does Fran, for example, feel mere satisfaction or a deeper self-approbation when she is there for her family? If she has to leave work and is rushing to get to her son's school play in time, does she feel fear or hope turning into relief or satisfaction? Or, rather, does she feel anxiety or self-assurance turning into self-affirming relief or self-approbation? These questions may not yet have determinate answers, insofar as there may not yet be a clear pattern of rationally connected felt evaluations to resolve the matter one way or the other, and hence no antecedent fact of the matter about the depth of import here. In the face of this indeterminacy, as revealed by self-interpretation, Fran may decide to delineate the relevant patterns in terms of non-reflexive rather than reflexive felt evaluations: although she cares about missing these important events in her children's lives, her bad feelings are merely the effects of a regrettable conflict given her circumstances rather than a failing of herself as a person.

Once again, this decision is a matter of simultaneous invention and discovery. It is a discovery insofar as the evaluative judgment it involves is one that must be held accountable to the subsequent felt evaluations Fran comes to have, and so the resulting rational patterns that constitute the import things have for her. It is an invention insofar as, by making this judgment, Fran is coming to articulate more clearly the kind of import at issue in her felt evaluations, for to do this is to shape the broader rational patterns in these felt evaluations by resolving antecedent indeterminacies and thereby to commit herself to (and exert rational pressure on) her subsequent felt evaluations, which are beholden to these patterns. It is only out of these mutual readjustments of felt evaluation and evaluative judgment, each rationally accountable to the other, that a single evaluative perspective and the import it constitutes can be simultaneously invented and discovered.

Consequently, an articulation of import by self-interpretation can be faithful to the patterns in one's felt evaluations only because these patterns are rationally structured; insofar as interpretation is to be possible at all, it cannot be interpretation of what Taylor calls one's "unstructured sense" of import. Moreover, it is also only because of this structure of rationality in felt evaluation that we can understand how self-interpretive judgments are able to shape the subsequent course of feeling: by articulating in judgment the patterns in one's felt evaluations, one

220

thereby delineates more precisely what those patterns actually are; since one's felt evaluations are beholden to this pattern, this delineation of past patterns *ipso facto* imposes rational pressure on one's subsequent felt evaluations to conform.

7.4 DELIBERATION AND RATIONAL IMPROVEMENT OF IMPORT

This account of the way in which self-interpretation can shape the patterns of our felt evaluations and so what has import to us is not by itself an account of how we can reason about value. For, according to my account so far, self-interpretation enables us to identify and resolve indeterminacies in what has import to us simply by achieving increased coherence in the rational patterns of felt evaluations and evaluative judgments. The trouble is, there may always be multiple ways to do this, and only some may count as an improvement. Yet nothing has been said about the standards according to which such a change is intelligible as an improvement, and so the account of the discovery of import as it stands is inadequate for solving the deliberative problem. Moreover, the discussion so far can seem quite limited by focusing merely on how to resolve antecedent indeterminacy in the import things have to us, for deliberation about import can obviously proceed even when there is no current indeterminacy. My aim in this section, therefore, is to overcome these limitations by expanding the account of simultaneous autonomous invention and rational discovery from §7.3 to include deliberation proper so as to achieve an account of the invention and discovery of import that underwrites a conception of ourselves as able freely, but nonetheless rationally (and so defensibly and non-arbitrarily), to decide what shape our lives should take.

Justification in general is a conceptual affair. Even if all I do to justify something is to point, my pointing succeeds as a justification only if you thereby come to see things in a particular way, through the application in perception of particular concepts. The justification of a certain evaluative perspective, which includes an understanding not only of what things have value, but also of the priorities among these values, therefore, must proceed in light of certain evaluative concepts. Part of the question as we deliberate in search of a justification for such an evaluative perspective must concern what evaluative concepts are most relevant and how to apply them.

One way to justify the application of certain concepts is by *elucidating*

221

them: by articulating their rational, inferential connections within a broader nexus of concepts in such a way as to make good sense of their subject matter and so of our experiences of and responses to that subject matter.[15] Such an elucidation need not involve an *analysis*, that is an articulation in other vocabulary of precisely the role a particular concept has in our inferential economy. Nonetheless, it does require being able to say in particular cases both why the concept applies and what inferences it licenses. Doing so may reveal inconsistencies or confusions in our understanding of particular concepts, and part of the task of elucidating concepts is to refine this understanding or even, in extreme cases, to come to see a concept as untenable and so as one we should reject. In the case at hand, such a refinement will be a refinement not only of our intellectual understanding of import, but also, insofar as our felt evaluations are informed by these concepts (cf. §5.3), of our entire evaluative perspective and therefore of the import this evaluative perspective constitutes. The question is: how in detail does this elucidation work, and what is the source of the standards of refinement at issue?

So far, this is just a reworking of the deliberative problem, and the familiar problems of simultaneous invention and discovery and of the risk of vicious circularity remain. Nonetheless, we are now in a position to see how the elucidation of evaluative concepts in the context of self-interpretation can help us overcome these problems and so achieve a conception of how the justification of an evaluative perspective as an improvement over its alternatives is possible. I shall proceed by presenting two examples, one of the justification of a particular value (in §7.4.1) and the other of the justification of priorities (in §7.4.2).

7.4.1 Justifying value

Assume that George has been brought up in a culture in which men are expected to be strong and dominant, especially in their relationships with women. Consequently, by virtue of the patterns he displays in his reflexive felt evaluations and evaluative judgments, he comes to value and so identify himself with a certain machismo. Thus, he is shamed by any display of weakness of his own or even of his friends, proud of

---

[15] Cf. John McDowell's "Projection and Truth in Ethics," in Darwall, Gibbard, and Railton, eds., *Moral Discourse and Practice*, pp. 215–25, at p. 220; and David Wiggins' "A Sensible Subjectivism?" and "Truth, and Truth as Predicated of Moral Judgments," both in *Needs, Values, Truth*.

himself for standing up for himself and protecting those weaker than himself, and frequently makes such judgments as: "only a wimp would do that!" However, as he tries to convince his younger brother to "be a man," he is forced to justify the value of machismo and finds himself with astonishingly little to say. Although he may have the sense that its value lies in a certain kind of distinctively masculine strength and self-confidence, grounded in honor and virility, exactly what kind of strength, self-confidence, honor, and virility are at issue here, and how do these justify the value of machismo? Here, the elucidation of concepts is a necessary part of justifying that import.

The elucidation of machismo and related concepts must involve, in part, an examination of particular cases and an articulation of what it is about these cases that gives them import. In this context, where it is the value of machismo that is in question, the answer cannot simply be that something has import because it is macho; rather, the answer must partially elucidate the concept of machismo by identifying in other language what makes each particular case be an instance of machismo in a way that manifests its value: as, for example, proper self-respect and courage in the face of harassment or as self-confident virility and social ease in dealing with women. Of course, it may be a non-trivial accomplishment to articulate a case of machismo in one of these ways, perhaps requiring much discussion and argument with others he loves and respects. Moreover, it need not be that the result of articulating in other terms what is macho in a broad range of cases will be an analysis of the concept of machismo, for there may be no systematic convergence of these articulations that we can identify across the whole range of cases except in terms of machismo itself. Thus, for example, there may be no way of articulating what kind of self-respect and courage are proper in the face of harassment without eventually appealing to the concept of machismo. In spite of such circularity, we can nonetheless gain some clarity concerning the concept of machismo by roughly locating its place not only within a rationally interconnected scheme of concepts, for this would provide only a formal understanding of machismo, but also and essentially within the patterns of our felt evaluations.[16]

In the articulation in other terms of particular instances of machismo we can find the beginnings of a justification of the value of machismo,

---

[16] Cf. McDowell's "Projection and Truth in Ethics," p. 220; my claim here is an extension of McDowell's insofar as I require that the elucidation of evaluative concepts like machismo requires locating it also within a pattern of felt evaluations.

for such an articulation reveals non-contingent overlap between the concept of machismo and other concepts whose value is not now in question, such as strength, honor, or virility. For, by revealing overlaps among these concepts, one is also, because of the way in which felt evaluations are conceptually informed, thereby revealing overlaps among the various patterns of felt evaluations one has. Thus, if an instance of machismo is so because it is the manifestation of honor of a certain sort, where honor is itself the focus of a pattern of felt evaluations (and evaluative judgments), we can understand and so justify the value of at least this instance of machismo in terms of the value of honor. Nonetheless, insofar as the concept of machismo is not analyzable in terms of these other concepts of strength, honor, virility, etc., the appeal to these other concepts must fall short of a justification of the value of machismo itself, even though they may serve to justify the value of particular instances of machismo.

Of course, the value of strength, honor, virility, etc. can themselves be questioned: the deliberative problem is hard in part because in principle any value can be questioned and so stand in need of justification. Indeed, the initial questioning of the value of machismo may ramify widely throughout other things one values precisely because of the way in which the concept of machismo gets elucidated. Nonetheless, it cannot ramify too widely lest we lose entirely the necessary background of value against which alone deliberation is possible. As the image of Neurath's boat being rebuilt at sea suggests, we need at least a temporary foundation upon which to reason, even if that foundation itself can (later) come into question, albeit only from the perspective of another temporary foundation. Deliberation about values is in this way a kind of dialectic, always potentially advancing but never with an absolutely secure foundation in values we accept essentially without question.[17]

There is more to an elucidation of the concept of machismo than simply the articulation of what it is about particular cases that makes

---

[17] *Pace* Adrian Piper, who claims that at least part of what is required for valuing something is that the reasons one appeals to in making the relevant evaluative judgment be reasons one accepts without question. This means, she thinks, that there must be "terminating criteria" for deciding which reasons are good ones, criteria that cannot themselves be called into question. (See her "Two Conceptions of the Self," *Philosophical Studies*, 48 [1985], pp. 173–97.) However, it is not clear exactly what such terminating criteria could be for value judgments, and Piper's appeal to mere dispositions in this context is unworkable: dispositions on their own cannot ground reasons unless the dispositions themselves are antecedently intelligible as rational. (This is essentially the same criticism I offered in §7.1.1 of cognitivist accounts of value.)

them be cases of machismo. For concepts are identified and individuated also by the inferences their application licenses. For example, we might think, if someone or some action is macho, it follows that it is admirable in men (but not women), and that its opposite, a kind of wimpishness, is worthy of disdain. (Notice that what is at issue here is not merely the inferences an application of the concept of machismo licenses, but also the felt evaluations to which those inferences commit one. I shall return to this point below.) This means, in part, that a specification of what it is about a particular case that makes an action or person be macho, as, say, a particular kind of honor, virility, self-confidence, etc., must make clear how these inferences are warranted. The reverse is also true: precisely which inferences a concept ought to license depends, in part, on the sense we have of how that concept applies to particular cases and of the way in which it overlaps other concepts in such cases. This means that our understanding of a concept may seem to be pulled in different directions by (a) our sense of how the concept applies to particular cases, (b) an articulation of those features of such cases that warrant the application of the concept, and (c) the inferences that application licenses. Consequently, the attempt to elucidate a concept like machismo can reveal hitherto unnoticed complexity, such as distinctions that until now have not been made or seen as relevant, distinctions which might prove important for the purpose of understanding the value of machismo.

For example, one of George's friends may take a very controlling (though well intentioned) attitude towards women, especially his wife and daughters. Thus, he may try to prevent them from associating with others he disapproves of, shield them from disturbing news, and generally guide their lives in ways he thinks appropriate. All of this is a manifestation of the friend's strength, power, and virility, and he intends it as a way of protecting them from unnecessary harm. Indeed, George has always admired his friend's power and virility as a manifestation of his machismo and has sought to emulate him. Nonetheless, now in the context of an attempt to elucidate the concept of machismo so as to justify its value, George finds himself confronted with the question of the kind of power and virility that machismo involves and so that warrants respect and admiration. This means, in part, that he must clearly distinguish the kind of distinctively masculine exercise of power that both is central to machismo and makes it intelligible as admirable from clearly abusive exercises of power, such as that involved in his boss's underhanded attempts to maintain his superiority over his workers or even that involved in the clearly unjust oppression of slaves. Nonetheless, he recognizes, there is a slippery slope from the exercise of strength and power in order to benefit and protect to such an exercise in order to control and subjugate.

The question now arises for George for the first time as to how much of this slippery slope can be understood as worthy of respect and admiration, and so how to draw the line between genuine and merely apparent cases of machismo. In part, this is a question for self-interpretation, for the question of what warrants respect and admiration in others (or pride and self-approbation in oneself) is, in part, a question of what the rational patterns in his felt evaluations are, insofar as these patterns help define the relevant conditions of warrant. Of course, the question is not what things the current pattern does now find admirable, but rather what the pattern should find admirable: the current pattern can go wrong in ways deliberation aims to discover, and so self-interpretation cannot be the whole answer. Nonetheless, insofar as the standards of discovery here are partially internal to the subject's evaluative perspective, self-interpretation of these patterns will have a role in such deliberation.

Interpretation in this case, however, may not be straightforward insofar as the distinction between appropriate protection of the weak and subjugating control has thus far been blurred in his conception of virility and, therefore, of machismo. Before he raised this question, the focus of his admiration of his friend was simply machismo. Insofar as George would not then have understood the relevance of making a distinction between appropriate and inappropriate exercises of power to determining whether a case was macho or not, the question of whether the kind of exercise of power by his friend is macho or not was for him largely settled by its involving a particular style: a certain masculine swagger and self-confidence. Given the manifest differences on this score between his friend's self-confident, masculine exercise of power and his boss's underhandedness, he would have rejected out of hand any suggestion that the two cases are relevantly similar. Consequently, there was antecedently no indeterminacy in the focus of that admiration or of the broader patterns of felt evaluations of which it is a part.

Now, however, having begun to elucidate the concept of machismo, and so having at least begun in his own mind to see the relevance of carefully delineating appropriate from inappropriate exercises of power

226

(for which the mere appeal to style is inadequate), the question can be pressed. As a result, George has made possible a kind of indeterminacy in his felt evaluations that was not there before: insofar as he did not previously see this distinction as relevant, the past pattern in his felt evaluations underdetermines precisely how much of this slippery slope from protection to oppression is relevant to machismo. He is now faced with an interpretive decision that might enable him to refine his understanding of machismo in new ways, thereby refining his sensitivity in felt evaluation to both machismo and, consequently, its import. Further explanation is needed of how this works.

What reasons can George have for elucidating the concept of machismo one way rather than another? That is, what reasons can he have for drawing the line in one place rather than another between appropriate and inappropriate cases of those exercises of power relevant to machismo? Assume, first, that George is not willing to give up the inferential connection between machismo and respect and admiration: that if something is macho, it is *ipso facto* worthy of respect and admiration. Also assume that George concludes that a particular exercise of power – his friend's attempts to shield his wife from disturbing news – is inappropriate. For, he now comes to think, in spite of his friend's bravado in stark contrast to his boss's lack of self-confidence, the two cases are nonetheless more similar than dissimilar in the relevant respects: each is an overreaction to the fear of losing control and so stems from a cowardly aversion to the risks implicit in trusting others. This conclusion has implications for his understanding of other potential cases of machismo, for he now has come to see bravado and manifest self-confidence as much less central, and courage and protection of honor much more central to machismo than he previously thought.

This is an attempted refinement of his conception of machismo that purports to achieve a better understanding of what is admirable about it. Consequently, it enables George to understand the past pattern of his felt evaluations focused on machismo as involving a degree of confusion. Thus, he may conclude that, although he did not realize it at the time, his felt evaluations focused on machismo were in some cases confused responses to a kind of virility now manifest as cowardly domination or as merely self-serving puffery and bluster. As such, he now concludes, these felt evaluations were unwarranted because they were not properly responsive to what really is macho, even though they seemed at the time to fit into a pattern of felt evaluations focused on machismo and partially

227

constitutive of its import. Moreover, he can now understand his current value of machismo as an improved continuation of the pattern of felt evaluations he felt all along because of its dissociation from such inappropriate exercises of power. As such, he has apparently achieved a new perspective on import that commits him to feel subsequent felt evaluations (and make subsequent evaluative judgments) in accordance with this refined pattern, thereby imposing rational pressure on these felt evaluations to fall in line.

Whether this is the correct way to refine his understanding of machismo depends in part on whether George's felt evaluations end up conforming to his new evaluative judgments. For, as I argued in chapter 5, the pattern in our felt evaluations can correct our evaluative judgments by failing to conform to these judgments insofar as such a failure provides reason to reconsider, because the pattern constitutes a continuing evaluative perspective inconsistent with that provided by judgment. Now we can see that such a correction can amount to a correction of the elucidation of concepts as well, for this alternative, inconsistent evaluative perspective provides reason to reconsider not only the deployment of such evaluative concepts in particular cases, but also the understanding of those concepts that purports to license such a deployment. Indeed, by virtue of the way in which our felt evaluations can correct our evaluative judgments, the sensitivity to import implicit in our felt evaluations can in some cases be revealed as ultimately finer and more discriminating than that made explicit in our earlier evaluative judgments.[18] Consequently, in the face of consistent recalcitrance in his emotions focused on machismo to conform to this new elucidation of the concept, George has reason to reconsider not only the content of those judgments, but also the conception of machismo they involve, potentially forcing further revision of his understanding of machismo. In this way, his newly elucidated understanding of machismo and its import is subject to rational constraint from within the evaluative perspective afforded by his felt evaluations.

As before, however, we should not understand such recalcitrance in his felt evaluations as leaving George with nothing to say on behalf of his judgments and his changed understanding of the relevant concepts; evaluative judgments are not merely beholden to our felt evaluations. Recalcitrance in his felt evaluations may simply be the result of habits of

---

[18] Cf. Martha Nussbaum's "The Stoics on the Extirpation of the Passions," in *The Therapy of Desire*, pp. 359–401, at p. 380.

feeling ingrained in him along with his earlier misunderstanding, and often considerable effort and perseverance is required to overcome this source of irrationality. Through judgment, he can bring these conceptual resources self-consciously to bear on his evaluative perspective so as to articulate his reasons for a refinement of that perspective, and he can thereby impose rational pressure on his felt evaluations to conform. As I argued in §7.3, insofar as his understanding of machismo depends, in part, on the sense it is able to make of his past pattern of felt evaluations focused on machismo, such rational pressure is applied partially from within his felt evaluations. Moreover, through such self-interpretation George can try to explain away apparently anomalous felt evaluations by re-interpreting their target, focus, or depth and in this way reduce or eliminate rational conflicts within his evaluative perspective.

In elucidating the concept of machismo in this way, therefore, George is providing himself with not merely an intellectual understanding, but one that ought to resonate with his felt evaluations. Thus, first, George is not only articulating what it is about particular people or actions that make them macho and so have the import they do, but also thereby identifying ways in which the pattern of felt evaluations and evaluative judgments focused on machismo ought to overlap those focused on these other features. It is, in part, because of such overlap that the articulation of why something is macho can make intelligible its having import: insofar as honor and self-confidence are themselves the focus of projectible, rational patterns of felt evaluations and evaluative judgments, the import such patterns constitute can support the import of machismo to the extent of that overlap, and vice versa. In this way, the import of machismo comes to depend on even those actions focused on one's honor, etc. that do not overlap, for such cases are essential to the evaluative perspective constitutive of the import of one's honor tout court. Moreover, the way in which George articulates the inferential connections between machismo and other concepts, such as that between machismo and merely self-serving and cowardly domination, also ought to show up in the patterns of his felt evaluations given the way these felt evaluations are conceptually informed. Thus, when George comes to see a particular exercise of power as a matter of self-serving domination rather than protection for the benefit of the weak, insofar as his conception of self-serving domination is not evaluatively neutral, it ought to evoke certain negative felt evaluations inconsistent with seeing such an exercise of power as simultaneously worthy of admiration because macho. Indeed, self-serving domination may come to have this negative import precisely because of the role that concept comes to play in opposition to that of machismo as the result of his elucidation of machismo.

This has some important consequences. On the one hand, if George does feel the appropriate negative felt evaluations (such as disdain) as the result of his self-conscious understanding of a situation in terms of cowardly domination or self-serving bluster, especially if this is true of his judgments and felt evaluations focused on cowardly domination or self-serving bluster quite generally, such a resonance of his felt evaluations with his evaluative judgment provides reason to think that both are correct and so that he has reason not to feel admiration at what is now revealed not to be machismo at all. Indeed, as I argued in §5.3 in the example of Cassie, it is precisely this sort of resonance between his evaluative judgments and broader patterns of felt evaluations that makes those judgments intelligible as his considered view, and so the evaluative perspective they help form as genuinely his. (Of course, George may continue to respond to such cases of cowardly domination with admiration and in this way be ambivalent, but it is clear in such a case that the source of irrationality that ambivalence brings is located within the pattern of felt evaluations focused on machismo rather than that focused on domination.) On the other hand, if George does not feel the relevant negative felt evaluations focused on what he identifies in judgment as cowardly domination, especially if this failure of feeling is consistent throughout those cases he also feels to be instances of machismo, such a failure of resonance serves to undermine his judgment and so provide reason to reconsider. With discord of this sort, as not occurring within a range of cases that is isolated relative to his considered view, it becomes unclear what George's understanding of machismo is and so what his reasons for feeling and judging are.

As I argued in chapter 5, a person's evaluative judgments rationally constrain his felt evaluations and are simultaneously rationally constrained by these felt evaluations. What I have now argued is that, by elucidating the relevant concepts in the context of self-interpretation, the resulting mutual readjustments of his conceptual understanding, his judgments, and his felt evaluations can properly be understood as a dialectic, the upshot of which can be not merely a change in the patterns of his felt evaluations and evaluative judgments, but also his coming to have reasons in terms of which such a change can properly be understood as an improvement. Thus, if George is able to achieve the sort of resonance just described between his evaluative judgments and his felt evaluations focused on cowardly domination, he now has reason to have a certain shape to the projectible pattern of felt evaluations focused on machismo, whether or not the pattern he now exhibits actually has that shape. This coming to have reasons for having a certain shape to one's felt evaluations therefore provides what was missing from the account of freedom of the heart in §6.4 and so enables us to make sense of evaluative judgment as able to impose genuinely rational pressure on one's felt evaluations to conform.[19]

Moreover, in light of this elucidation of the concept of machismo and related concepts, George can now explain why his previous tacit understanding of machismo was confused insofar as it failed to make appropriate distinctions between different kinds of exercises of power, and so he can explain why, in light of that confusion, portions of his previous experience of import in felt evaluation were mistaken. Such a dialectic therefore makes intelligible the possibility of the *discovery* of import of a sort that is more robust than that described in §7.3. For it is a discovery both of what really has import to him and of the concepts in terms of which that reality is more properly described. (I say "more properly described" here to indicate that what one has discovered is an improvement of one's concepts and so of one's cares and values, thus leaving open the possibility (or even inevitability) of further refinement and improvement.) Consequently, the appeal to machismo as the object of his understanding (and previous misunderstanding) is an appeal to an *evaluatively thick property:* an evaluative property that both is intelligible as an object of discovery and is therefore that by virtue of which we ought to assess and regulate our evaluative perspective.[20]

At this point, several objections might be raised. First, one might

---

[19] This account of how the achievement in evaluative judgment of a new perspective on import by means of the elucidation of concepts, and the way in which such an achievement can impose this sort of rational pressure on felt evaluation, fills in the final piece of my account of how evaluative judgment involves active assent to import and so is to be distinguished from the passive assent characteristic of felt evaluation.

[20] In this account of the importance of the role of elucidation in deliberation about import, I am indebted to Wiggins' discussion in §9 of "A Sensible Subjectivism?" However, Wiggins does not provide much of an account of the nature of our evaluative attitudes, and consequently his talk of "holding" such an attitude "relatively fixed" is merely metaphorical. In effect, I have tried to spell out this metaphor in terms of the way in which elucidation reveals overlaps and oppositions among the patterns in our felt evaluations and evaluative judgments.

think that this account of the elucidation of evaluative concepts is restricted to merely clarifying concepts the subject already possesses, so that the reasons for valuing she comes to have by virtue of such elucidation are unacceptably relative. For it may be that what she ought to value can only be articulated in terms of concepts she does not possess. In reply, nothing I have said about George's case presupposes that the concepts he elucidates are concepts he already possesses. Trivially, it might be that as the result of conversation with others he comes to learn new concepts the elucidation of which better enables him to achieve the requisite rational coherence among his evaluative judgments and felt evaluations. More interesting, however, is the possibility that successive refinement of existing concepts can enable George to reveal and over-come misunderstandings that were not merely the result of failing to grasp a concept everyone else understood all along. Indeed, as the process of refining his concept of machismo continues, it might no longer be clear what is left of the original concept of machismo, and the result may be a new concept: not merely new to George, but new for anyone. Thus, the account of deliberation about values I have given is not relative in this way to one's current concepts.

Second, one might object that this account of how to deliberate about import is merely a matter of attaining internal coherence among our felt evaluations and evaluative judgments and so presents an account of discovery that is no better off than that of the non-cognitivist. For, it might seem, non-cognitivists can avail themselves of all this talk of the elucidation of concepts and of the rational conflicts between emotions and judgments, even the quite complicated sort I have discussed. How, therefore, does my account of discovery avoid the criticisms offered of non-cognitivism in §7.1.2?

Part of what I have claimed in this account of the discovery of evaluatively thick properties is that they are potential objects of experi-ence, about which we can be right or wrong in a way not intelligible for non-cognitivism: it is these properties themselves, I claim, that are the standards of warrant for our felt evaluations and evaluative judgments. (Such a claim is not one non-cognitivists can make given their assertion of the rational and ontological priority of our conations over the values things have.) Part of what legitimizes this understanding of the discovery of evaluatively thick properties (as opposed to the mere attainment of internal coherence) is that we can make sense, on my account, of how the discovery of import can result in an overall decrease in rational coherence, even in the long run. Thus, assume that, before George began to elucidate the concept of machismo, his evaluative judgments and felt evaluations focused on machismo for the most part cohere together and mutually reinforce one another. After that elucidation, however, George continues to have felt evaluations focused on machismo in cases (of cowardly domination, say) that he now recognizes not to have the import machismo has. These recalcitrant felt evaluations, though isolated by his broader understanding of import, decrease the overall coherence of his evaluative perspective. Indeed, insofar as these felt evaluations may be the result of deeply ingrained habits of response of which he may be unable entirely to rid himself, that decrease in coherence may be permanent. Part of the question, therefore, is how we can understand this sort of change in his evaluative judgments and (some of) his felt evaluations to be rationally justified even when it results in an overall decrease in coherence.

A non-cognitivist might try to make sense of this by appealing to the idea that some kinds of rational coherence or incoherence are more important than others: it is more important in this case for George to maintain the coherence of his evaluative judgments (and so of a particular way of elucidating machismo) with his felt evaluations focused on cowardly domination than with those focused on machismo, and it is that greater importance that makes intelligible why the resulting increase in the number of overall instances of rational conflict nonetheless can be rationally required. Yet, how do we draw the line here between those kinds of coherence or incoherence that are more important and those that are less? The answer can only be that the rational conflicts that are less important are those that stem from confusion or misunderstanding of what really is macho – of the evaluatively thick property that defines the standards of warrant for this pattern of felt evaluations; indeed, this is precisely what gets revealed through George's elucidation of the relevant concepts. For, having elucidated these concepts, he is now able to give reasons for why his former understanding of machismo was confused and so for why the recalcitrant felt evaluations ought to change, even if he finds himself unable to change them: because they are not properly responsive to what is really macho. That is, the only way to identify when a change in one's overall evaluative perspective that results in a decrease in coherence is rationally required is by appeal to evaluatively thick properties. To presuppose, as the non-cognitivist does, that the evaluative properties things have are ontologically and rationally posterior to our conations, perhaps as shaped by conversational pressures, is to rule out the possibility of such properties as evaluatively thick: as that by which we are to regulate our evaluative responses in terms of their warrant.

So far I have argued for a way of making sense of evaluatively thick properties as potential objects of discovery by means of a certain dialectical process of deliberation. Of course, as I have argued, these evaluatively thick properties cannot be understood as ontologically and rationally prior to our evaluative perspective, for they are intelligible only as constituted by such an evaluative perspective; the idea of discovery articulated here does not require the cognitivist conception of discovery whereby the object of discovery must be wholly independent of the particular evaluative perspective of the subject. In order to solve the deliberative problem, however, we need to understand not only how rational discovery of value is possible, but also and simultaneously how value can be the object of autonomous invention such that we can have a say in what values it is worth our having and so the kind of person it is worth our being. At this point, a third source of objection might seem to arise: how is an account of autonomous invention compatible with this account of evaluatively thick properties?

The answer lies in the way in which evaluatively thick properties depend on our evaluative perspectives as perspectivally subjective, a dependence which provides a foothold for understanding the role of autonomous invention in the very process of coming to discover these evaluatively thick properties. As I have argued, George's elucidation of the concept of machismo is successful only to the extent that it enables him through self-interpretation to make good sense not only of the past patterns of his felt evaluations but also of the way in which these patterns project into the future. However, the very questioning that leads to the elucidation of concepts, I argued, creates indeterminacy in the pattern of felt evaluations he feels. The element of autonomous invention therefore enters first in the process of self-interpretation, which essentially involves making decisions that resolve this indeterminacy by delineating these patterns in new ways. Such delineation in the case of George's pattern of felt evaluations focused on machismo is a matter of refining his concept of machismo, and such refinement may require all of his originality and imagination to extend or restrict the concept by articulating both its inferential connections to other concepts and how it applies in particular cases.

234

Of course, we cannot simply elucidate these concepts any way we please, for they must remain true to our experience of import in felt evaluation, which has the potential to correct our evaluative judgments and the conceptual elucidations we provide. Nonetheless, our autonomy has a role here as well insofar as, in the face of recalcitrant felt evaluations, we can actively shape our felt evaluations by exerting rational pressure on behalf of our evaluative judgments and our understanding of the relevant concepts so as to get them to fall in line – in short, by exercising freedom of the heart. Indeed, we can now see that freedom of the heart is really one aspect of our autonomy. When an exercise of such rational pressure is successful, both in creating a new understanding of the relevant concepts and in exercising control over one's evaluative perspective, one has thereby had a say not only in how it is appropriate to refine one's sensitivity to import, but also in what the evaluatively thick properties are that this sensitivity as thus refined enables one to discover. It is precisely in this way that we can make sense of George as *autonomous* and so as having a say in what these evaluatively thick properties are.

At this point, the third objection can be stated more precisely. Concepts are potentially public matters: others can come to share the concepts George has a say in elucidating, and by sharing them offer criticisms not only of these concepts, but also of the evaluative perspective he comes to adopt as a result. In this way, disputes about evaluative concepts are also simultaneously disputes about the evaluatively thick properties there are, and vice versa. This means, the objection continues, that, once we get the evaluative concepts right, there is a single evaluative perspective on the world that everyone should adopt; this, however, makes unintelligible the idea of autonomy – that each of us can have a say in the kind of person it is worth our being. So, it might seem, insofar as my account enables us to make sense of the discovery of values, that account is, like the cognitivist's, unable to offer a satisfactory account of autonomy and therefore fails to escape the paradox of simultaneous invention and discovery.

I can concede, as the objection suggests, that some evaluative concepts, such as those articulating moral values, are *universally valid* in the sense that the standards for correctly understanding and applying such concepts in both denotation and inference are independent of any particular person's evaluative perspective. Thus if, as we might think, the moral concept of oppression is universally valid, it provides a constraint on how anyone can properly understand machismo in a way that manifests its value. Assume, contrary to the case described above, that George had understood any sufficiently swaggering exercise of power to be macho no matter what its effects on those subject to that power. Such an understanding of machismo would be defective in ways we can point out in terms of the concept of oppression, and this defect is one that George himself ought to recognize, given the universal validity of the concept of oppression.

The objection, however, ignores two ways in which the relevant evaluatively thick properties, like machismo, are perspectivally subjective. First, such moral constraints on how it is permissible to understand machismo or other evaluative concepts does not exhaust their content: not all perspectivally subjective concepts need be universally valid. Rather, we can make sense of evaluative concepts that are *subjectively valid* in terms of the account just given: the standards by which we can criticize concepts expressive of personal values emerge out of the kind of dialectic just described in which one elucidates these concepts from within one's own evaluative sensibilities, in part, by means of self-interpretation. Indeed, if we continue to assume that moral concepts are universally valid, this distinction between universal and subjective validity helps make sense of the intuitive distinction I have appealed to between moral and personal values.[21]

Second, there is some room for disagreement even among reasonable people about how to elucidate the concept of oppression and apply it to particular cases: there is no sharp line between morally permissible and impermissible exercises of control over another, even though there are many clear cases on either side. It is in terms of the possibility of such clear cases that the concept of oppression can properly be understood as universally valid. Nonetheless, in the borderline cases, where there is no clear fact of the matter whether something is or is not an instance of oppression, we must each depend on our evaluative sensibilities to help us make sense of such cases, and there can be room for autonomy here as well. Indeed, for this reason the borderline between universally valid concepts and subjectively valid concepts is itself not sharp. (This leaves open the possibility that the line between moral and personal values is not particularly sharp in a way that figures into an Aristotelian concep-

---

[21] Precisely how we are to make sense of the relevant standards of universal validity is not something I can address here, which is why I am limiting my discussion primarily to personal values. I shall, however, briefly discuss how my account of personal values can be extended to accommodate moral values in chapter 8.

tion of virtue. Nonetheless, all my argument requires is that there be clear cases of subjectively valid evaluative concepts, such as that of machismo.)

Nonetheless, that a concept is subjectively valid does not mean that it is valid only for a particular individual or that how this individual understands the concept simply determines its content. For even concepts that are subjectively valid are shareable and so are potentially open to criticism. Given the subjective validity of these concepts, however, such criticism can take place only from within the relevant evaluative perspective. To see this, consider the following analogy. A native Japanese speaker will say that the color of both a clear sky and tree leaves is *aoi*. I cannot, however, offer a valid criticism of her concept of *aoi* by insisting that the sky and leaves are clearly of different colors, for, given the system of color concepts and perspective on the world they provide, she can rightly point out that I am simply blind to the similarity in their color she articulates with the concept of *aoi*, a blindness she can remedy in part by teaching me the relevant system of concepts and so to see colors from her perspective.

Likewise, to those who criticize his concept of machismo without making any real attempt to understand his evaluative perspective and the patterns of felt evaluations that inform it, George can respond that they are blind to the import this evaluative perspective reveals, a blindness that, given the role values have in constituting his identity, is, in part, a failure to understand him. What justifies such a response is the way in which the standards for correct elucidation of subjectively valid evaluative concepts depend essentially on the sense these concepts as thus elucidated are able to make of the subject's patterns of felt evaluations (once these felt evaluations are appropriately informed by these concepts). Remedying a critic's blindness requires, in part, training her to see things from this perspective and so at least to understand, if not actually to have, the patterns of felt evaluations George does. Such a sympathetic critic can therefore work with George as he deliberates, offering alternative interpretations of his patterns of felt evaluations in light of alternative ways of elucidating the relevant concepts, potentially getting him to see that such alternatives are improvements. Nonetheless, the responsibility for the conclusion of such deliberation, and so for the evaluatively thick properties that emerge, lies with George, insofar as self-interpretation and the active attempts to control his felt evaluations, attempts which self-interpretation both presupposes and makes possible, are fundamental to such deliberation. Consequently, that the conclusions of deliberation about value and the resulting elucidations of evaluative concepts are open to criticism from others does not undermine our autonomy in the way the objection suggests.

In short, deliberation about values requires the mutual adjustments to each other of our felt evaluations, our evaluative judgments, and our understanding of the relevant evaluative concepts. Thus, on the one hand, deliberation can have two kinds of effects on our patterns of felt evaluations, and so on import. First, by elucidating our concepts so as to understand what has import and why, we can reveal relevant complexities in our concepts to which we were not previously attuned. Such complexities may well give rise to an indeterminacy in the focus of the relevant patterns of felt evaluations, an indeterminacy that was not antecedently there and that makes possible a refinement of these patterns of felt evaluation and so of the imports things have for us. Second, we can deploy these newly elucidated concepts in deciding how to resolve the resulting indeterminacy. Such a decision, in turn, institutes a new pattern of commitments that rationally constrains our future felt evaluations. It is in part because of the elucidation and deployment of concepts that this process of shaping our felt evaluations is properly understood as deliberation.

On the other hand, in each of these stages we are involved, in part, in self-interpretation in an attempt to understand ourselves and what has import to us. Consequently, the way in which we elucidate evaluative concepts and deploy them, both in creating indeterminacy and in arriving at decisions about how to resolve it, must ultimately be answerable to how much sense this elucidation is able to make of import and our felt evaluations in response to import. Insofar as our felt evaluations do not cohere with the pattern of commitments as we have understood it, we have reason to rethink this understanding and so the relevant elucidation of concepts. It is for this reason that it is proper to understand such deliberation as being partially from within our evaluative sensibilities.

This account of how deliberation about value is possible is, therefore, circular, but not viciously so. For such a circle is vicious only if we assume that either the values things have or our evaluative perspective is ontologically and rationally prior to the other. Having rejected such priority, the circularity inherent in my account of deliberation about values, therefore, is the inoffensive, non-vicious circularity of a dialectic, such that genuine improvement (and not merely the attainment of internal coherence) is possible without stepping outside the very evaluative perspective that is thereby at issue. What was missing from Wiggins', McDowell's, and Taylor's discussions, and what I have now provided, is the sort of explicit account of the precise nature of the interconnections between evaluatively thick properties and our evaluative perspective that makes such a rejection of priorities intelligible.[22] By virtue of this rejection of ontological and rational priority, it would be misleading to understand evaluatively thick properties as objects of either discovery or invention insofar as the notions of invention and discovery in their ordinary usage imply such priority one way or the other. Nonetheless, as I have argued, this account maintains the intuitions behind these notions of the invention and discovery of value by providing an account of evaluatively thick properties both as that by which we ought to regulate our evaluations, and as simultaneously shaped by exercises of our autonomy. Consequently, we might say in light of this rejection of priority, evaluatively thick properties are *disclosed* by such a process of deliberation. The apparent paradox of simultaneous invention and discovery is thereby dissolved.

7.4.2 Justifying priorities

This account of how we can deliberate about values can be readily extended to handle cases of deliberation about priorities. Priorities, recall, are reflexive preferences – preferences we value, and so the having of which is a component in the kind of life we find worth living. We can, therefore, think of deliberation about priorities as a special case of deliberation about values, such that the value in question is our having not a certain care but a certain preference. The task, therefore, is to achieve a proper elucidation of certain evaluative concepts in terms of which we can justify why we ought to value a certain preference – why, for example, a contrary preference would be shamefully petty or ignoble. Of course, as I argued in §7.4.1, such an elucidation in turn depends on the way in which these concepts as elucidated enable us to make sense of

---

[22] Indeed, this explicit account of the nature of felt evaluations can also make sense of McDowell's claim that these evaluatively thick properties are the objects of perception, a claim for which he has been widely criticized. (See, e.g., Simon Blackburn's "How to be an Ethical Antirealist," *Midwest Studies in Philosophy*, 12 [1988], pp . 361–75.) For such evaluative properties are a kind of import and as such are intelligible, in light of our overall evaluative commitments, as impressing themselves on us in felt evaluation.

our evaluative perspective quite generally and so the rational patterns in our reflexive felt evaluations and evaluative judgments. Consequently, deliberation about values is, in general, possible in virtue of the three-way rational interconnections among our felt evaluations, our evaluative judgments, and the concepts that inform each. Nonetheless, when what we value is having certain preferences, the relevant rational interconnections must include as well those defining the dampening relations among felt evaluations.

Once again, an example will help clarify this account. Consider a somewhat modified version of the cases of Martin from §6.4 and Fran from §7.3.2. This time, however, imagine that Harry has been with a philanthropic organization for many years, gradually moving up in the hierarchy and so gaining increasing responsibility. The organization has treated him well, and he has become a loyal employee – and indeed prides himself on his loyalty. Now, however, he is offered yet another promotion that will require him to spend even longer hours at work and to go on frequent business trips, often for weeks at a time. Already faced with some tension at home over how much he is working, Harry comes to see his acceptance or rejection of this promotion as a question of where his priorities really lie: with his career, as a career that involves doing good, or with his family. How can he justify his decision one way rather than another?

Part of what makes this decision difficult for Harry is his ambivalence: although he is convinced of the importance of his work and so is excited by the opportunities the promotion presents, he also feels some concern and hesitation about the effects accepting the promotion would have on the rest of his life, a concern which dampens his enthusiasm. After some consideration, however, he finds himself inclined to accept the promotion, and he articulates his reason this way: to refuse it would be selfish, putting his own private interests ahead of the greater good – the work of the philanthropic organization. Nonetheless, his understanding of his reasons here does not change his initial ambivalence, and he remains concerned about losing touch with his family. As he imagines what his life would be like if he accepts the promotion, with long days at work and business trips preventing him from having more than minimal contact with his children and from being present during important events in their lives, he comes to feel a kind of regretful loss outweighing his pride in his work. (Of course, there are risks involved in using imagination, for imagination can be unreliable for many reasons. Yet, by using imagination in this way, one can come to have a sense of one's broader evaluative perspective that includes one's felt evaluations without already having made the choice. I shall therefore make the idealizing assumption that Harry's imagination is perfect; nonetheless, the example could easily be rewritten so that he does accept the promotion and actually feels these emotions, potentially resulting in his deciding to look for a less demanding job.)

In the face of this recalcitrance in his felt evaluations, Harry tries to exercise freedom of the heart, telling himself that he should not feel this way, that to do so is to fail properly to appreciate the relative importance of doing good for others in a way that manifests a broader selfishness on his part. So, as he imagines his life, he focuses his attention on the good of his work even as doing that work takes him away from his family. He imagines, for example, that he is about to embark on an important business trip, a trip that ultimately proves successful, and so tries to get himself to feel the enthusiasm, anticipatory excitement, and subsequent pride this ought to bring. Yet he finds that his regret, his sense of loss, is still undiminished, undampened by these judgments of priorities; to the contrary he finds his enthusiasm, excitement, and pride to be weaker than he thinks they ought to be. Thus, the sense of priorities implicit in the dampening relations among his felt evaluations seems consistently to conflict with the evaluative perspective he makes explicit in judgment, making it rational for him to rethink his priorities.

In trying to reassess why he thinks refusing the promotion would be shamefully selfish, he begins to think of various social and political activists whom he has admired for not being selfish, such as Gandhi and Mother Theresa. Yet he also finds himself thinking about his mother: that her devotion to family is admirable in a similar way for her giving so much of herself to others, even if her devotion is deeply personal. He comes to realize that what is shameful about selfishness should not be characterized, as he now realizes he has until now implicitly thought, simply in terms of undue concern with matters that are private in the sense that they are personal as opposed to public; rather, at least in some cases, even the most personal, intimate concerns – such as those for his loved ones – can be admirable. He thus comes to distinguish two ways of describing what might be admirable counterparts to selfishness: *selflessness*, which involves concerns that are public and impersonal, and *unselfishness*, which involves concerns for others, even when this concern is intensely personal.

The distinction Harry makes here between selflessness and unselfishness is not simply a matter of carefully defining these ordinary English words, and so we need not think Harry is confused in a way that can be cleared up simply by consulting a dictionary. Rather, what is at issue is the proper understanding of how to make out a contrast with selfishness in such a way that this contrast is valuable and so a proper part of the kind of life it is worth his living; this is what I mean in speaking of the "admirable counterpart to selfishness." Although Harry had implicitly understood this admirable counterpart to selfishness to be (what he can now articulate as) selflessness, given this distinction, he can now ask which is the proper object of his admiration. Insofar as this question has not yet been settled, it may be indeterminate how best to understand the foci of his patterns of felt evaluations and the dampening relations among them; resolving such indeterminacy therefore calls for self-interpretation.

Given Harry's admiration for his mother's personal and intimate devotion to and concern for her family, it seems natural to understand unselfishness rather than selflessness as properly describing his priorities. Whether this is justified depends on the way it enables him to make sense of his overall evaluative perspective, in particular the patterns of dampening relations among his felt evaluations and of reflexive felt evaluations focused on the preferences these dampening relations disclose. Thus, first, this understanding of unselfishness rather than merely selflessness as valuable enables him to reinterpret his earlier negative felt evaluations in response to his imagined acceptance of the promotion as not merely regret at not being there for his family but, more strongly, shame at not exhibiting the preferences he feels he ought to have. Such a reinterpretation, of course, imposes commitments on what other felt evaluations he ought to feel in relevantly similar situations.

Second, this new understanding enables Harry to exploit new inferential connections among unselfishness and related evaluative concepts so as better to justify his felt evaluations as he now understands them. For example, Harry previously would have argued that his acceptance of the promotion could not result in his neglecting his family because, in the context of his former understanding of his personal concerns as selfish relative to his public concerns, he did not see his relative inattention to his family as a matter of failing to give attention to something that has a legitimate overriding claim on him. Now that Harry has come to see that concern for his family is not only compatible with being unselfish but demanded by it, however, he can see that to accept increased responsibility at work would be precisely to neglect his family; he can reinterpret his feelings in response to his (imagined) acceptance of the promotion as not merely shame but also as guilt for this neglect. Consequently, finally, he is now able to make sense of the relative import of his family as properly dampening that of his job in these circumstances. For, given this understanding of unselfishness, the import of his missing important events in their lives because he is away on business is now intelligible as having high severity (because neglectful) in the context of his having only minimal contact with his family, and this makes intelligible the relative intensity of his feelings of loss compared with his enthusiasm for and pride in his work.

Insofar as Harry is able to come to have this kind of unity within his overall evaluative perspective, including his perspective on priorities, he now has a justification not merely for this way of elucidating his concept of the admirable counterpart of selfishness as unselfishness, but also for the priority his family has for him over his work, at least in this instance. For he can now articulate, in light of the inferential connections between unselfishness and neglect, how he was formerly confused and so why the choice to accept the promotion would be neglectful and so shameful. In this way, we might naturally say that his priorities here are a proper object of *discovery*, as that by virtue of which he is to assess and regulate his evaluative perspective. Nonetheless, just as with deliberation about values, deliberation about priorities depends on our exercising freedom of the heart so as actively to shape our overall evaluative perspective in light of an explicit understanding of the relevant evaluative concepts. We can, therefore, make sense of Harry as simultaneously *autonomous* and so as having a say in what his priorities are. Consequently, as with evaluatively thick properties, it would be better to say that priorities are neither simply invented nor discovered but *disclosed* by such a dialectical process of deliberation.

7.5 CONCLUSION

The account offered in §7.4 of the disclosure of evaluatively thick properties and priorities solves not only the deliberative problem, but also the motivational problem, and shows the two to be essentially connected. Thus, my account of how deliberation about value is possible has an essential role for the exercise of control over felt evaluation so as autonomously to achieve an elucidation of evaluative concepts that appropriately informs and makes good sense of those felt evaluations; the deliberative problem, therefore, cannot be solved independently of the motivational problem. Moreover, only in light of this account of the disclosure of evaluatively thick properties and priorities as what provide reasons for making certain evaluations can we properly understand the nature of the rational control we are able to exercise over our felt evaluations so as to make possible freedom of the heart. Indeed, as I have argued in §§7.3–7.4, the nature of the rational control we are thus able to bring to bear on our felt evaluations is considerably broader than that articulated in §§6.3–6.4 once it is understood as a part of the processes of self-interpretation and the elucidation of evaluative concepts central to our deliberation about value. The motivational problem therefore cannot be solved independently of the deliberative problem. Once again we have encountered a kind of circularity: deliberation about value and the resulting attainment of reasons to value are possible only through the possibility of exercising control over our hearts, and such an exercise of control is possible only through the attainment of reasons to value. Yet this circularity is none other than the sort of non-vicious circularity characteristic of a dialectic that I have already vindicated. The motivational and deliberative problems are therefore solved.

8

Persons, friendship, and moral value

I began this book signaling sympathy with the idea that to be a person is
to be a rational animal. My aim since then has been to offer an account
of at least part of the kind of rationality characteristic of persons, namely
the sort of practical rationality involved both in deliberating about value
and in motivating ourselves to act accordingly. In the context of a
sustained attack on the cognitive–conative divide, I developed as a
replacement for the notion of conation an account of disclosive assents to
import, articulated in terms of a distinctive kind of rationality characteristic of the rational interconnections among evaluative judgment and felt
evaluations. This new conception of rationality therefore enables me to
present a more refined conception of what it is to be a person.

To see this, consider Harry Frankfurt's account of the distinction
between persons and mere animals, or "wantons," as he calls them.[1]
Wantons, on the one hand, have beliefs and desires and are able to reason
about how best to fulfill these desires, but they "not only . . . pursue
whatever course of action [they are] most strongly inclined to pursue,
but [they do] not care which of [their] inclinations is the strongest"
(p. 17). Wantons, therefore, can have a kind of freedom, but this is
merely freedom of action. *Persons*, on the other hand, can care about
their motives for action. This means that for a person, but not for a
wanton, there is the potential for a difference between the motives for
action he in fact has and those he thinks he ought to have, and this opens
up the possibility of freedom of the will. Given this much, Frankfurt
claims:

A person who . . . enjoys both freedom of action and freedom of the will . . .
has, in that case, all the freedom it is possible to desire or to conceive. There are
other good things in life, and he may not possess some of them. But there is
nothing in the way of freedom that he lacks. (pp. 22–23)

[1] "Freedom of the Will and the Concept of a Person," in *The Importance of What We Care
About*, pp. 11–25.

245

This is mistaken. As I have argued, freedom of the heart is distinct from freedom of the will, and it is therefore a dimension of personhood that Frankfurt simply ignores. Nonetheless, Frankfurt's fundamental idea is sound: we can distinguish persons from mere animals in terms of the kinds of freedom that are possible for us but not for them. Thus, in terms of the notion of freedom of the heart, we might make a further distinction between persons and what we might call "emotional wantons." Although *emotional wantons* can care about things in the world, they do not concern themselves with what they care about – about where their hearts lie. Persons, on the other hand, because they can concern themselves with their hearts and can deliberate about what hearts to have, have the potential for a difference between the heart they think worth having and the heart they in fact have, thus opening up the possibility of freedom of the heart. Frankfurt is therefore right in that what distinguishes persons from animals is not merely our capacity to step back from and reflect on the mental states we actually have – not merely the capacity for this sort of self-consciousness. Rather, the capacity for self-consciousness is important because it underlies the kinds of freedom that are more fundamentally distinctive of persons.

Of course, the kinds of capacities characteristic of wantons are the very same as those characteristic of emotional wantons. For a creature is intelligible as having the capacity for desire (and so as being a wanton) only if it is intelligible as having the capacity for felt evaluation quite generally, and that brings along with it the capacity to care about things. Nonetheless, the importance of insisting on the difference lies with the conception of the kinds of rationality that make these capacities possible and so in the precise understanding of the capacities at issue. The same is true of the kinds of capacities characteristic of persons: even though having the possibility of freedom of the will presupposes also having the possibility of freedom of the heart and so the capacity to deliberate about value and vice versa, and so, even though the set of what Frankfurt thinks are persons is coextensive with the set of what I think are persons, the importance of my insistence on freedom of the heart lies with the conception of rationality that makes intelligible the way in which freedom of the heart is distinct from freedom of the will. What distinguishes us persons from animals is our ability to reason non-instrumentally about import and so to have control not merely over what we do but also over who we are. It is, therefore, this rationality of import, as not merely either instrumental or epistemic (as the cognitive–

conative divide would have it), that underwrites this richer conception of personhood.

If, as I have alleged, the assumption of the cognitive–conative divide is at the root of serious misconceptions of human practical reason, why has it been so widely accepted in both philosophy of mind and moral psychology? The answer, I think, can be found in an all-too-neat division of philosophy into the subdivisions of philosophy of mind and moral psychology. On the one hand, philosophers of mind, focused on the mind–body problem, have been narrowly interested in problems of intentionality and consciousness. By ignoring broader issues of moral psychology and human practical reason – the kinds of thinking that characterize our everyday lives – they are led to think these problems can be treated separately by appealing to seemingly independent notions of direction of fit and to qualia. This means, in particular, that they are blind to the problem of import and so are led to a kind of account that, I argued, can provide neither a solution to the problem of import (cf. §2.4), nor an adequate account of emotions or of pleasures and pains more generally (cf. §§2.3, 3.6). On the other hand, moral psychologists inherit from philosophy of mind this conception of our mental states and capacities, thinking they can straightforwardly extend this account of cognition and conation to account for our autonomy and evaluative rationality. Yet, given the problem of import, it is not surprising that this approach cannot provide adequate solutions to the motivational or deliberative problems (cf. §6.2 and §7.1, respectively). The result is an inadequate understanding of the kinds of control we can have not only over our actions but also over our values and our selves.

In short, it is the mismatch between the aims of philosophers of mind and those of moral psychologists that is partly responsible not only for the widespread acceptance of the cognitive–conative divide, but also for the invisibility of a distinctive rationality of import characteristic of felt evaluations; these are mistakes that jointly prevent our ever finding adequate solutions to the sort of problems characteristic of moral psychology. We cannot, therefore, offer theories within either philosophy of mind or moral psychology without considering from the beginning the implications these theories have for the other: there is no neatly circumscribed division between these two sub-disciplines of philosophy.

At this point, however, it might seem strange that, in offering a new theory of practical reason, I have tried as much as possible to focus narrowly on personal values and how we can deliberate about them, frequently setting aside questions about both the ontological status and the rationality of interpersonal values, in particular the sort of interpersonal values that underlie friendship and morality. For such interpersonal values and the ways in which we can reason about them are also central to a full understanding of what it is to be a person, and cannot be neatly divided off from the problems of personal value that I have been addressing. The adequacy of my account, therefore, must depend in part on its ability to shed light on these issues. I shall, therefore, briefly describe some implications my account has for these broader issues, with the hope of stimulating fruitful work in these areas.

In my solution to the deliberative problem, I already (in §7.4.1) broached the way in which others can collaborate with one in deliberating about value: insofar as deliberation about personal values involves subjectively valid concepts elucidated partially from within one's own evaluative perspective, a collaborator must be a sympathetic critic, able, at least hypothetically, to adopt that evaluative perspective so as to criticize it from within. Such internal criticism can consist in offering new ways to understand the central evaluative concepts and so new ways to reinterpret the subject's felt evaluations so as, potentially, to shape them in order to achieve a justification of that understanding. Of course, others can be not merely sympathetic critics; they can also offer "*moral support*" as the subject tries actively to shape the habits in his felt evaluations to accord with a proposed elucidation of the relevant evaluative concepts and so with his evaluative judgments. Such moral support can take the form both of helping him remember his evaluative judgments, and so attend to features of his situation relevant to these judgments, and of providing external sanctions for proper or improper responses to these situations.

Yet a deeper sort of collaboration with others in deliberation about values is possible: that characteristic of the sort of love, trust, and respect involved in relationships of friendship.

Aristotle describes (character) friendship as a relationship in which each friend loves the other for her sake and as "another self." At least part of what is meant by this claim that a friend is another self is that friends share a conception of how it is best to live – of *eudaimonia* – such that each can attain *eudaimonia* only by helping the other. Translated into the sort of language I have been developing, we might say that friends must share a particular evaluative perspective not merely in the relatively shallow sense of happening to agree in their evaluative judgments, but more deeply in that their evaluative judgments and felt evaluations together form a single projectible, rational pattern constitutive of their shared values. (Of course, not all their values need be shared in order for them to be friends, for friends may agree, perhaps tacitly, to respect and even cherish certain differences between them. Yet the overlap of shared values must be non-trivial in order to make sense of how their relationship can have the kind of depth and intimacy distinctive of character friendship.) Consequently, at least within the limits of this shared evaluative perspective, the kind of commitment one undertakes in judgment or felt evaluation is one that imposes rational pressure not merely on one's own subsequent evaluative judgments and felt evaluations, but also on those of one's friend. Thus, assume that my friend has devoted herself to giving her time and money to various charities and so values being this kind of person. Insofar as this value is a part of our shared evaluative perspective, I have reason to judge and feel accordingly: to be proud of her, to want to contribute myself, etc. Conversely, that my felt evaluations are resistant to this sort of rational pressure gives her reason to reconsider the value she places on it.

That friends have and sustain such a common evaluative perspective is, therefore, far from accidental, but is rather an essential feature of their relationship as friends. Friends must trust and respect each other's judgments and feelings not merely as one would trust and respect a thoughtful and sympathetic advisor, but in a rich and deep sense that might properly be understood as a kind of *love:* love of your friend for her sake and as another self.[2] Deliberative collaboration in friendship, therefore, is a way of exercising your autonomy as persons together. Helping a friend become a better person is a matter of offering not merely external moral support – reminders and external sanctions – but support and guidance from within what is an essentially shared projectible, rational pattern of disclosive assents that constitutes your joint evaluative perspective, such that you together take pleasure in and feel pain at each other's successes and failures. Indeed, it is only by virtue of this kind of loving relationship we have that it makes sense to say that my friend is ashamed of my lack of charitable giving: since shame is a reflexive emotion, it makes sense only as a response to what is, in a non-

---

[2] For an interesting analysis of the notion of trust in terms of the giving and accepting of reasons along something like these lines, see Edward Hinchman's "Trust and Reason," Ph.D. thesis, University of Michigan (2000).

trivial sense, a part of one's self; a mere acquaintance might be disappointed in my lack of charity, but not ashamed.[3] The evaluative concepts that friends elucidate in the process of such deliberation, therefore, should be understood to be *intersubjectively valid*, rather than merely subjectively valid.

This sketch of an account of the kind of love, trust, and respect that makes intelligible the kind of interpersonal values characteristic of friendship can, I believe, be extended to make sense of the kind of interpersonal values encountered in morality.

As a first step, we might extend this account of interpersonal values to include broader groups of people with common values; call such a group a *community of valuers*. As with friends, what characterizes a community of valuers is not merely that its members share certain values by coincidence; rather, by virtue of the kind of interpersonal rational interconnectedness I have been discussing, they must have their evaluations regulated by the shared evaluative perspective that attunes each to these values. (Unlike friends, however, the shared values within such a community can be focused on a relatively narrow range of issues, such as certain political causes, that need not encompass even most of the values defining the kind of person its members are.) Deliberation within the community, it might seem, can proceed in roughly the same way I have articulated for deliberation about personal values, and sketched in the case of the interpersonal values of friends, by means of the elucidation of evaluative concepts so as to make better sense, through interpretation, of the evaluative responses of the community as a whole. An individual, therefore, is a member of such a community just in case there is a *de facto* pattern of reciprocity in the way in which that individual and the rest of the community treat each other's evaluations as rationally connected to the shared evaluative perspective. (Of course, there is considerable looseness in this sketch of membership in such a community, in part because the relevant pattern of reciprocity has not been well defined, and in part because there ought to be room for individuals to be more or less central to, or more or less on the fringe of, the community.)

This brief sketch of a community of valuers is clearly not yet a sketch of a *community of moral agents*, for moral values seem universal rather than merely intersubjective, and membership in a moral community (and so the adoption of this shared evaluative perspective) seems therefore

---

[3] Cf. Charles Taylor's "Self-Interpreting Animals," in his *Human Agency and Language*, pp. 45–76, and Gabriele Taylor's *Pride, Shame, and Guilt*.

rationally required rather than merely the result of *de facto* reciprocity. Precisely how this should be spelled out is, of course, a general problem in meta-ethics, though the account I have offered so far affords at least the beginning of an answer.

Moral communities are distinctive in part in that the concept of the kind of being that is a member of the community – i.e., of a person – is itself one of the concepts to be elucidated within the community as a part of the delineation of its shared evaluative perspective. In part, this means tying the concept of a person not merely to the possibility of freedom of the heart, as I have done above, but also to notions of responsibility. Following the kind of account I gave in chapter 7 of deliberation about personal values, we might expect such an elucidation of the concepts of personhood and responsibility to be justified only in light of the way in which it makes intelligible the relevant aspects of our human experience, including what might come to be seen (in virtue of further elucidation of their formal objects) as distinctively moral felt evaluations, such as sympathy, resentment, remorse, guilt, and moral (dis)approbation. In light of this justification, therefore, those who are already members of this moral community, and so who share its evaluative perspective, have reason to act and mold their hearts accordingly, even when they do not realize they have such reasons.

For the norms defined by this evaluative perspective to be universal, however, they must apply as well to those who are not already members of the moral community. Consider two cases: one of a moral agent who claims to be a member of a different moral community and so who tries to reject membership in this one, and the other of a moral skeptic who rejects membership in any moral community whatsoever. In the former case, the one moral community might well be able to show that its evaluative perspective is better justified in virtue of the way it makes sense of human experience, thereby providing reason for the other to change accordingly; or it might be that, in the face of confrontation with another moral community, each might find ways in which it ought to modify its evaluative perspective, thereby bringing their evaluative perspectives closer together. (Indeed, in such cases, it may be unclear to what extent these are clearly two moral communities rather than one with some conflict internal to its evaluative perspective, and this is part of what sustains the idea that the relevant evaluative concepts are universally valid.) Of course, if it turns out that multiple shapes to human experience, as it is delineated by the relevant evaluative concepts, are

251

equally justifiable, then moral norms would be relative to particular moral communities. Consequently, it is a contingent fact, if it is a fact at all, whether or not there are any universal moral norms, dependent as they must be on the kind of valuers we can justifiably get ourselves to be.

What, then, can be said of the latter case of a moral skeptic who rejects any such characterization of human experience as definitive of interpersonal values? In what sense can we say that moral norms apply to her? To be such a creature, we might think, is to refuse to acknowledge an evaluatively rich conception of what it is to be a person, and so is to live an impoverished life as no longer really a person at all. Here, perhaps, the best we can say is that she is simply missing out on the kinds of goods that come with being a person in this richer sense of being a moral agent – goods such as friendship, trust, and love. She therefore has reasons to be different than she is, even if she is, by virtue of the kind of evaluative perspective she currently has, wholly blind to these reasons.[4]

This sketch of an account of both friendship and moral values is, of course, all too brief. Nonetheless, it does provide a reorientation to our conception of properly moral psychology. For we might think of what happens when a creature comes to be a moral agent, by virtue of her having a proper upbringing or of her undergoing a kind of conversion from moral skepticism, as her becoming a *friend of humanity* and so a member of this most general community of valuers. Consequently, it begins to provide some insight in light of the nature of such friendship into the way in which we can deliberate with each other about value and so assert moral claims on each other. For a central and legitimate part of such conversations can be attempts to play on and mold one another's sympathies; this is the sort of conversation about values non-cognitivists like Allan Gibbard and Simon Blackburn are after,[5] though we can now understand it to be not merely arational manipulation but rather a part of the give and take of reasons within relationships of mutual respect and trust.

---

[4] Cf. John McDowell's "Might there be External Reasons?" in J. E. J. Altham and Ross Harrison, ed., *World, Mind, and Ethics: Essays on the Ethical Philosophy of Bernard Williams* (Cambridge University Press, 1995), pp. 387–98.

[5] Gibbard, *Wise Choices, Apt Feelings*; Blackburn, *Ruling Passions*.

Select bibliography

Altham, J. E. J., "The Legacy of Emotivism," in Graham Macdonald and Crispin Wright, eds., *Fact, Science, and Morality: Essays on A. J. Ayer's Language, Truth and Logic*. Oxford: Blackwell, 1986, pp. 275–88.

Anderson, Elizabeth, *Value in Ethics and Economics*. Cambridge, MA: Harvard University Press, 1993.

Armstrong, D. M., *The Nature of Mind and Other Essays*. Ithaca: Cornell University Press, 1981.

Blackburn, Simon, *Ruling Passions: A Theory of Practical Reason*. Oxford: Clarendon, 1998.

   Spreading the Word: Groundings in the Philosophy of Language. Oxford University Press, 1984.

   "How to Be an Ethical Antirealist," *Midwest Studies in Philosophy*, 12 (1988), pp. 361–75.

Boyd, Richard, "How to Be a Moral Realist," in Stephen Darwall, Allan Gibbard, and Peter Railton, eds., *Moral Discourse and Practice*. Oxford: Clarendon, 1997, pp. 105–35.

Burnyeat, Miles, "Aristotle on Learning to Be Good," in Amélie Rorty, ed., *Essays on Aristotle's Ethics*. Berkeley: University of California Press, 1980, pp. 69–92.

Buss, Sarah, "Weakness of Will," *Pacific Philosophical Quarterly*, 78 (1997), pp. 13–44.

   "Autonomy Reconsidered," in *Midwest Studies in Philosophy*, 19 (1994), pp. 95–121.

Churchland, Paul, *A Neurocomputational Perspective: The Nature of Mind and the Structure of Science*. Cambridge, MA: MIT Press, 1989.

D'Arms, Justin, and Jacobson, Daniel, "Sentiment and Value," *Ethics*, 110 (2000), pp. 722–48.

Davidson, Donald, *Inquiries into Truth and Interpretation*. Oxford: Clarendon, 1984.

   Essays on Actions and Events. Oxford: Clarendon, 1980.

Davis, Wayne, "The Two Senses of Desire," *Philosophical Studies*, 45 (1983), pp. 181–95.

Dennett, Daniel, *The Intentional Stance*. Cambridge, MA: MIT Press, 1987.

   "Why You Can't Make a Computer that Feels Pain," *Synthese*, 38 (1978), pp. 415–49.

Dillon, Robin, "Self-Respect: Moral, Emotional, Political," *Ethics*, 107 (1997), pp. 226–49.

Dray, William, *Laws and Explanation in History*. Oxford University Press, 1957.

Dynes, J. B. and Poppen, J. L., "Lobotomy for Intractable Pain," *Journal of the American Medical Association*, 140 (1949), pp. 15–19.

Elithorn, A., Glitherno, E., and Slater, E., "Leucotomy for Pain," *Journal of Neurology, Neurosurgery, and Psychiatry*, 21 (1958), pp. 249–61.

Frankfurt, Harry, *Necessity, Volition, and Love*. Cambridge University Press, 1999.
  The Importance of What We Care About: Philosophical Essays. Cambridge University Press, 1988.
  "The Faintest Passion," *Proceedings and Addresses of the APA*, 66 (1992), pp. 5–16.

Frey, R. G., *Interests and Rights: The Case Against Animals*. Oxford: Clarendon, 1980.

Gaus, Gerald F., *Value and Justification: The Foundations of Liberal Theory*. Cambridge University Press, 1990.

Gibbard, Allan, *Wise Choices, Apt Feelings: A Theory of Normative Judgment*. Cambridge, MA: Harvard University Press, 1990.

Gordon, Robert, "Review of *The Rationality of Emotion* by Ronald de Sousa," *Philosophical Review*, 100 (1991), pp. 284–88.
  The Structure of Emotions: Investigations in Cognitive Psychology. Cambridge University Press, 1987.

Graham, George, *Philosophy of Mind: An Introduction*. Oxford: Blackwell, 1993.

Greenspan, Patricia, *Emotions and Reasons: An Inquiry into Emotional Justification*. New York: Routledge, 1988.
  "Emotions as Evaluations," *Pacific Philosophical Quarterly*, 62 (1981), pp. 158–69.
  "Emotions, Reasons, and 'Self–Involvement'," *Philosophical Studies*, 38 (1980), pp. 161–68.

Hall, Richard, "Are Pains Necessarily Unpleasant?," *Philosophy and Phenomenological Research*, 49 (1989), pp. 643–59.

Helm, Bennett, "Integration and Fragmentation of the Self," *Southern Journal of Philosophy*, 34 (1996), pp. 43–63.
  "The Significance of Emotions," *American Philosophical Quarterly*, 31 (1994), pp. 319–31.
  "Significance, Emotions, and Objectivity: Some Limits of Animal Thought." Ph.D. dissertation, University of Pittsburgh, 1994.

Hempel, Carl, "Aspects of Scientific Explanation," in *Aspects of Scientific Explanation and Other Essays in the Philosophy of Science*. New York: The Free Press, 1965, pp. 331–496.

Hinchman, Edward, "Trust and Reason," Ph.D. thesis, University of Michigan, 2000.

Hursthouse, Rosalind, "Arational Actions," *Journal of Philosophy*, 88 (1991), pp. 57–68.

Keats, A. and Beecher, H., "Pain Relief with Hypnotic Doses of Barbiturates and a Hypothesis," *Journal of Pharmacology and Experimental Therapeutics*, 100 (1950), pp. 1–13.

Kennett, Jeanette and Smith, Michael, "Philosophy and Commonsense: The Case of Weakness of Will," in Michaelis Michael and John O'Leary-Hawthorne, eds., *Philosophy of Mind: The Place of Philosophy in the Study of Mind.* Boston: Klewer, 1994, pp. 141–57.

Kenny, Anthony, *Action, Emotion, and Will.* London: Routledge & Kegan Paul, 1963.

Korsgaard, Christine M., *The Sources of Normativity.* Cambridge University Press, 1996.

Kripke, Saul, *Naming and Necessity.* Cambridge, MA: Harvard University Press, 1980.

Jaggar, Alison, "Love and Knowledge: Emotion in Feminist Epistemology," *Inquiry*, 32 (1989), pp. 151–76.

Lyons, William, *Emotion.* Cambridge University Press, 1980.

Marks, Joel, "A Theory of Emotion," *Philosophical Studies*, 42 (1982), pp. 227–42.

McDowell, John, "Projection and Truth in Ethics," in Stephen Darwall, Allan Gibbard and Peter Railton, eds., *Moral Discourse and Practice.* Oxford University Press, 1997, pp. 215–25.

"Values and Secondary Qualities," in Ted Honderich, ed., *Morality and Objectivity: A Tribute to J. L. Mackie.* London: Routledge & Kegan Paul, 1985, pp. 110–29.

"The Role of *Eudaimonia* in Aristotle's Ethics," *The Proceedings of the African Classical Associations*, 15 (1980).

"Virtue and Reason," *Monist*, 62 (1979), pp. 331–50.

"Are Moral Requirements Hypothetical Imperatives?," *Proceedings of the Aristotelian Society*, Supplement, 52 (1978), pp. 13–29.

Mele, Alfred, *Autonomous Agents: From Self-Control to Autonomy.* Oxford University Press, 1995.

"Internalist Moral Cognitivism and Listlessness," *Ethics*, 106 (1996), pp. 727–53.

Millgram, Elijah, *Practical Induction.* Cambridge, MA: Harvard University Press, 1997.

"Pleasure in Practical Reasoning," *Monist*, 76 (1993), pp. 394–415.

Nelkin, Norton, "Reconsidering Pain," *Philosophical Psychology*, 7 (1994), pp. 325–43.

Newton, Natika, "On Viewing Pain as a Secondary Quality," *Noûs*, 23 (1989), pp. 569–98.

Nussbaum, Martha, *The Therapy of Desire: Theory and Practice in Hellenistic Ethics.* Princeton University Press, 1994.

Oakley, Justin, *Morality and the Emotions.* New York: Routledge, 1992.

Peterson, Grethe, ed., *The Tanner Lectures on Human Values*, vol. 15. Salt Lake City: University of Utah Press, 1994.

Pettit, Philip and Smith, Michael, "Practical Unreason," *Mind*, 102 (1993), pp. 53–79.

Piper, Adrian, "Two Conceptions of the Self," *Philosophical Studies*, 48 (1985), pp. 173–97.

Pitcher, George, "Pain Perception," *Philosophical Review*, 79 (1970), pp. 368–93.

Railton, Peter, "Moral Realism," *Philosophical Review*, 95 (1986), pp. 163–207.

Roberts, Robert C., "What an Emotion Is: A Sketch," *Philosophical Review*, 97 (1988), pp. 183–209.

"Shaped Passions: An Essay in Moral Psychology." Unpublished.

Searle, John, *Intentionality: An Essay in the Philosophy of Mind.* Cambridge University Press, 1983.

"Minds, Brains, and Programs," *Behavioral and Brain Sciences*, 3 (1980), pp. 417–24.

Sellars, Wilfrid, "Empiricism and the Philosophy of Mind," in Herbert Feigl and Michael Scriven, eds., *Minnesota Studies in the Philosophy of Science*, vol. 1, Minneapolis: University of Minnesota Press, 1956, pp. 253–329.

Shaffer, Jerome, "An Assessment of Emotion," *American Philosophical Quarterly*, 20 (1983), pp. 161–73.

Smith, Michael, *The Moral Problem.* Oxford: Blackwell, 1994.

Solomon, Robert, *The Passions.* University of Notre Dame Press, 1976.

Stephens, G. Lynn and Graham, George, "Minding Your P's and Q's: Pain and Sensible Qualities," *Noûs*, 21 (1987), pp. 395–405.

Stocker, Michael, *Valuing Emotions.* Cambridge University Press, 1996.

Taylor, Charles, *Sources of the Self: The Making of Modern Identity.* Cambridge, MA: Harvard University Press, 1989.

Human Agency and Language: Philosophical Papers 1. Cambridge University Press, 1985.

Taylor, Gabriele, *Pride, Shame, and Guilt: Emotions of Self-Assessment.* Oxford University Press, 1985.

Tye, Michael, *Ten Problems of Consciousness: A Representational Theory of the Phenomenal Mind.* Cambridge, MA: MIT Press, 1995.

"A Representational Theory of Pains," *Philosophical Perspectives 9: AI, Connectionism, and Philosophical Psychology* (1995), pp. 223–39.

Velleman, J. David, *Practical Reflection.* Princeton University Press, 1989.

"The Possibility of Practical Reason," *Ethics*, 106 (1996), pp. 694–726.

"The Guise of the Good," *Noûs*, 26 (1992), pp. 3–26.

Watson, Gary, "Free Agency," in Gary Watson, ed., *Free Will.* Oxford University Press, 1982, pp. 96–110.

Wiggins, David, *Needs, Values, Truth: Essays in the Philosophy of Value*, 2nd edition. Oxford: Blackwell, 1991.

"Deliberation and Practical Reason," *Proceedings of the Aristotelian Society*, 76 (1975–76), pp. 29–51.

Williams, Bernard, *Moral Luck: Philosophical Papers 1973–1980.* Cambridge University Press, 1981.

Wolf, Susan, *Freedom Within Reason.* New York: Oxford University Press, 1990.

Index

257

deliberative problem (*see* deliberation, problem of)

Dennett, Daniel, 2n.1, 31n.1, 93n.25

desire, 30–32, 81–89, 117–19 (*see also* felt evaluation, desire as)
  as pleasant or painful, 87, 109
  first-order, 103 (*see also* felt evaluation, non-reflexive)
  intensity of (*see* felt evaluation, intensity of)
  long-term, 87–88
  occurrent, 85–87
  perverse, 82–84
  second-order, 54, 103 (*see also* felt evaluation, reflexive)
  strong, 38–39

Dillon, Robin, 154n.26

direction of fit, 4–5, 7, 82–83 (*see also* cognitive–conative divide)
  mind-to-world, 4–5, 82
  world-to-mind, 5, 83

disclosive assent (*see* assent, disclosive)

discovery (*see* deliberation, problem of; import, objectivity of; value/valuing, as evaluatively thick property)

distinct existence (*see* cognitive–conative divide, and distinct existence)

Dray, William, 3n.2, 76n.10

eliminative materialism, 76n.10

elucidation, 221–22, 223–31, 234–38

emotion, 6, 80 (*see also* felt evaluation)
  as felt evaluations (*see* felt evaluation, emotions as)
  as pleasant or painful, 33–36, 60–61, 80–81, 109
  backward-looking, 68
  cognitivist account of, 6, 37–46, 58
  expression of
    arational, 75
    rational, 77
  forward-looking, 67–68
  intensity of (*see* felt evaluation, intensity of)
  judgmentalism about, 41–42, 45–46, 65
  negative, 68
  passivity of, 34, 65–67, 72–74 (*see also* assent, passive)
  positive, 68
  and problem of emotionality, 38–41, 42n.12, 46–48, 81

and problem of rational conflict, 41–46, 47, 65
  anti-judgmentalism about, 42–45, 65
  rationality of (*see* rationality, of felt evaluation)

evaluation (*see also* evaluative perspective; felt evaluation; judgment, evaluative)
  complete, 180–81
  constituting, 37, 51–53
  discovering, 37, 49

evaluative perspective
  fragmentation of, 137, 142
  integration of, 159
  singleness of, 144–45, 148, 152–53, 158–59, 177–78

feeling (*see* emotion, as pleasant or painful; emotion, passivity of; felt evaluation; pain; pleasure)

felt evaluation, 74, 80
  and attention to import, 72–74, 78
  and conflict with evaluative judgment (*see* rationality, and conflict between felt evaluation and evaluative judgment)
  and motivation, 43–45, 75–80, 85–86, 109–10
  as attunement to import, 72–73, 79, 88–89, 115
  as conceptually informed, 155–56
  as constituting import, 72–74, 78–80, 86
  as exerting rational pressure, 71, 113, 249
  bodily pleasure and pain as, 89–96 (*see also* pain; pleasure)
  desire as, 85–87 (*see also* desire)
  emotion as, 74, 80 (*see also* emotion)
  focus of, 69–70, 118–19, 215–19
  formal object of, 34, 62–64, 69, 75–76, 83–85
  intensity of, 108–11, 114
  non-reflexive, 103, 219–20
  pattern of (*see* pattern)
  rationality of (*see* rationality, of felt evaluation)
  reflexive, 103–06, 219–20
  target of, 34, 69
  warrant of, 34–36, 51–58, 64–65, 70–71, 85, 108–11, 112–14

focus (*see* felt evaluation, focus of)

formal object (*see* felt evaluation, formal object of)